MORE ADVANCE PRAISE FOR *TAKING THE SEA*

"A remarkable book, well written and thoroughly researched—one of the best reads of the decade."

—Michael G. Walling, author of *Bloodstained Sea, the U.S. Coast Guard in the Battle of the Atlantic, 1941–1944*

"Dennis Powers dives deeply into the long-forgotten tales of ingenuity and bravery in search of what was thought lost to Neptune . . . . Rivals Bella Bathurst's *The Wreckers* and Henry Kittredge's *Mooncussers of Cape Cod* as the definitive work in this area."

—John J. Galluzzo, Executive Director, U.S. Life-Saving Service Heritage Association

"A page-turning story that readers of all ages will find both interesting and exciting . . ."

—Floyd Shelton, Commissioner of Ports, State of Oregon; Harbor Commissioner of Astoria, Oregon, and Redwood City, California

"With a skillful and intriguing narrative, the author explores a facet of maritime history that's little explored . . . . This belongs in every maritime library."

—Bill Kooiman, Porter Shaw Library, San Francisco Maritime Museum

TAKING THE SEA

TAKING THE SEA

Perilous Waters, Sunken Ships, and the True Story of the Legendary Wrecker Captains

BY DENNIS M. POWERS

AMACOM AMERICAN MANAGEMENT ASSOCIATION

New York • Atlanta • Brussels • Chicago • Mexico City • San Francisco
Shanghai • Tokyo • Toronto • Washington, D. C.

This publication is designed to provide accurate and authoritative information
in regard to the subject matter covered. It is sold with the understanding that the
publisher is not engaged in rendering legal, accounting, or other professional
service. If legal advice or other expert assistance is required, the services of a
competent professional person should be sought.

Library of Congress Cataloging-in-Publication Data

Powers, Dennis M.
Taking the sea : perilous waters, sunken ships, and the true story of the legendary
wrecker captains / by Dennis M. Powers.
    p. cm.
Includes bibliographical references and index.
ISBN 978-0-8144-1353-1
1. Salvage—United States—History.   2. Shipwrecks—United States—History.
3. Ship captains—United States—History. I. Title.

VK1491.P69 2009
387.5'80973—dc22

2008021002

Printing number
10 9 8 7 6 5 4 3 2 1

CONTENTS

PREFACE

As I worked through the voluminous files in writing my last book, *Sentinel of the Seas*, I became curious about the vessels used in the building of the St. George Reef Lighthouse—and especially with one man who owned the ships in the construction. Starting in 1883, Captain Thomas P. H. Whitelaw leased out the schooner *La Ninfa* as the building crew's quarters, as well as the steamer *Whitelaw* that towed it and supplies to the reef. I wondered, what kind of a man would rent out good ships in such a risky venture? In answering this question, I discovered a new world: the adventurous times of Captain Whitelaw and the master wreckers.

The premier ship salvager of his day, T. P. H. Whitelaw watched as ships and their designs changed. He and his crews pulled tall-masted ships from reefs, refloated steamers whose hulls had been slashed by rocks, and salvaged schooners from the bottom of bays. I discovered that over time, Whitelaw had become a large shipowner, in addition to owning huge maritime used-parts lots.

Whitelaw had arrived in San Francisco at age sixteen with a quarter in his pocket. By age forty-five, he was extensively engaged in mining and real estate ventures, operated a stock ranch of 43,000 acres, and had accumulated substantial holdings of land. Internationally recognized, Whitelaw had become regarded as "The Master Wrecker" and "The Great Wrecker of the Pacific." His world encompassed the other important ship salvagers that operated across the United States, and his career spanned the era from sailing ships to steamers and from wooden to steel-hulled vessels.

Wrecking as a livelihood originated along the rugged coastlines of Europe, which had been a haven for wreckers and smugglers, and immigrants to the United States brought along the traditions. Wreckers in the nineteenth century built the town of Key West, Florida. When ships foundered, the first mariner on the scene—from a flotilla of streaking schooners—was designated the master of that wreck and ran the operation. Salvors later received their cut as a share of the auction proceeds, a part of the saved goods, or some "in kind" payment. Abuses and calls for reform led to this rough-and-tumble world becoming regulated and eventually maturing into a competitive business for hire.

The United States had its share of standout salvors starting in the late 1860s, including the East Coast's Captain E. R. Lowe and Israel J. Merritt, as well as Captain Thomas A. Scott and William Chapman. Like Whitelaw, they were about salvage—not plunder. They saved ships and people, putting together ventures to refloat sunken or beached ships for a fee. Or they might buy the salvage rights to what could be saved. However, the wrecker who stood out with success, respect, and publicity was Captain T. P. H. Whitelaw.

Whitelaw came from a poor Scottish family, and at age twelve apprenticed himself to a British vessel that traveled the East India trade. When this ship docked a few years later in 1863 in San Francisco Harbor, he decided to stay. With charisma, persistence, and brilliance, Captain Whitelaw started and built up his operations. He was an avid reader of the Greek classics, a self-taught philosopher, and a literary genius. And he worked on different nationally recognized efforts to save wrecked ships. One of his most noteworthy was the raising of the steamship *Umatilla*, which sank in Esquimalt Harbor, British Columbia, in 1884. This feat resulted in the British Admiralty giving international accolades to Captain Whitelaw.

"A terrible, always hungry monster, with long white teeth is the sea," observed the Captain. "It is a smiling witch one day—a terrible monster the next." He understood the incredible, combined powers of the winds, waves, currents, and tides that reduced the sturdiest vessels to piles of splintered wood and shards of steel plates. For Whitelaw, "Ships have individuality, each leading its own life, sometimes against the will of man.

Some ships survive almost incredible disasters, as do some men, while others leave their wood and steel bones on the first reef."

For decades, ships of all sizes and shapes dominated the movement of goods and people. Before railroad networks and airplanes or trucks and buses crisscrossed this country, these were the times when ships ruled the transportation world. Owing to inadequate charts, lack of warning lighthouses, and limited weather forecasting, however, vessels continually slammed into reefs, were thrashed by storms, and rendered helpless by strong currents. I became awed by the stories of these shipwrecks, the courage of the men and women, and the epic salvage efforts of the wreckers.

Using pontoons, powerful tugs, and strong steam engines on huge wreck ships, salvagers saved sunken ships—and under terrifying conditions. When performing their work, they were confronted by the same capricious seas and frightening winds that had caused the disasters in the first place. The accounts of the most memorable incidents—and the bravery the salvagers showed in the face of death—are detailed here.

Operating from his San Francisco base, Captain Whitelaw's ventures took him to Mexico and then north along the lengthy West Coast to British Columbia and the Bering Sea. Countries overseas and the U.S. government alike called upon him for his expertise. His counterparts on the East Coast, such as Merritt, Chapman, and Scott, also rose in importance as they steamed into savage waters to save ships and passengers. Their experiences and operations are part of this story as well.

This book is about the era when shipping was the dominant form of transportation throughout the world. It pictures the savage seas and times that Whitelaw and other wreckers faced, their human failures, and their triumphs. The stories are about courage, achievement, and the historical challenges of these times.

ACKNOWLEDGMENTS

The writing of *Taking the Sea* required a blend of sources in bringing together the stories of adventure, courage, and heartrending wrecks that spanned from the mid-1800s into the twentieth century. I wish to thank everyone connected with this project—maritime museum curators, librarians, experts, and researchers—for their gracious help, suggestions, and information.

The San Francisco Maritime Museum, and especially Bill Kooiman of its Porter Shaw Library, were invaluable resources with their historic pictures and extensive files on Captain Whitelaw and his ships. Bill helped to track down important details and found a treasure trove of files on T. P. H. Whitelaw that brought out his family life and philosophies. In this regard, I also thank Steven Canright, Park Curator-Maritime History, and David Hull, Principal Librarian, for their insights and input on this work.

Maritime museums deserve special recognition for their help in tracking down information about vessels, their captains, and maritime life. Dave Pearson and Jeff Smith of the widely respected Columbia River Maritime Museum greatly helped by opening up their files and pictures on the Oregon connection. Thanks also go to Jim Delgado and Susan Buss at the Vancouver Maritime Museum for supplying vital photographs and information about Whitelaw's ventures in Canada. Julie Greene of the Bridgehampton Historical Society was very helpful regarding the *Circassian,* while Amy German and Wendy Schnur with the Mystic Seaport Museum in Connecticut provided their extensive files on captains Merritt, Chapman, and Scott.

Jim Gibbs, the informative and well-regarded maritime author, provided welcomed background on shipping. John J. Galluzzo—the respected maritime historian, writer, and executive director of the Cape Cod Maritime Research Association and United States Life-Saving Service Heritage Association—also gave appreciated help.

Experienced librarians are always a key to successful research. Anna Beauchamp, the coordinator of interlibrary loans for Southern Oregon University, was very helpful in tracking down old publications and articles. Researcher Kevin Knapp did an excellent job in the same respect, and the History Center at the San Francisco Public Library (Tim Wilson, librarian) was very generous with its files of newspaper clippings on the times and wreckers. A diver, historian, and Great Lakes maritime expert, Brendon Baillod (www.ship-wreck.com), gave appreciated assistance with that region's background and sea stories, as did Dr. Richard J. Boyd, who has similar expertise with that region.

In historical research, pictures are important in supporting the personal accounts. Reviewing the archived pictures of wrecks, cities, and Captain Whitelaw's family gave as much accuracy to this story as any other resource. In this regard, the aforementioned maritime museums were very helpful, as were the Puget Sound Maritime Historical Society and the Royal British Columbia Museum in Vancouver. Tim Campbell of the San Francisco Maritime Museum also went beyond the call in helping me to find the necessary pictures to put these stories together.

I wish to give special thanks to Sandy Clunies, who provided very valuable historical and genealogical research, as well as Stan Wakefield and Andy Ambraziejus of AMACOM Books for their continual positive attitude, insights, and professional suggestions. Chris Murray also gave welcomed suggestions and thoughtful comments, as did two friends of mine, Chris Honore and Jim Simms. My literary agent, Jeanne Fredericks, deserves a special mention, not only for her support, but also for being a constant friend throughout the years.

My wife Judy accompanied me on trips involving this project and, without any question, made the difference in this book becoming a reality and being enjoyable. I am fortunate in being able to do what I truly enjoy, and I am grateful for those who join me in this quest.

CHAPTER ONE

EARLY YEARS

The *Sydney* steamed into the straits of the Golden Gate, the mile-wide gap in the coastal mountain chain leading to San Francisco's docks. On the bridge, the harbor pilot suggested a different course to the captain, and the vessel slowly turned into another heading through the wide expanse between the green-and-brown hills. Numerous small islands of rocks littered the entrance, "lifting their moss-grown heads above water, and beat by the eternal surges of an ocean ten thousand miles wide," according to one voyager's observation. The year was 1863.

Dense black smoke poured from the ship's smokestack as the winds sweeping in from the ocean quickly twisted the thick trail into grotesque swirls. A curving wake of blue-white froth trailed behind the vessel toward the horizon and seemingly back to the other side of the world where the seamen had once been. On board, young Tom Whitelaw smelled the sharpness of the sea—even with his years spent on the ocean—as the rocking, staggering steamer pushed into another port.

San Francisco's harbor was one of the finest in the world. Landlocked by surrounding hills and points, the bay was large enough to give shelter to all the fleets of the globe some said. As the ship moved through the expansive strait that connected the enclosed waters with the Pacific Ocean, on the left, or port side, six promontories of land projected from the higher ground. On the right, or starboard side, an arena of hills appeared with the browning amber colors of early summer.

The sixteen-year-old seaman felt the tremors from the freshwater currents flowing out of the bay that met the ocean in a massive vortex of energy. Hauling in weighted measuring lines, seamen yelled out that the water depths were now decreasing from the initial 300-foot soundings outside the entrance. The water would soon become much shallower, averaging twenty feet inside the bay's deep interiors.

The *Sydney* passed scores of huge sea lions, weighing one ton and up, as the closest seals rose up mightily on their flippers to bark at the passing vessel. They acted like a pack of dogs protesting the stranger ambling by their neighborhood. Staring intently at the scene unfolding in front, Tom became amazed at the long, stretching wharves that reached hundreds of feet into the cove, filled with different-shaped ships.

Clipper ships with masts that reached high into the sky were anchored or docked next to large riverboat paddlers and steamers, some with wisps of smoke rising from their stacks. The *Sydney* slowly passed the large black hulk of a paddleship steamer at anchor, ten-story sails fore and aft, with three-story paddle wheels. Small lighters with fat smokestacks behind enclosed pilot cabins chugged toward the docks with off-loaded goods. Horns sounded, bells clanged, overhead gulls squawked, and steam whistles blew. The harbor teemed with activity as the windy city of hills and structures appeared.

A crewman had told him this country was in the throes of a terrible civil war, but he couldn't see any evidence of that. He was curious about this new land. "Tom! What's the problem! Get movin'!" The rough yell startled him and spurred Whitelaw into action. He quickly began hauling ropes and moving goods around the deck like the larger, beefy men who surrounded him.

The captain telegraphed the engine room's crew to cut the ship's power, and the vessel began its glide toward one spot of densely wooden structures and ships. The long arm of a wharf stretched toward them as the steamer approached the docks with the city's streets and hills dotted by wood, brick, and stone buildings behind. When the deep-throated rumble of the engine pounded in reverse, the large ship slowed dramatically. The sounds then ended abruptly. Another long grumble and the ship nudged against the protective fenders of the wharf now two-stories down.

Crewmen tossed down light lines with heavy "monkey fist" tops. After tying each end to a thick hawser and bowline, dockworkers pulled the heavy rope to them and made the ship fast to the bollards, the large mushroom-shaped iron posts on the dock. The crews shouted to one another as the gangplank was maneuvered into place and then helped the passengers disembark.

A tentacle of wharves stretched away from either side of the ship. Wall-less, wood-roofed shelters were by gates and ticket booths with multicolored flags, all connecting to streets and buildings that teemed with people and horse-drawn trolleys. Three-story, box-like structures with signs announcing hotels, restaurants, and shops angled from the wharves to where avenues swept away. Bales of wool, boxes of tallow, wine casks, copper ingot stacks, and goods of every size and shape were heaped on the dock from ships being off-loaded.

Stevedores in frayed corduroys with rough, open-necked shirts sweated while they worked, and passengers walked away or toward them to board an adjacent clipper ship. Bearded men in three-piece suits with wide lapels, high-necked collars and thick bowties strolled with women wearing plump-sleeved, high-collared dresses with bustles and tight bodices in bright colors. The men wore bowlers and stovepipe hats, while the women carried shawls or held an umbrella. The less-well-to-do wore beaten hats and dungarees with their wives dressed less stylishly in plain cotton dresses.

Rebuilt after the destructive fires of past years, impressive buildings with Corinthian columns and marble facades rose majestically. Four and five stories high with iron-fenced patios that encircled the windows, these grand residences and ornate commercial structures lined the cobblestoned streets, filled the level areas, and then swept up the hills. Black wrought-iron streetlights enclosed oil-burning lamps on tall stands, and clopping horses with strolling pedestrians shared the streets.

Looking forward to their leave after months at sea, Tom and the seasoned seamen swarmed about the *Sydney* to move off the luggage, barrels, and crates. A century before huge container ships and cranes plied the oceans, ships carried cargo bundled in rope nets and crates, and the difficult and dangerous task of unloading a heavy ship could take two or more weeks. As no one knew when a ship would arrive in port, owners didn't employ full-time workers, but instead only hired laborers when they needed them for a particular job. The shipowners walked along the docks yelling, "Men along the shore!" These cries led to the name "longshoreman" for someone who loaded or unloaded a ship.

Those on the *Sydney* had a particularly difficult voyage this time when the ship had steamed around the Horn. In the decades before the Panama Canal was constructed, Cape Horn at the southernmost point of Chile and Argentina was the course taken to sail between the Atlantic and Pacific Oceans. The strong winds and large waves had nearly capsized the vessel, and the size of the huge icebergs that the ship had to dodge still stood out in Tom Whitelaw's mind.

Whitelaw was born in Irvine, a coastal town in North Ayrshire, Scotland, on August 21, 1847. Located on the Atlantic Ocean, Irvine was a major seafaring port for western Scotland and handled a large flow of goods destined for the industrialized city of Glasgow. He grew up there with his brothers, and with the closeness of the ocean, they fished, sailed, and knew the seas.

He was from a poor family, and youths didn't have the opportunities of education as they have now: Children were thrown early on upon their own resources to survive. Having a natural love for the power and beauty of the ocean, Whitelaw shipped out to sea at an early age. As a twelve-year-old lad, Tom began singing sea chanties as a "midshipmite," or apprentice seaman, when he signed onto the *Sydney* in Glasgow on its voyages to the Far East and India.

Being a young person on a ship with rough seamen was not an easy time for anyone. Stories abounded about the rites of initiation for the "newbies," who were forced to take on the most dangerous of tasks during the worst storms and endure verbal and physical abuse. Whatever happened stayed with Whitelaw, but he sailed on the *Sydney* for four years, growing up in the company of tough men and times, while also rising to the position of "able body seaman."

Whitelaw finished helping the crew move the baggage, goods, and people to the dock and joined the men on the wharf. When asked if he was going to head off with them into the city, he told them that he'd catch up later. As his term of apprenticeship had expired, Tom Whitelaw had decided to stay. He had only one quarter in his pocket.

Tom was a small man who weighed at most 125 pounds. His Scottish brogue would last his lifetime, but he was also energetic, good-natured with a strong positive outlook, and blessed with a fine intuitive mind. He strolled off on his own, as was his nature, to see and learn for himself what San Francisco and this new country was about—despite his tiny amount of funds.

❦ ❦ ❦

OVER 100,000 people resided in the San Francisco area in the 1860s, which made it the largest and most populous city on the West Coast; by comparison, New York City was eight times as large. Travel was by stagecoach and ship, since interconnecting railroads between San Francisco, neighboring Oakland, and Los Angeles had not yet been built. Cars, electric streetcars, or even cable cars were not in existence, and sending news depended on where the closest telegraph line was located. The telephone wouldn't become a reality for another fifteen years.

The region would still be remote and sparsely populated had it not been for the discovery of gold and the historic California Gold Rush. Once the news about the glittering, valuable metal was out, the population of San Francisco exploded from a sleepy town of 2,000 folks in February 1849 to a booming, lawless place of 50,000 in two years—joining other burgeoning cities and towns in Northern and Central California—and these populations increased greatly each year. Almost every immigrant who came by sea passed through this port, as did most of the goods imported from the outside world. And the rowdy city, crowded with hotels, saloons, brothels, and gambling houses, was the place to which the weary, dirty miners came to spend their hard-earned wealth. When women, families, and the law finally settled into governing San Francisco and its neighboring cities, more respectable opera houses and libraries quietly began replacing the "dens of iniquity." By the late 1850s, San Francisco had left much of its tumultuous times behind and had taken on the look of a major cosmopolitan city.

In 1861, the horrific Civil War began to rage between the states. A million Americans died or were wounded by the time it came to a merciful end four years later. Although San Franciscans enlisted and generally supported the Union cause, due to their fortunate isolationism they were spared the destruction that rained down on much of the country. The San Francisco Mint continued to coin multimillions of dollars in gold for its wealthy residents' accounts, and steamers routinely sailed through the Golden Gate with a million dollars of gold dust, bars, ingots, and coins destined for the East Coast.

The noted San Francisco historian of the times, Charles B. Turrill, wrote:

And during all of the time [of the Civil War], the wheels were revolving here at home. Ships were being built, streets improved, new and better homes were being built, and larger and more sumptuous hotels erected. Fires removed structures and better ones took their places.

After seeing San Francisco, however, Tom Whitelaw then left the city. He headed to Samuel Brannan's vineyards at Calistoga, located in the Napa Valley seventy-five miles north of San Francisco and near the city of Santa Rosa. Tom had met the owner on board the *Sydney*.

Sam Brannan was born in 1819 and lived for seventy years. He was a famous Mormon apostate, who had his hand in nearly every aspect of early California State history, and helped develop the wine and brandy industries in the upper Napa Valley. He concentrated his efforts in this valley and named its "urban" center Calistoga, hoping that his investment there would make it the California counterpart of New York's resort spa in Saratoga. Calistoga still exists today as a small town in the Northern California wine country.

Brannan had sailed to France and sent home 20,000 cuttings of French grape varietals, which was a sizable importation of European vines. When Brannan's grapevines were en route to San Francisco, he and Tom became acquainted, and the vintner had offered a job to the young seaman. After nine months of working the vineyards, however, Whitelaw regained his yearnings for the sea, left Brannan, and headed back to San Francisco.

Tom secured a position on the steamer *George S. Wright* with Western Union Telegraph Company's expedition to conduct surveys for a telegraph cable route across the Bering Sea into Asiatic Siberia. The Bering Sea covers more than three-quarters of a million square miles and is bordered on the east and northeast by Alaska, on the west by Russia's Siberia, on the south by the Alaskan Peninsula and Aleutian Islands, and on the north by the Arctic Ocean. This voyage was to discover the best route to lay a competitive telegraph cable "the long way" through the United States, across Alaska, underneath the Bering Sea, and then overland through Siberia and Russia to Europe. This region was also one of the world's richest fishing and sealing grounds.

The experiences that young Whitelaw had on board the *George S. Wright* would be very helpful in his business career. He saw the problems and inner workings of another steamer. With an inquiring mind and confident manner, he learned how ships weathered storms and needed repairs, as well as about voyages on the Bering Sea. Later in his life, he looked at the Bering Sea as another business opportunity for sealing and whaling, knowing the trade well from his early travels.

The Western Union expedition selected the best cable approaches and landings inside the protected harbors. The party recorded numerous soundings of the bottom, and the relatively moderate depths and soft beds were considered advantageous. Floating ice fields were prevalent and dangerous, however, even during the early summer months. The team leaders continued on, however, disregarding the threat of icebergs ripping apart the ship and any laid cable. "Ice flows into the Arctic Ocean—not from it," one report concluded in justifying their decision.

With the survey completed in 1865, Whitelaw returned to San Francisco and apprenticed himself to the shipwright firm of Middlemas & Boole to learn the ship-carpentering trade. One year later, he learned that the completion of the great transatlantic telegraph cable from Newfoundland to Ireland had ended Western Union's trans-Siberian dream. Its crews had by then buried 300 miles of cable under Alaska, 350 miles through Siberia, and 400 miles in the Canadian wastelands, but all had to be abandoned. The venture eventually sold the line's glass insulators to Siberian peasants to use as teacups.

Meanwhile, Sam Brannan set up a distillery and later shipped his Calistoga Cognac around the Horn to New York City. In the 1870s Brannan's economic world fell apart, and creditors eventually foreclosed upon his Calistoga estate. He lived out his years in obscurity in Southern California.

●　　●　　●

TOM WORKED hard to learn his trade at Middlemas & Boole on San Francisco Bay. He had come to love the city and its maritime ties with the sea. With names such as Clarke's Point, Vallejo, Shaw, Central, and Flint, numerous wharves jutted out into the huge cove, ensuring more than enough work for the locals on the ships that came to port. As an apprentice ship's carpenter, Whitelaw worked on the California Drydock Company's construction of the Hunters Point drydocks in southeastern San Francisco, and what is now Oakland rose across the bay from the point. Finally completed in 1868, the yard encompassed 638 acres of waterfront and the site of the first commercial drydock on the West Coast. (Once a vessel is inside the structure, pumps force the seawater from the enclosure, allowing workmen to work on the ship; after the vessel is repaired, water is forced back inside, allowing the vessel to be towed out.)

During this time, "Cappie" Whitelaw, as he later would become known to his friends, built his own sailboat, the *Put-Up-or-Shut-Up*. In the days when the nearby Hay Wharf was used to offload hay, the young men docked their boats there and raced them on the bay. A keen rivalry had developed between the lads with different dares and challenges. Although Whitelaw didn't own even a sailboat, he "put chisel and saw to work" and built a boat of his own design. Once finished, he named it in a way typical of these competitions. The men wagered as much as six dollars a race, which was a good sum when a day's wages were a quarter and this amount represented nearly one-month's wages. He did well. "Whitelaw cleaned them all up," one newspaper reported later.

When he was twenty-one years old at Middlemas & Boole, Tom was nearing the end of his apprenticeship and work on the drydocks. After the company's diver was injured, Whitelaw later said, "I, though I never had put on a diver's suit, applied for his place." Tom went to the foreman and sold himself as someone "who could do what the diver had not yet completed and do it as well." He argued that the diver couldn't do what Tom did, because the man wasn't a carpenter, and while Tom wasn't a diver, he was certainly an excellent carpenter. "Blowing weather" must have done well by him, for the little bluff he ran on the foreman worked. He was "permitted to try it," as Whitelaw subsequently relayed, and put on a diving suit for the first time.

Tom headed out that day on a steam-tug for his first wreck dive. The injured diver had been working on the underwater repair of the sunken schooner *Golden Rule,* which had collided with a steamer and quickly sank from the holes in its side. Once the tug anchored over the spot, Whitelaw eyed the gleaming bronze air-pump with its upright wheel that rested on the deck from where he would descend. A rotating drum stood nearby—also ready to be turned by the attendant or driven by a hoisting engine—to haul him back to the surface.

His crude diving outfit consisted of a canvas-and-leather diving dress, breastplates of lead weighing twenty-five pounds each on his chest and back, and heavy lead shoes. (Natural India rubber would be used later for the diving dress.) The air-line hose attached to the back of his weighted copper helmet with wire-protected glass faceplates in front and all sides for peripheral vision. A thick rope wrapped around Tom's waist and underneath his arms to haul him back.

The heavy shoes and weights were needed to counterbalance the natural buoyancy of his inflated suit and helmet. Moving underwater was very limited in this gear; however, when a diver spread his arms, the suit inflated more and he could rise some feet to float over underwater objects. A signal line was also tied to the diver's wrist to let people on top know what was going on by a series of pre-agreed, Morse-code-like tugs. Depending on the number of pulls, different messages were sent, such as "Pull me up immediately," "I'm coming up," or "Send down another diver." Since telephone (or radio) communication with divers wouldn't be possible for decades, they operated with these crude ways of communication, regardless of the storms that suddenly raged above or currents that ripped below.

Whitelaw hung his canvas haversack over one shoulder. This bag held his chisel, tools, a water compass, and all-important knife in case of trouble. He tightened the wrist straps that kept the ocean from rushing into his suit. Tom donned his helmet and, with a last word to his tender, tucked his chin inside the opening and waited for the attendant to screw on his faceplate. Inhaling several times, Whitelaw confirmed by a nod from inside the glass that life-giving air was pumping in. He made a final check and then stepped down the crude ladder into the sea. Letting go of the final rung, Tom Whitelaw entered a new world.

As Tom sank down, he kept his arms close to his body and pressed his knees together; the attendant had told him that this position forced the excess air from his suit through a valve in the helmet. The thick lead soles of his shoes kept his feet down and head up, while the breastplates steadied his descent. As Whitelaw plummeted down, the ocean took on a filtered look with decreasing light amid the tiny plankton and algae in the water.

He watched long strands of sea kelp stretching toward him and felt their bulbs pass by his legs. Seeing a large rock quickly loom up, Tom instinctively arched his body, missed the obstacle, and landed on a soft bottom. Looking around, he found dark sand kelp bobbing in the currents, irregular boulders, fish darting in schools, and tiny crabs scuttling about. Off to one side, the large shadowy hulk of the schooner loomed up, its sails and rigging moving with the currents in the surrealistic gray darkness.

Tom felt an excitement rise within at these sights. He had dived before without equipment into the ocean, but this time he could stay and study what was there. Feeling a sharp tug on his wrist, Whitelaw pulled back on his lifeline and signaled to the top that his landing had gone well. His visibility at the bottom was initially good—not a very common experience, especially at deeper depths.

Next, he had to learn how to move about in the suit. Walking on the seafloor took effort, and he needed to figure out how to manipulate the air inside his suit to rise or stay on the bottom. Whitelaw quickly learned that a diver's apparatus was not made for maneuverability: The weights were designed to bring divers down and moor them on the bottom. Visibility then lessened, the water was colder below, and the currents were noticeable. However, he headed to the *Golden Rule* after his first trial walks.

While his air bubbled out from the valve, small fish darted around in front of him. As Tom came closer, the ship's silhouette lost its shape and its hull dominated his view. He touched its slipperiness and continued around the vessel to where he discovered the gashes in its side. Feeling around the ship's holes where the first diver had worked, he quickly decided on what had to be done. After making his inspection, he moved back and tugged on his lifeline. The winch quickly hauled him back up to the surface. As the schooner had settled in relatively shallow water, Whitelaw didn't have to take time and stop at different levels to avoid the bends, the painful buildup and bubbling of nitrogen in a diver's blood, which has deadly effects. Once topside, he was elated over the solitude, adventure, and total control that he had when below.

On his next dive, Tom took a hammer and nails. The workers on top sank rough boards down to him on weighted lines. Positioning himself again by the schooner's side, he tried to hammer a plank against one small hole. He found that moving and working in the water while fully dressed in the diver's suit was difficult, especially when he had to use his tools underwater. Tom experimented and discovered how to make sharp wrist cracks with short strokes on a pre-positioned nail and drive it into the wet wood.

Although warned not to stay down longer than two hours—and risk exhaustion, mistakes, dizziness, or even unconsciousness from the buildup of carbon monoxide—he continued working on. After the tugs on his wrist insisted that Whitelaw return, he reluctantly decided to ascend. Above the ocean's surface, the only sounds heard were the wheezing of the air pump and the swish of the lifeline cutting through the seawater as Tom "told" his attendant by his short tugs to haul him up. Whitelaw would learn later the complete code of short and long tugs, whereby divers could communicate with their land partners on a variety of points.

Once back on land, the attendant screwed off his faceplate and helped him take off the lead breastplate and backplate. Whitelaw stepped out of the lead-soled shoes and finally removed his diving suit. He didn't feel tired, as he loved what he was doing and looked forward to the next day.

Although the weather was foggy, he didn't have to contend with sixty-mile-per-hour winds and harsh waves. However, even given this decent weather, working inside the Golden Gate wouldn't be an easy task. The tides flow strongly through the bay four times a day—twice surging in and twice withdrawing. The quantity of saltwater in motion each day between the high and low tides alone averaged 400 billion gallons.

The flows of tides and rivers coursing out made work difficult, and he learned that the currents underneath the sea could sweep him about just as they did on the surface. Depending on how deep a diver was, the water temperatures were chilling, despite the thick clothing and diving suit with its heavy canvas wrapping. The lack of light made visibility near impossible. The currents swept unknown objects against him, and he had to fight past his initial worries over roving sharks or octopuses hiding inside the cold, dismal darkness.

The following day the Scottish lad geared up once again. This time he felt around in the shadows and currents to accurately measure the size of the largest punctures in the *Golden Rule's* side. After he gained an idea of their shape, he signaled for the attendant to haul him back. Once on board the hovering mother ship, he drew a diagram of a patch plate and the cofferdam that needed to be constructed. This watertight, wooden compartment is built to keep out the sea when there is a large hole in a ship. The cofferdam can surround the entire vessel (if the bottom is very shallow) or, as is usually the case, it is nailed underwater to a ship's hull to cover a jagged opening. When the water is pumped from the sunken ship, these chambers hold out the seawater so the vessel can rise to the surface. Once permanent repairs are underway on land, workers dismantle the cofferdam.

With his carpentry skills, Tom knew what would work and then could precisely cut the planks and wood plates. The initial design concept and procedures were important and might involve nailing large planks or first sending in divers to work inside and shore up broken beams. It wasn't necessary that the patching be completely watertight, as steam-driven pumps could handle minor leaking. What was important was that the design worked, could be completed on time, and would hold until permanent repairs were made.

The noise from saws on hard wood, hammers on long nails, and grunts of hard labor sounded out. The patch plate was soon ready to be sent down with the attached lead weights. Whitelaw then descended and nailed the wood plate over another opening. Next, he nailed a key door and openings shut so that the pumps could remove enough seawater to give the drowned ship sufficient buoyancy to rise.

Whitelaw knew that a downed ship didn't need to have all of the ocean inside its hull drained—if that was even possible—and there were always pockets of air trapped inside compartments. Enough areas had to be made watertight, however, so that the pumps could drive out a "sufficient weight" of the sea to enable the vessel to rise by its own equilibrium. This meant divers had to work inside the ship and seal off areas, as ship designs back then didn't call for watertight compartments. Determining what needed to be done and how required an expert, and Whitelaw had to be that from the very beginning.

The braced, wooden-box cofferdam was finally readied and lowered down on its weighted line. Whitelaw guided the compartment to the large hole and then nailed it to the sides. Given his experience in ship and dock carpentry, Whitelaw felt optimistic that his design was workable. But this was the first time he had been both a diver and the lead carpenter. There are different ways to raise a ship—if it was possible at all—and Tom had selected just one approach. The question was whether this would work.

When "all that could be done was done," including shutting or sealing portholes, hatches, and doorways, the coal-driven engines fired up. As the steam built up with the engines clanging noisily, men activated the pumps that sucked the water from the sunken ship. Two six-inch canvas hoses snaked out to the surface over the mother ship's sides and quickly sprang taut when powerful jets of saltwater spewed back into the ocean. The men waited anxiously for some sign of success. Then the main mast of the sunken ship pierced the ocean's surface with the sounds of rushing water.

The vessel continued rising toward the gray sky, muddy water pouring off its trimmed sails and spars, followed by smaller masts, the raised afterdeck, forecastle, and gunnels. Rust-colored seaweed, debris, and bric-a-brac coated the vessel's spars, deck, and hull as seawater drained away in a symphony of heavy rivulet sounds. The men shouted out cheers, while the ship bobbed back and forth with the ocean's swells.

A surfboat quickly rowed out to the bouncing, unmanned vessel so that a crew could take charge. The closest man quickly pulled himself up and threw a rope ladder down to the waiting men. The ship seemed cold and forbidding, and what once had teemed with men and bustling action now was dripping mud, creaking, and smelled like rotting fish. The vessel, however, seemed to be otherwise in repairable shape.

Replacing the patches and cofferdam later with supporting ribs and planks of the same thickness, workmen completed the permanent repairs in a drydock. The men cleaned down the schooner, replaced machinery that had rusted, changed the rigging and canvas sails, and refurbished the ship for a fraction of its initial cost. *The Golden Rule* soon sailed away on another voyage.

Tom worked hard on this particular repair project. As he remarked later, "I found the hardest part of the job to be driving nails underwater. I mastered this and in three weeks had the position permanently." Tom Whitelaw was now a diving carpenter and had helped to float his first ship.

He also received a bonus of $250 on top of his usual wages of less than a dollar a day. This reward for his performance was a good amount of money, the most he had ever seen at one time. He also saw the opportunity to start a business that he could do—and did very well.

Whitelaw remarked later:

This was the turning point in my life. For when I received that bonus, I said to myself, "I'm going to be a ship salvager." I purchased a diver's suit with that money and became what was then known as a "wrecker," afterward converted to the higher-sounding term of a "ship salvor."

Tom Whitelaw became a salvor at a time when the risky crudeness of nineteenth-century wrecking clashed head-on with the complexities of salvaging the faster, larger fleets then in development. He and others would be part of this maritime history—and also experience a changing world.

CHAPTER TWO

THE WRECKER CHRONICLES

For centuries, the rugged coastlines of Europe and England—particularly Cornwall with its treacherous rocks and strong winds—were a haven for wreckers and smugglers, and these activities reached a peak in the eighteenth century. Seizing the opportunity to ease their miserable lives a little, ordinary folks and even a few clergy plundered wrecked ships to smuggle the "saved" goods with unchecked enthusiasm. When one man interrupted a Sunday service to shout that a ship had just wrecked on the nearby rocks, the vicar was said to have begged his congregation to remain seated until he could take off his cassock "so that we can all start fair." English authorities actually caught one rector possessing four casks of wine that had been looted from one wreck.

What was taken from shipwrecks and not declared was viewed by authorities as smuggling; this was equivalent to running goods into the country past customs. And millions of pounds of tea and gallons of brandy were smuggled into the country each year. Smuggling was a dangerous business, and the penalties for being caught were harsh, including heavy fines and even death. One memorial epitaph is in Talland Church and concerns the sad death of one such man, whom custom officers shot and killed in 1802:

In prime of life, most suddenly,
Sad tidings to relate;
Here view my utter destiny,
And pity my sad state.
I by a shot which rapid flew,
Was instantly struck dead.
Lord pardon the offender who
My precious blood did shed.
Grant him to rest, and forgive me
All I have done amiss;
And that I may rewarded be
With everlasting bliss.

In Cornwall, smuggling and wrecking were popular pastimes, and numerous folks sought to enhance their lives by collecting the booty from wrecks or engaging in a bit of dealing in contraband. There are two popular misconceptions about shipwrecks in Cornwall. The first is that the wreckers caused most of the wrecks by hanging lights from the cliffs at night or building bonfires as misleading beacons. They didn't have to go to these extremes because the frequent squalls, raging ocean, and deadly rocks produced a continuing string of shipwrecks. They acquired this reputation because they plundered the wrecks that came onto their coastline with such regularity.

The second mistaken belief is that the wreckers killed shipwreck survivors so they could loot what was on board. Although violence was at times a by-product of smuggling, the townsfolk were more interested in booty than they were in murder. Far more deaths occurred from drowning than from the conflict in grabbing goods.

The custom officers (or "preventive men") sent to deter this looting nonetheless did bring violence to the times. It wasn't rare for people to break into the officers' warehouses—after these officials had taken and safeguarded the cargo from both the seas and the wreckers—and take back what they felt were theirs by right. Wreckers and custom men died alike in these battles. Moreover, little was left to salvage after the wreckers left: Not only did they take away as much of the cargo as possible, but the scavengers also stripped the railings, anchors, sails, rigging, equipment, and even timbers from the vessel. Custom officers were also known to include themselves in the action when the pickings were especially good.

All sections of society seemed to think the wrecks were fair game with hundreds of people at times following a troubled ship along the coast in hopes of finding a rich score. Decades were to pass before this pastime finally became a regulated, for-profit industry. The ship and cargo would remain the property of the original owners—subject to the wrecker's agreement—and all of the salvaged articles were to be reported to England's Receiver of Wrecks and its governing rules. With the large influx of European immigrants to the United States in the decades before the mid-1800s, however, it was natural that they would take along their ways of earning a living from the sea.

❦   ❦   ❦

FROM THE VERY beginning, ships crashed onto the reefs of the Florida Keys in the New World. Vessels ripped their hulls out on the rocks or collided with others and sank; winds, tides, and downright captain error beached more. The early square-rigged merchant ships were often overloaded and difficult to control, and they did not sail well into or with the winds. Navigation charts were quite inaccurate and often failed to show the location of dangerous rocks, reefs, or currents. Reliable navigation equipment was nonexistent; more accurate weather forecasting had not yet been created; and guarding lighthouses had not been built.

The Florida Indians were the first wreckers. The Spaniards, for example, hired them to help salvage the Spanish fleet that wrecked in 1622 in the Marquesas Keys some thirty miles west of Key West, of which the *Atocha* and *Santa Margarita* are the better known galleons (discovered in 1985 by Mel Fisher with over forty tons of silver and gold valued at $450 million); the Indians spent eight years assisting the Spaniards in this salvage. Dutch mariners frequently harassed the Spanish salvagers, and it's likely the native Indians profited by working for both in their diving for the sunken gold and goods. The Bahamians also were on the hunt for shipwrecks, which meant that competing wreck claims had to be decided at Nassau, Havana, or other locations the disputing parties agreed on.

The word *wrecking* referred to the saving of crews, ships, and/or cargoes—hopefully in that order. Payment or a rich "reward" for these services was not only demanded, but unconditionally expected. When Florida became a United States territory in 1821, no federal statutes governed these practices and only the maritime Common Laws at Sea and a Bahamian Admiralty Court existed to police these activities. From the very beginnings in old England, opinions differed and arguments resounded over the morality and reasonability of wrecking—but people had to find ways to earn their living.

Wrecking, sponging, fishing, and turtling were early industries in the Florida Keys, along with farming, cigar making, salt and charcoal manufacturing, and supplying the military's needs. Of these livelihoods, wrecking and farming significantly shaped the early settling of the Upper Keys. Although nearly all of the wreckers worked as spongers, turtlers, or fishermen, or undertook other endeavors that placed them close to the scene of a wreck, the Key West fishing fleet became a centerpiece for wrecking, and this activity was a major industry in the Florida Keys through much of the nineteenth century.

During the golden age of sail, at least a hundred ships passed each day by Key West, and the waters they sailed through had some of the most treacherous reefs in this country. At least one ship wrecked each week somewhere along the Florida coast. Wreckers watched the reefs day and night from observation towers along the shoreline, some of which were over eighty-feet high. They anchored their crafts for the night, but then sailed quickly away at daylight to cruise the reefs on the lookout for distressed vessels. The fleet was not only prepared to put to sea upon receiving the first news of a disaster, but depending on the seas and storm conditions, wreckers anticipated the misfortunes of others, since they knew that coming upon the right ship could yield fortunes.

The wrecking operation was simple enough: Get aboard the distressed ship, contract with the captain for the "reward," and then salvage the cargo. When a wreck was spotted, the cry of "Wreck ashore!" echoed over the islands as men scrambled to their boats to join the race for the foundering vessel. The ever-ready fleet of some 150 small schooners and sloops then quickly sailed off in "glorious haste and hope." The waterfront would be alive with excitement while spectators crowded the wharves to eagerly await the news of the ship's name and its cargo.

This was a race to the swiftest, since the first wrecker aboard from the flotilla of boats was the one who made the contract with the bewildered skipper. He controlled the salvage operation and gained the largest share of the prize as the "master wrecker." The captain's ship could be water-logged on a reef, the seas breaking wildly over her deck, or the vessel might be stuck high and dry on a rocky shoal. She could be listing on the beach or rolling on a reef in the boiling surf miles out to sea. The crew could have hastily abandoned her, in which case the ship was considered to be a derelict with enormous salvage value—and there would be no trouble from a recalcitrant captain or the owners. Or the crew might be still aboard, either desperate to be taken off or equally fearful of the wreckers and their pirate reputation.

Regardless of winds or seas, men took chances to get their score. On a near daily occurrence, they found wrecks and made their "agreement" on how to divide the saved goods. The seamen then worked feverishly day and night to salvage the ship, hopefully before bad weather drove her far-ther onto the rocks or caused her to sink to the bottom. The wreckers saved cargo by working in ocean up to their necks or by diving into the relatively shallow seas. Since they didn't wear diving suits, the oceans raged, sharks and other predators menaced, and the watered-down cargo, whether it was sugar or guano, covered their bodies.

Wreckers used different tools and equipment in these operations. They carried heavy anchors, strong chains, long hawsers, and large fend-ers to secure their vessels in rough water. For cargo recovery, they equipped their boats with a large number of blocks, ropes, tackle, and hooks to move the large cotton bales, kegs, and other goods that might be recovered. They wielded sledgehammers, axes, and saws to cut away broken sections of the wreck, open hatches, and save people and goods.

The ship's captain could choose whomever he wanted to be the master wrecker. Other than a simple low-tide grounding, however, the selected captain usually needed help as soon as he had cut the deal. At times the agreement was being hammered out as other men jumped on board from pursing schooners. Ideally, only part of the cargo had to be removed to float the ship free at the next high tide. In practice the situations were more difficult, often requiring the assistance of other wreckers, who then divided the contracted share. The salvagers received their agreed cut later in kind or from a share of the Key West auction proceeds. The wreckers also rewarded their "agents" from their cut, such as the fishermen who first reported the shipwrecks to them. The richest cargoes of the world, whether they be fine laces, silks, wines, or silverware—in fact, everything that the commerce of the world afforded—reached Key West in this way.

One folktale was that wreckers would rig a line between two mules, hang ship lights on the rope, and walk the mules along the beach at night to give the impression that a ship was sailing by a treacherous reef. Although enforced laws didn't rule these times, there is little evidence this was the practice. Like others before them, Key West wreckers had no hesitation in taking advantage of the misfortune that befell others.

Wreckers built the town of Key West, and shipwrecks occurred everywhere. In the Upper Keys, Carysfort Reef was an especially dangerous reef, and the waters around Tavernier Key became a favorite anchorage where salvagers waited for wrecks to occur on the shoals. (In early times, the name "Carysfort" was frequently used as a generic term to include all of the reefs in the general area.)

Owing to outcries over the unchecked abuses, the Territory of Florida in 1823 passed a wrecking act. To rectify this law's limitations and to prevent shipwreck spoils within U.S. coastal limits from being spirited away to foreign ports, Congress passed the Federal Wrecking Act two years later. Among other provisions, this law mandated that all property shipwrecked in these seas had to be brought to a U.S. port of entry.

In 1828, the federal government established a superior court in Key West with maritime and admiralty jurisdiction. During these early territorial times, disputes over the ownership of a "ship in distress" or its goods could be resolved by agreement or arbitration, and this practice continued over time. The court's decision was required when an agreement couldn't be reached. It wasn't rare for a ship's owner to disagree later with the captain's contract, which may have been made under "perilous" circumstances, or with how the salvager actually worked under that understanding.

The first case tried in the Key West court concerned the *Nanna,* which had run aground on Carysfort Reef. Three salvagers anchored in deep water, lightened the ship's cargo by unloading 450 bales of cotton, and then, as the tide rose, pulled the stranded ship off the reef by their capstans (a rotating spool-shaped device used for pulling). The typical dispute arose over how much should the wreckers be awarded.

The percentage paid for salvage varied according to the circumstances; the more difficult the wreck and weather conditions, the higher the amount received. It mattered whether a dangerous gale was blowing, if the ship ran aground or became impaled on a reef, and whether the cargo could have been easily off-loaded by simply throwing it overboard. In the Nanna case, the salvaged cotton was valued at $60,000, of which the judged awarded the wreckers $10,000 for their efforts. Earlier court decisions seemed to favor the owners and underwriters, although the salvagers were always compensated and abuses still occurred.

A case that went the other way involved the Bahamian fleet. In 1855, the *Crescent City* washed ashore on the northernmost point of the Bahamian reefs. The "Black wreckers," as they were described, saved $90,000 of the cargo before the vessel broke into pieces under terrible storm conditions. The court set their salvage award at 65 percent of what they saved, or about $60,000, which was then a very good sum. After deducting the salvage award, governor's and legal consul's claims, and the auctioneer's fees, the owner and insurers were left with only $4,500, or 5 percent.

In addition to fixing compensation when no agreement could be reached, the courts applied thirteen rules governing wrecking—and most were complex. These regulations dealt with collusion, licensing, discrimination, bribery, price fixing, unreasonable charges, the rights of the master wrecker, and other areas. Judges oversaw the issuance of wrecking licenses and the wreckers' conduct under these laws. Infractions of the rules resulted in license suspensions, and if found guilty of looting, the guilty party could even lose his license to practice this trade. "Errors in judgment" resulted in fines for those mistakes, as the rule of law began to rope in the wayward practices.

In one Carysfort Reef wreck, a wrecker grabbed cargo that he didn't later turn over in Key West; he stopped instead at his home on the Keys and the goods disappeared. For this infraction, the judge denied him and his crew the entire salvage for the four vessels used in the effort and revoked his license. In another case, the salvager delayed three days before requesting needed assistance from the underwriter or other wreckers. The judge ordered his cut be reduced from "50 or 60 percent" of the saved goods to 35 percent. When a beer-laden ship was salvaged, the wreckers consumed a considerable amount of the cargo in the process. The court decided no additional fees were owed, ruling that the men had already drunk their compensation. Another time, the wreckers ate a large amount of food from the wrecked ship, and the judge deducted this amount from the salvage award.

The embezzlement of wrecked goods, voluntarily running a vessel aground under the pretense of piloting her, scheming with the captain of a wrecked ship, or "corrupting" the captain, such as by making an unlawful present or promise, were additional causes for withholding or revoking a wrecker's license. Depending on the judge and circumstances, however, these rules were either enforced or overlooked.

Wreck vessels were separately licensed along with the captain. The judge of the Admiralty Court of Key West had to be satisfied that a vessel was "reasonable to be used," sufficiently fitted, and reasonably equipped for the purpose of saving property. The judge also had to make a finding that the master was trustworthy. In 1858, forty-seven vessels averaging fifty tons and carrying eight men each held wrecking licenses. Since their income fluctuated widely depending on what was found, one-half of these boats were also used in commercial fishing.

● ● ●

DESPITE THE rules and licensing oversight, even the barrel of a gun or gleam from a knife didn't seem to deter a wrecker once he climbed aboard. One salvager calmly looked down the barrel of the captain's revolver for the entire time needed to get a salvage contract on the desired terms. They also showed little sympathy for the unfortunate captain. "The buoy was half a mile out of place!" complained one disgusted skipper to account for his bad predicament. "What do I care?" shrugged the wrecker in response. "If it hadn't been out of place, then you and I wouldn't be here."

Long ago, one anonymous "old wrecker-master" told this story:

With the great gale, a friend of mine in Cuba telegraphed me about a wreck with only a general idea of where she might be. Seven schooners took off with us, and we crossed the Gulf Stream to the Bahamas in twelve hours. It was a long search down the coastline, but we found her at last, hard and fast like a rock on a point beyond Bahama Shoal, in a smother of soapy green water churned up thick and white from the coral bottom. It was a nasty place. There wasn't any lee to protect us from the winds, and the anchor wouldn't hold in the gale that was blowing. There was nothing to do but to run to Saw Key for shelter until the sea went down. Lord, but we hated to leave her! The wreck represented hundreds of thousands of dollars to the underwriters and tens of thousands to us. She had been abandoned, too, and there was nothing to do but start and save her cargo. It was the easiest kind of salvage, but this looked as if it might not come our way.

There was more than a high sea to consider, as the Black Fleet from the Bahamas had to be taken into account. Nobody loves the Black Fleet, as they are tough customers and no friends of the Key West Wreckers. We lay in the shelter of Saw Key until we couldn't stand it any longer; then twelve of us decided to get aboard anyhow, to hold possession, and let the fleet follow. We got aboard between the seas and scrambled along the rail to the cabin, where we stayed for two days, as the waves crashed over us. With the first storm clearing, sure enough, the Black Fleet came driving along the Bahamas with a fair wind like a flock of vultures. It looked like we'd have a fight.

However, in this case the wrecker and his crew made like the crew of the ship. He got some greasy overalls from one of the cabins and donned one of the captain's hats. And the bluff worked. They stood off to the order, meek as you'd like, and sang out offers to save us, asking one-third. When the Key West fleet came by, the Black Fleet knew they had been duped and were angry. There was "half a gale of wind" blowing and the sea was running high, but when one of their bowsprits raked a mainsail of a Bahaman craft, the fight was on: knives for the Blacks and "pump-handles" for the Key Westers.

Knowing that the Blacks could get more men as backups before the Keys could get theirs in place, the master wrecker offered to split the salvage: They would work one side, while the Key Westers had the other. And it was agreed. A red-paint line was drawn down the middle and that's the way both groups worked. Although close calls and fights were always near, finally along came customs, the underwriters, and a British gunboat to arrange the landing of the cargo in Key West. Not all of the cargo arrived there, however, and it never seemed to do in a case like that. There are too many leaks on the way to port, and the Keys make good hiding places for anything from a bale of cotton to a bottle of rum. This time it was easy.

Lloyds and other marine underwriters employed representatives who were known as marine surveyors. These men quickly sailed to the wreck to represent the insurers' interest, and it was natural that surveyors and wreckers didn't trust one another. When one surveyor left the wreck for shore, he turned his head and said sarcastically to the wreck master, "Well, Jim, leave the [smoke] stacks in her until I get back." The master snorted back, "I'll guarantee nothing."

It was said that no one sailed more recklessly in their small crafts than the Key West wreckers when going after a shipwreck. They were on the scene whether the strongest gales or the worst calm prevailed. One fleet of wreckers was anchored during the "steady blows of winds for fourteen days." Another time, three schooners and their crews were lost in a bad storm. One great wind wrecked half a dozen vessels, blew the ships out of Key West Harbor, and submerged the outlying keys with four feet of breaking water. And yet the salvagers continued on.

Residents estimated that half of the wealth in early Key West days came from the wreckers. They felt that a cargo of phosphate was near worthless. Appreciating the finer things of life, these men valued much higher the bottles of ale, champagne, goods such as clothing and shoes, and general cargoes that could be consumed by the people. Steam-powered wrecking tugs weren't typically used at Key West: A steam vessel with its greater "usefulness" would have been awarded more salvage for its use, which meant there would be less to share among the various sloops that were usually around.

When a vessel became a total loss, the wreckers stripped the ship for the underwriters. Like the townspeople off Cornwall, Key Westers took everything: the anchors, chains, brass fittings, copper pipes, railings, and engines from steamers; sails, masts, rigging, ropes, and equipment from schooners. Using chisels, they even stripped away the copper sheathing from hulls.

Until the 1850s, the majority of salvage vessels off the Florida Keys were sloops, whose low drafts allowed them to maneuver alongside wrecks in very shallow reef waters. By 1860, the wreckers had traded in these boats for schooners. Although these vessels displaced more water, they had larger cargo holds to store their finds.

As for the Bahamians, who made a living diving for wreckage, the old master-wrecker observed:

> The Black divers dive without equipment. It takes about three minutes for one of them to release a sheet of copper, then up he comes to the surface, grabs a lifeline, and is hauled aboard, where he lies gasping until minutes later, he's ready to go down again. He is usually good for six hours of this work. Working on these copper sheets, warding sharks away with a chisel, and then streaking up when out of breath doesn't sound like fun to me—whoever does it.

An 1874 article in *Harper's Magazine* outlined one experience on the Keys:

A small fishing smack soon came close to us, and from it appeared a rough specimen of humanity, who said he was the master of the smack and then boarded us. He also held a wrecker's license. He was, therefore, not regarded very favorably by us, and more especially since he had been seen to come to us from the direction of the Tortugas Light [a wrecker's haven]. He came upon our deck by the starboard bulwarks, and we saw a stout, burly, red-faced, sunburned sailor, whose only clothing consisted of a Guernsey shirt, pantaloons rolled up to his knees, a slouched, weather-beaten hat, and no shoes or stockings. With some stretch of fancy, Bryon's description of the meeting of Gabriel and Satan fairly represents the cold civility that took place when the smack's skipper and our worthy captain met: "Between His darkness and His brightness, there passed a mutual glance of great politeness."

The sunburned skipper made offers of assistance, but the captain refused them, not only because the charge was high, but also—and chiefly because—our captain feared (perhaps wisely) that he might be drawn into even greater danger with the wrecker. The skipper of the smack left us, but evidently with the conviction that his opportunity would soon come.

All the crew's ingenuity and skill that could be mustered was used to try and save the ship, as the time of high tide was approaching. A kedge anchor was carried out astern, and all hands placed at the windlass [a rotating drum that can raise an anchor]. They pulled mightily on the anchor at high water to move the ship from the rocks. As was hoped, but hardly expected, the ship floated! Everyone on board—passengers and crew alike—were joyful. The sails were trimmed and all of the crew at their post, but unfortunately it was impossible to fetch by the reef. The ship grounded again, this time driven onto it even further. Everyone spent another night on board the ship.

Another day came by, but the winds rose, and the waves thumped savagely against us. The captain decided to lighten the vessel by throwing everything possible off and at high tide try to sail over the reef. Again, the wrecker came on board, and in answer to the captain's questions, gave his advice as to where to find a place of anchorage.

The heavy press of sail and a strong wind then carried the ship over the rocks, but during the passing, the reef smashed the rudder into uselessness. By trimming the sails, the captain was able to steer the schooner to the anchorage pointed out by the wrecker, but the vessel came too close. During the next night, the winds rose to half a gale and before morning, the ship again struck bottom. With its anchor dragging along the bottom, the vessel came to a rest with its stern buried in the sands of a lee shore.

With the waves whipping the ship against the beach, the wreck was driven stern-first until it became broadside upon the key. The wrecker returned with his smack that day. His opportunity had arrived. With much difficulty he succeeded in taking off all of the passengers with their luggage and landed them on Dry Tortugas Island. It was after dark when everyone landed.

According to the rules of "professional" wrecking, the voyage had now ended. Although the ship belonged to the underwriters, the wrecker who "first came" had to be "first served" as to the saved property. Although any goods, fittings, anchors, sails, or equipment saved were ostensibly for the benefit of the underwriters, they were usually as much for the wreckers. This smack captain and his crew of three fishermen controlled the entire prize. As other wreckers arrived, he decided who did what and received what in return. When the public sale of the wrecked goods took place later under the eyes of the admiralty court, the "savings" of each wrecker or association of wreckers were kept distinct from what was left for the underwriters and owners.

The cry of "Wreck ashore!" meant a loss for someone, whether of lives, cargo, or ships. The captain of the lost ship worried about his stranded vessel, lost freight, and having to hunt for another job if the wreckers failed to float or free his vessel without damage. When a vessel was lost, the salvage schooner brought the captain back to Key West, where he then sailed home as a passenger. The schooner then "lazily put to sea again, bound turtle-fishing or sponging or something, but all of the while keeping one eye out for another wreck."

● ● ●

HUMAN ERROR, compounded by unforgiving tides, currents, and storms, caused most wrecks. In late 1862, *California Nautical Magazine* published an "old salt's" reflections. He listed the errors as:

> Neglect of the leader, bad lookouts, being shorthanded, navigating by dead reckoning, neglect of tides, or ignorance of their direction, mistaking the land, collision, employment of pilots who are not seamen . . . and shaving headlands too close in rounding them with an onshore wind.

Boards of inquiry convened to investigate the causes of a particular disaster. Sometimes called the Board of Pilot Commissioners, this official inquiry had the power to point blame. Although they typically deferred to a captain's testimony—especially when terrible sea conditions were present—boards did find fault and censured, suspended, or revoked a captain's license when especially bad circumstances of neglect were present.

Weather conditions, of course, greatly contributed to these disasters. Whistling winds and ferocious ocean currents quickly captured ships and drove them onto rocks or beaches. Vessels wrecked on reefs that couldn't be seen until it was too late. Hidden by thick fog or stormy seas, coastline consisted of towering rocky cliffs, reefs, and unforgivable terrain with no harbors for safe refuge when the hurricane winds and gales howled. The winter storms that suddenly blew in caught captains unaware with their terrifying power.

Warning lighthouses would be constructed first off Florida and the East Coast. The first lighthouse built in the United States was Boston Light in 1716 at the entrance to Boston Harbor. Spaniards constructed

Florida's first coastal navigational aid earlier than that, in 1586 at St. Augustine, but the first true lighthouse was the seventy-three-foot harbor light built there in 1824. Thirty years later Alcatraz Lighthouse, the first sentinel constructed on the West Coast, shone its light onto San Francisco Bay. (It wouldn't be until the Civil War that Alcatraz would be first used as a prison.) From the late 1800s to the early 1900s, the United States constructed lighthouses at an astonishing rate up and down the West Coast. However, even with the building of these protecting sentinels, captain errors, treacherous weather, and uncharted rocks continued to claim one ship after another.

The West Coast was generally spared Florida's wrecking experience because its total population was sparse with limited shipping until the California Gold Rush. The unprecedented migration westward sparked by the rush caused a great increase in maritime commerce, as ships continually brought in prospectors, farmers, and goods, then sailed away with gold and agricultural products. The unprecedented growth in seafaring activity created a strong need in turn for salvagers and reclaiming the ever-increasing number of wrecked vessels.

On the East Coast, seamen seemed to operate under their own "law of the sea" and salvage rules. Although its wintry, rocky environment discouraged sailing around in search of wrecks, this region had its problems with wreckers. In 1860, the Board of Marine Underwriters of New York City decided to solve the problem of mounting shipwreck losses and the unorganized, amateurish state of salvage along the Atlantic seaboard. The underwriters formed the Coast Wrecking Company and placed the mustached sea captain, Israel J. Merritt of New York, as its head. Merritt's goal was to save a vessel from sinking, and if he and his crew couldn't, then he would salvage as much of the ship and its cargo as possible. He selected a black horse galloping over a field of white as the company's flag. This icon was a tribute to the agents in isolated areas who raced on horseback to the nearest telegraph station to notify the Coast Wrecking Company of a ship in distress, and these underwriter agents were later referred to as the "Pony Express of the Beaches." All of the salvage vessels that Merritt used for this company flew the symbolic black horse flag on their mastheads.

During the Civil War, Captain Merritt had raised on the Pacific Coast the large, heavily timbered *Aquila,* which also carried at the time the disassembled Union ship *Camanche.* As a monitor-class warship, the *Camanche* was built with a shallow iron hull, an overhanging ironclad "raft" deck, little superstructure, and a cylindrical gun turret. Although these ships were to operate only in sheltered coastal waters, two had already sunk in stormy weather off the East Coast while attempting ocean passages.

Wanting an ironclad ship to guard the Pacific Ocean and San Francisco Bay, the Union Navy loaded the parts of the 1,335-ton, disassembled *Camanche*—including its hull, turret plates, guns, ammunition, anchors, chains, and surfboats—on board the *Aquila.* The large sailing ship bore its heavy cargo for six months past stormy Cape Hatteras and around Cape Horn to California. However, owing to officer error, the ship berthed in 1863 directly over a rock in San Francisco Harbor. When a gale roared through the bay, the ship pounded against the rocky bottom and sank with a twenty-nine-foot-long gash along her bottom. With the *Aquila's* stern jutting from the bay at low tide, the ship lay underwater with the broken-up *Camanche.*

When a local sea captain couldn't raise the ship after trying for three weeks, the New York underwriters with $600,000 of insurance on the vessels dispatched its Coast Wrecking crew. Two months after the sinking, Israel Merritt, four "wreckers," and ten divers arrived on the scene from New York. They shipped the necessary wrecking equipment and materials overland by wagon from the East Coast. After contractors built a derrick on the wharf, the workers removed the heavy iron plates and 200 tons of "live" shot, shells, two fifteen-inch guns, and other war cargo.

Winter storms delayed the work, but the divers finished reclaiming the *Camanche's* last pieces by the following June. They patched the gash in the *Aquila's* hull. After chaining "enormous pontoons" to the hull, Merritt's workmen pumped the water from her holds and with the floats' buoyancy raised the large sailing ship. Once workmen completed the repairs and refurbishment, the *Aquila* sailed to the Atlantic Coast while the monitor's salvaged parts were being reassembled in a nearby shipyard.

Just after the Civil War ended, the *Camanche* became fully operational. Until the later arrival of a larger twin-turret monitor, this vessel was the navy's only ironclad warship stationed on the Pacific Coast. Merritt and his Coast Wrecking Company meanwhile continued their salvage work on the East Coast.

Competition inevitably developed later when William E. Chapman, a salvager in the same mold as Merritt, formed the Chapman Derrick & Wrecking Company of Brooklyn. This company specialized in lightering (shuttling goods ashore in smaller boats), hoisting, and the salvaging business, also in the flourishing port of New York City. His company acquired three large derricks that could lift smaller ships from the harbor bottom, and the ensuing rivalry between the two companies became keen, even hostile at times.

With an office in New York, Captain E. R. Lowe operated as a coastal wrecker who also gained exposure and experience during the Civil War. When the federal fleet sailed into Mobile Bay, the captains discovered the Confederate Navy had "thickly" planted explosive torpedoes (or mines) in the harbor. Since it was difficult to remove them safely, Lowe decided to drag the bottom with a hawser made of steel wire. As the cables pulled the torpedoes from their moorings, the mines exploded at a relatively safe distance. Although two tugboats were blown up during these supposedly "safe" efforts, he cleared the harbor so federal ships could attack the guarding forts.

The Union gunboat *Osage* was a single-turreted monitor used in an 1865 attack on a fort near Mobile, Alabama. After ramming into a torpedo, the ensuing explosion sent the gunboat to the bottom and Captain Lowe secretly sent in his divers. The men courageously explored the vessel's insides in full range of the artillery from the forts and shore batteries. They discovered that the blasts had "stoved in" the starboard bow and badly shattered the first bulkhead. Under the cover of darkness, they removed all of the shot and shells from the *Osage*. After the fort fell, his workmen constructed a temporary bulkhead to replace the broken one, and strong pumps forced the water from her holds. After the vessel was raised, she was fitted out and put back into service. Lowe also continued his operations after the war's end.

❦   ❦   ❦

THOMAS A. SCOTT was another notable wrecker who operated on the East Coast. Scott's lifelong love of the sea started at age fifteen, when he and a friend near his hometown traded wood for oysters and clams. Born in Snow Hill, Maryland, he shipped out as a seaman in 1852 on the schooner *John Willetts*. Within three short years he had become master and part-owner of the vessel. After a few more years Scott sold his interest in the schooner and moved his family to New Jersey, where he opened a general store. Store life wasn't for him, and two years later he earned money by salvaging the cargo from a steamer that sank near Fort Lee. He decided to earn his living by doing what he loved, and Scott went back to the sea.

Captain Scott's quick thinking and penchant for taking risks were shown when he was the master of the Off-Shore Wrecking Company's tug *Reliance*. On January 30, 1870, the Hoboken-Manhattan ferryboat *Union* was slowly crunching her way through floating ice floes in the Hudson River, her paddle wheels nearly clogged with crusted ice. The ship's decks were choked with hundreds of men, women, children, and teams of horses, congregated "near solid" against the railings and gates. An ocean tug suddenly appeared by the ship's gunnels that early morning, veered in an attempt to miss the *Union,* but instead crashed into her side. Screams and shrieks pierced the cold air, and the collision's force slashed a great V-shaped gash below the waterline while people and horses were slammed forcibly against the deck.

Weaving her way cautiously up the New Jersey coast to take on coal, the wrecking tug *Reliance* was within 200 yards of the collision. While the ocean tug reversed her engines to back away from the shattered ferryboat's wheelhouse, Captain Scott maneuvered his tug toward the stricken vessel. He ran the *Reliance's* bow along the ferry's rail, gave the command to another, and dropped "like a cat" onto the ferry's deck. Scott first ordered everyone to stand to the starboard side to right the listing craft. The increased weight on the high side gradually righted the stricken boat until she nearly regained an even keel.

Racing down into the engine room, he met the engineer halfway up the ladder and ordered him to turn around. With other crewmen, the two men dragged the mattresses from the crew's bunks, stripped away the blankets, and took whatever could be found—from racks of clothing, overalls, and cotton waste to "rags of carpet"—and crammed them into the long gash. Chilling cold water continued to rush through the rent in the ferry's side, even as the men crammed whatever they could into the space. Finally each broken plank was covered. One area continued to flood, however, and allowed "great spurts" of green water to surge through the opening. The sea poured into the ship, deluging the floors and washing down the gratings into the hold below. As Scott surveyed the scene, he knew that everything that was loose, even oily rags, had been stuffed into the slash.

He quickly ordered the men to take their coats and vests off and shove them into the gap. Each time they forced wet clothing into the opening, the water burst out from another place, like holes in the proverbial dike. Without hesitation, Captain Scott threw his own body into the gap with one arm dangling outside into the drifting ice. Although his human plug stopped the rush of water into the stricken ship, one hour passed before another tug could tow the crippled ferry back to a slip at Hoboken, New Jersey.

Scott was unconscious and barely alive due to the exposure, severe blood loss, and broken ribs that he had suffered from his actions. The water had "frozen his blood," and the surface ice had torn hunks of flesh from his exposed arm. When he regained consciousness, Captain Scott's first words were to ask if any of the babies were hurt. Five weeks passed before he regained his strength, and his arm healed to where he could even put on his coat. Scott then went back to work on the *Reliance*.

Unbeknownst to him, the Off-Shore Wrecking Company presented its bill to the ferry company for salvage, claiming that the reason for the safe return of the ship and passengers was due to the actions of its employee, Thomas Scott. The ferryboat owner refused to pay the invoice, and the wrecking company sued over its demand. The president of Off-Shore next called Scott into his office and told him, "We're going to have some trouble getting our pay for that ferry job." He handed him a lawyer-drawn affidavit that Scott was to sign.

Captain Scott refused and when the president asked why, he answered:

Because I ain't so darned mean as you be. Look at this arm. Do you think I'd got into that hellhole if it hadn't been for them women cryin' and the babies a-hollerin'? And you want them to pay for it?

Scott walked out, answered a newspaper advertisement the following day, and within one week took charge of the construction work at Race Rock Lighthouse off the west end of Fishers Island in Long Island Sound. He moved his family to New London, Connecticut, so that they could be closer to him during this time. Seven years later in 1878, the long and seemingly impossible construction of this lighthouse was finally completed, and Scott stayed in New London to start his wrecking operations.

CHAPTER THREE

SAN FRANCISCO BAY TIMES

W ith his trademark focus and persistence, once Tom Whitelaw made his decision to be a salvor and run his own salvage business, he directed all of his energies toward this goal. His decision to make San Francisco his home base was easy, not only because he felt comfortable there, but work was plentiful with the expanding port activities.

When gold was discovered, the hulk of an old iron steamer, the *James K. Polk*, was beached at the foot of the bluff near Clarke's Point at the bottom of Telegraph Hill and used as the first, prime passenger landing point. A substantial wharf that was 750 feet long and 60 feet wide was erected later so that deep-water ships could dock. Other wharves followed, from the lower ends of Broadway and Clay streets, as well as other dirt ways that became streets.

In the first year of the gold rush, the captains and crews of hundreds of ships beached and abandoned them in the tidal flats of the Yerba Buena cove as they joined their passengers in racing away to search for the fabled fields of gold. A blanketing forest of masts rose from these ghost fleets of forgotten vessels that eventually filled the inlet. Numerous ships ran aground and later became parts of the city.

Named for the Central Wharf in Boston, the great Central Wharf in San Francisco was built in 1849 at the end of where Commercial Street now runs. Two years later, this dock had "ten times" more business than it could handle, and numerous new wharves were built into the bay to handle the huge inflow of shipping. They had names associated with the streets that ended there: Market, Sacramento, Washington, California, Clay, Jackson, and the Pacific Street wharves, some of which changed names and routes over the years. The numerous wharves along the northern waterfront would eventually disappear with the building of the San Francisco seawall, the land filling, and modern piers that came much later.

Two docks of notice then projected out from the foot of Taylor Street: McMahon's Wharf and the larger Meiggs Wharf. They had T- and L-shaped extensions, respectively, the former being a landing for wood and charcoal, while the 2000-foot Meiggs Wharf later became the landing for the Sausalito Ferry from Marin County.

Henry Meiggs was one of the biggest hustlers in San Francisco during the early 1850s and a pioneer promoter of his day. He built a road around the base of Telegraph Hill to Clarke's Point on the north shore, where he had invested large sums of money in the real estate. Meiggs constructed his wharf from what was the foot of Powell Street, named it after himself, graded the area, extended the streets, and started a real estate boom. However, he overspeculated in his ventures, sold forged notes, and was forced to flee to Chile in 1855 to avoid prosecution. Three years later, he started building a railroad across the Chilean coastal range; before his death in Lima, Peru, the irrepressible Meiggs had caused the building of much of the railroad track in Peru.

San Francisco was then a wharf city of wooden planks and structures always at risk from devastating fires. One-half of the early city was built on trembling wharves, as the residents didn't at first appreciate the scrub-filled, sandy hills surrounding them with their "few abodes and scattered tents." When the early docks and wobbly buildings fell into the bay, the waterfront was a jumble of abandoned ships and rickety piers. Looking for solid buildings and houses, contractors built new structures when they expanded onto the surrounding hills.

The U.S. economy was in boom times in the later 1860s due to the massive reconstruction efforts underway after the Civil War's end and the construction of the ever-expanding spider webs of railroad-track networks in the Midwest and East Coast. Adequate roadways for cars and trucks were decades away, however, and railroad tracks were basically nonexistent on the West Coast (although this situation would change). Horse-drawn wagons were limited in their ability to move people and goods.

Since many towns and cities were built by rivers and bays, boats were the prime movers of commerce. These vessels carried most of the food, mail, and even household needs, and ships sailed back and forth between countries on the Pacific and Atlantic with more goods and passengers. Seamen were the truckers of the nineteenth century, and as the maritime industries abounded, so did the ever-increasing needs for the salvors' services.

At the age of twenty-one in 1868, Whitelaw became a U.S. naturalized citizen with the name of "Thomas Patrick Henry Whitelaw." His grandson, Kenneth, later observed:

> His middle name of "Patrick Henry" was different. [Patrick Henry was a prominent figure in the Revolutionary War and remembered primarily for his "Give me liberty or give me death" speech. The name was well known, since this history was still fresh in people's minds.] He selected his middle name, because he just liked it and thought it would integrate him into America. People would be curious when they heard it. When someone asked him what the "P. H." stood for, he could just tell them.

Whitelaw had made his decision to be part of this country and its growth. Without the capital to buy steam wreckers and cranes or to hire crews to work on refloating vessels, he first worked as a diver for hire. Leaving Middlemas & Boole that same year, Tom hired onto the crews that worked on salvaging ships. He parlayed the first two years of those efforts into buying, exchanging, and trading services to buy the parts of wrecked ships.

He had an eye for what was salvageable and usable. Vessels needed constant maintenance, not to mention the repairs needed after windstorms had shredded lines, rigging, spars, and sails. Ships lost anchors, masts, surfboats, hawsers, booms, and capstans (anchor winches). Steam engines continually needed parts, brass fittings and railings wore away, and steering wheels had to be replaced. Whitelaw started up his used-parts business for ships, just as later entrepreneurs saw the same need with cars. His timing couldn't have been better.

Dating back to his youth, Whitelaw had a continuing fascination with the beauty, lure, and spirituality—even the ever-present danger—of the sea. This allure carried to his death. Working long and hard hours, he built up his business and marine inventory by diving, hiring others to work with him, and bidding on small wrecked fishing boats and schooners for the salvage rights. He plowed back every cent he earned into iron boilers, chambers, valves, compressors, pumps, and whatever else had resale value. His rented warehouse and office became crammed with the parts of ships and scrap.

About this same time, a "pretty young lass" from a seafaring family left Ayrshire, Scotland, and immigrated to the United States. Fifteen-year-old Miss Elizabeth Ryce arrived in 1867 with her family in San Francisco. Tom met her through his friends and get-togethers of the Scottish families in the area. Under the protective eyes of her parents, Tom soon was spending his free time with Elizabeth. They fell in love. Three years later, Elizabeth became a naturalized citizen, and the couple married that year when Tom was confident that his business would flourish and he could support a family.

The U.S. Census for that year listed Thomas P. H. Whitelaw, age twenty-two, and his bride Elizabeth, eighteen, as living in the "9th Ward, San Francisco" with James Whitelaw, age twenty-one, all from Scotland. James and Tom noted that they were "junk dealers" who bought and resold what was salvaged from wrecks. James was more than likely Tom's brother, and it is believed that he returned later to Scotland. While Tom's marine operations grew, so did his family. His first son, Thomas Andrew, was born in 1871, and daughter, Daisy, two years later. Tom and Elizabeth's union bore four children, two of whom survived—Thomas A. and Margaret Elizabeth (Daisy).

In an early picture of the family, Tom and Elizabeth are holding their two infant children, Thomas A. and Daisy. Mrs. Whitelaw is dressed in a

Scottish-plaid front, flowing dark dress, while he wears a dark suit, white shirt, and bow tie. In this early portrait, she is a petite, slender woman and shorter than her five-foot-three-inch husband. She appears thin-lipped with bright sparkling eyes, a mischievous smile, sunny disposition, and ash blonde hair in tight curls (that would darken in later years). Whitelaw is thin and wiry and exudes strength. He has a serious and determined look, blue eyes, a luxuriant trimmed beard and mustache, and a thick, full head of hair combed back on the sides.

At his warehouse, Tom continued to trade, buy, and sell used-ship parts—from capstans and anchors to sails and steam engines—while he led divers down to patch up sunken ships. One of his noted ventures was with the steamer *Costa Rica*. In September 1873, the vessel struck the rocks at Point Diablo, north of the Golden Gate, which protruded 600 feet into the ocean from the Marin Headlands, and sank on the shoals. The ocean was calm with no wind, but the ship had steamed into dense fog. The captain was listening closely for the warning "fog-whistle," but he heard nothing when the "flood tide" washed in and suddenly grounded his ship. The skipper later was found not to be at fault, since the foghorn had been silent for "some days" due to the lighthouse running out of the freshwater needed to run its warning whistle.

The passengers left by lifeboat. The first boat drifted out to sea, however, with the ebb tide and disappeared. Another boat spilled its occupants into the water when the davits—the arms that hold the lifeboat to the ship—broke as it was being lowered. Crew members from the remaining lifeboats plucked up these scared, wet passengers, and a rescue vessel finally picked up everyone, including those from the first lifeboat. The first salvage order of business was off-loading the 4,100 kegs of sugar, 100 barrels of molasses, and 1,200 "green" hides, along with bags of coffee, "bunches" of bananas, casks of port wine, rice, peanuts, and other goods.

Whitelaw then led the divers and carpenters in building and inserting the wooden plugs and patches that temporarily closed one gaping hole and several large leaks. Hawsers connected three tugs to one another, with a fourth tug off to one side, and the combined strength of these four tugs then slowly hauled the *Costa Rica* off the rocks.

After the successful work of dragging the steamer from "her rocky bed," a tug slowly towed her to the dry docks at Hunter's Point—the same facilities that Whitelaw had helped to construct. Before opening the heavy floodgates, workers placed a "vast" number of supporting blocks in position to support the *Costa Rica*. Others threw hawsers across the dock, and then the bay's waters were "permitted" to flow into a boat basin that held millions of gallons of water. Starting the operation at high tide, nearly 5 million gallons of seawater were pumped or flowed in, which brought the water level to a height of twenty-six feet above the concrete floor. The ropes were attached to the ship, the donkey steam engines started, the tugs pushed, and the capstans rotated to slowly bring the *Costa Rica* into her dock. Once the ship was inside, workers closed the floodgates.

When dockworkers positioned the vessel over the blocks, the large steam-engine-driven pumps again chugged into operation, and the water slowly began receding from the dry dock. "Quite a number of people," according to the newspapers, were staring "with interest" at what was going on. In a short two hours, only three feet of water remained inside the dock and the ship was settling on its supports.

When the facility was dry, workers inspected the hull and the plugged "ragged hole" that was located near the keel about midship. Showing the destructive effects of the grounding, the propeller flanges were sheered off, indented plates and broken rivets ran for forty feet on the starboard side, and hull plates had given way on the port side. When the temporary plugs were "drawn out," a heavy volume of water noisily gushed from the holes onto the concrete. Workmen then completed the repairs in mere weeks, and the *Costa Rica* soon steamed away on another voyage.

As he accumulated capital, Whitelaw leased a wreck vessel with an eye toward eventually buying his own. He was at the point where he could undertake a large recovery operation with a known steamship operator. It would be a step up from his underwater diving jobs and work on sunken feluccas (Mediterranean-style, triangular-sailed fishing boats), scow-schooners (flat-bottomed sailing vessels), and other smaller craft.

Salvagers now entered into legally enforced agreements to refloat a distressed ship. If the vessel couldn't be saved, then they could buy the wreck for the salvage rights. When a ship was in an unsalvageable condition, the owners or underwriters sold the derelict on the spot for cash. Whitelaw saw this arrangement as a "win, win" situation: If he bought the rights to the wreck, he could own an operational vessel with a successful recovery. If the damage was too great to refloat the ship, then he salvaged what he could and resold the parts.

In his marine yard, he pulled apart ships that he had purchased and reclaimed to sell piecemeal. Steam engines, boilers, condensers, and other parts were seen as being as valuable as the masts, spars, and rigging. When these items were recycled into another ship under construction or repair, Whitelaw prospered as he bid for sunken ships at a set fee and sold the pieces for more.

Because of Whitelaw's solid reputation for good, honest work, the venerable Pacific Mail Steamship Company called upon him in 1878 to refloat the SS *Constitution*. This high-profiled and well-capitalized company was an important mover of goods and people along the West Coast and transpacific routes. Eleven years before, the company had launched the first regularly scheduled steamship service between San Francisco, Hong Kong, and Yokohama, with extended service to Shanghai, leading to an influx of Japanese and Chinese immigrants. Pacific Mail ran as many as twenty-three large steamships at once; for the company to use the services of Whitelaw on a big vessel was significant and indicated his standing.

The *Constitution* was a large, 3,575-ton side-wheel steamer. Built in New York in 1861 at a cost of nearly $1 million, she was the largest wooden steamer ever built at the time. This paddle-wheeler was first used to transport troops to the South during the Civil War. After later service in the Panama trade, her owners brought the ship to the West Coast. There was not enough business then for a vessel of this size to operate profitably, however, so the ship had sporadic use before being commissioned for this run to Victoria, British Columbia, and back.

The *Constitution* carried a half-million dollars in gold bullion (worth multimillions in today's dollars), along with its passengers and cargo. "Some sixty men, several ladies, and children" were on board with a twenty-four-man crew. The apparent spontaneous combustion of coal in bunkers underneath the ship's two steam boilers had caused the fires to break out. The crew discovered the blaze fifty miles outside the Golden Gate entrance. The alarm was immediately sounded, and the ship's fire brigade quickly trained its hoses onto the flames. Despite their hard work, the men were not successful. The intense heat and sickening smoke from a burning cargo of hops forced the passengers to the deck.

San Francisco was the headquarters for the Pacific Mail Steamship Company, and it instantly assumed control of the rescue and salvage operations after receiving the disaster news. The company quickly dispatched fireboats, lighters, and tugs to meet the oncoming *Constitution*. Engulfed in flames, the ship steamed slowly and erratically into San Francisco Harbor. Three tugs "took hold" and towed the side-wheeler around North Point, along the waterfront, and toward the mudflats at the Potrero ship-yards in Mission Bay.

As the word spread about the disaster, thousands of spectators raced to the wharves and overlooking hills to watch the spectacle of the burn-ing vessel. With high flames leaping to the sky and dense plumes of smoke billowing from every opening of the ship, the trapped, frightened passengers huddled together on the upper deck. A veritable "small fleet" of harbor craft hovered around the crackling, fiery *Constitution*—"the scene exciting and animated in the extreme"—while the small tugs slowly pulled the vessel by at half-speed.

With spasms of flames reaching the upper deck, the captain spun the steering wheel around to beach the steamer on the mudflats. The tide was high. A steam-tug raced alongside the stricken ship and positioned itself by the deck. Passengers climbed down, jumped, or were lowered to the awaiting tug. Meanwhile, fire tugs directed heavy streams of seawater onto the vessel to try and squelch the flames. With salt sprays drenching men and boats, a lighter chugged aside the smoking hull with water draining off its deck. Its wet crew leaped on board and began to remove everything of value that was movable, ranging from bedding and furni-ture to pantry items and kitchen equipment.

The captain ordered his remaining men to cut a large hole through the hull, which allowed the fire tugs to direct heavy volumes of water directly into the ship's insides. But nothing seemed to stop the flames. The skip-per next told his carpenter to scuttle the steamer by boring large holes below the waterline by the stern. Within a few hours, the ship sank to her railings from the gaping holes and was "pretty well cut up, fore and aft." Due to the vessel's position when settling into the ocean, security guards weren't able to reach the gold coins and bars.

The Pacific Mail company quickly contracted with Captain Whitelaw to raise the *Constitution*. After extinguishing the last of the smoldering embers, Whitelaw's men had to make the openings watertight and ready the ship for refloating. Because the vessel was so deeply embedded in the mud, patching could not be done from the outside. His crews had to "stop up" the ports, valves, and holes from inside, and due to the construction of the vessel's holds, passageways, and compartments, the effort was more difficult than anyone had anticipated. Divers needed to measure and attach planks or drive in plugs from small hallways in brackish water with no light—but they succeeded. Meanwhile, other crews removed the ship's cargo of Wellington coal, hops, and hides, all of which were "pretty well" insured.

Pumping the ship out and setting her afloat took more days. Patches and plugs didn't hold, and after more repairs, the pumping would start anew. Little by little, however, the large vessel rose from the bottom to where it could be towed away. One and one-half weeks after taking on the assignment, Captain Whitelaw delivered the salvaged ship to the dry docks for permanent repairs. Her valuable cargo of gold bullion was still safe, and "every cent" was there when the *Constitution* docked. He had personally guarded the treasure during the last days of the ship's raising and didn't sleep "a wink, day or night." Whitelaw commented afterward:

> I'll never forget that 'un. For five days and nights, I guarded that bullion, without one wink of sleep, mind you. When I got home, I slept thirty hours at a stretch to make up for it.

As one newspaper reported: "Being without money or influence, he began in a small way in 1868, but proving his adaptability by his successes he rapidly gained credit and position, and with his well-equipped plant entered the top rank, soon outstripping all competitors."

❀   ❀   ❀

ON MAY 10, 1869, the ceremonial driving of the golden railroad spike at Promontory Point, Utah, announced to the nation that California's Central Pacific line had joined the track built by the Union Pacific. The East Coast was now connected to the West. The Central Pacific started east from Sacramento, California, while the Union Pacific commenced building the track from Omaha, Nebraska, and the entire line traveled nearly 1,800 miles. Although initially only one train ran weekly from the east and another from the west, ship tonnage through San Francisco dropped in the next two years. The opening of the transcontinental railroad at first halted harbor development and the building of the seawall, but construction was restarted when it became evident that railroads could connect to the ports and increase business.

Sweeping north and south from the Golden Gate, San Francisco Bay was enormous. Protected by a peninsula, the enclosed waters swept southward from San Francisco to the growing towns of San Mateo and Redwood City. Oakland was eight miles directly across from San Francisco on the bay's far side, with the cities of Hayward and Fremont farther below on its southeasterly outline. San Jose was nestled inland at the bay's end.

The Marin Headlands, or Marin Peninsula, enclosed the northern part of the bay with the cities of San Rafael and Richmond on opposite sides. The waterway stretched even farther into another inland cove, called San Pablo Bay, where the flows from the Sacramento, San Joaquin, and Napa rivers eventually came. Draining almost one-half of the land area of California, the group of interconnected bays—often referred to as the San Francisco Bay—encompasses a staggering 1,600 square miles.

The West Coast—especially San Francisco and Oakland Bay—teemed with ships of all sizes and shapes. Stately square-riggers unloaded cargoes of coal and took away mountains of grain on the docks. With the large numbers of horses pulling carriages and cable cars, hauling wagons, and being ridden, vessels continually brought in shiploads of hay, off-loaded appropriately enough at the Hay Wharf. Steam schooners, iron-hulled steamers, side-wheelers, and large oceangoing ships carried passengers and cargoes of lumber, sugar, ores, and all types of goods to, from, up, and down the West Coast. Everything from coal and cement to dresses, farm tools, and even railroad cars was transported this way.

River steamboats, schooners, bay freighters, and launches based in San Francisco sailed the numerous connecting rivers—such as the San Joaquin, Sacramento, Napa, and Petaluma Creek—to interior towns and cities on their banks. Like Portland, Vancouver (Washington), and other urban areas reached from the Columbia River's mouth, the large inland cities of Stockton and Sacramento had thriving ports that connected with San Francisco's waterways and were eventually used by oceangoing steamers. (Stockton's port would not officially open until a few years before World War II.)

When the whaling grounds on the East Coast and Atlantic Ocean declined, San Francisco became the base for America's whaling fleet. With railroads connecting both coasts, trains could transport the whale oil and baleen (whale bone) to markets back east while the ships stayed on the West Coast for years. By the late 1870s, San Francisco was the whaling capital of the United States.

Surplus U.S. wheat production in the 1880s created a sizable export opportunity for the West Coast, which continued into the early 1900s. Nearly two-thirds of the ships—primarily square-riggers—came from Great Britain. These vessels sailed into the bay with holds filled with coal or manufactured goods that were replaced with 100-pound sacks of wheat. Many of the granite cobblestones that once lined San Francisco's streets came as the ballast on these ships. Meanwhile, the thick sprawl of redwood and Douglas fir throughout the Pacific Coast brought about ship construction and a strong export trade in lumber.

Following an era of high prices and business activity after the Civil War, a severe financial depression in 1873 had cut across the country. The overbuilding of railroad networks, a decrease in the nation's money supply, and the failure of large investment firms such as Jay Cooke and Company brought the U.S. economy to near collapse. One-quarter of the nation's railroads went out of business, and 18,000 companies failed over two years, as unemployment reached 14 percent by 1876. The value of U.S. bonds plummeted, people's savings were exhausted, and many banks went under.

The tensions between the country's workers and employing companies lingered on well after the depression finally lifted in 1879. Some years passed before businesses regained past sizes and employment levels. However, the West Coast, which was less dependent on eastern money and railways with its growth in shipping, was somewhat spared; in fact, T. P. H. Whitelaw prospered as demand increased for his services.

⚜ ⚜ ⚜

WHITELAW NOT only proved adept at salvaging vessels, he also created different maritime endeavors that included his own steamship line. He contracted for the building of the steamer *Continental* and placed it on monthly runs from San Francisco Bay to Port Kenyon, located inland on the Salt River and two-thirds up the coast of Northern California toward Oregon. The Salt River is a tributary of the Eel River, which was also navigable, but from the Pacific Ocean. Located also on the Salt River, the city of Ferndale was an important transportation center, the largest city and inland port in Humboldt County above San Francisco, and a center for dairy products.

Whitelaw's *Continental* carried mail, passengers, and cargo between San Francisco and these ports, which was soon followed by other ships making regular runs to Ferndale and Port Kenyon. (Due to different natural and man-made causes, the shipping channel at Port Kenyon shrank over time from being 200 feet wide with a depth of 15 feet to its present-day width of 20 feet and depth of just 3 feet.)

When the *Continental* worked its way over the Eel River bar in 1877 on one trip, her main steam pipe exploded, leaving the steamer at the mercy of the waves. The wreck finally grounded two miles from the entrance to the Eel River and became a total loss. Whitelaw then placed the steamer *Alex Duncan* on the route. Its cargo hold was large, as on June 4, 1878, the ship's manifest showed it was carrying to San Francisco 35,000 board feet of spruce lumber, 897 sacks of oats, 138 kegs of butter, 291 sacks of peas, along with sacks of wheat, bales of wool, boxes of eggs and butter, dried hides, and packages of calf skins.

Two weeks later on a Sunday afternoon, the *Alex Duncan* left a pickup point on the Salt River with one hour left before the prevailing high tides swept in. This gave the captain ample time to reach the Eel River entrance that led to the Pacific. Due to the pilot's error, the ship didn't make the turn and steamed straight into the south spit. The *Alex Duncan* had little difficulty in backing from the sands.

When the vessel reversed itself into the channel, however, large breakers broke broadside over the ship and drove her back onto land about fifty yards from the entrance. The ship was left high on the beach at low tide. Workmen safely off-loaded the cargo onto land, and the good news was that the steamer's structure was undamaged. With the help of a local resident, the vessel was floated off the beach when the tides shifted. But the career of the *Alex Duncan* on this route had come to an end.

After this experience, the "energetic Mr. Whitelaw" went to work and designed a vessel specifically for the Port Kenyon voyage. As one critic wrote in the *Ferndale Enterprise:* "He probably had many sleepless nights modeling that wonderful steamer, and as it turned out, figuring and summing up the profits that he could pull from the pockets of Eel River valley farmers." The writer apparently had shipped produce on the vessels that the business-oriented Whitelaw placed on this route.

While Whitelaw & Company put another ship in service to meet the area's needs, he commissioned the building of the steamer *Thomas A. Whitelaw.* Named after his son, the ship was built during the summer of 1878 in San Francisco. Although he had the Eel River trade in mind, Whitelaw designed in flexibility for other uses. Constructed at a cost of $40,000, she was a "staunch vessel," a little large for the Eel River trade, and had two decks with accommodations for twenty-six first-class passengers. The ship was 136 feet long, 26 feet wide, with a depth of just over 13 feet, and could carry 400 tons.

In keeping with the industry's practices, T. P. H. brought in minority partners. He owned a 13/16th interest in the *Thomas A. Whitelaw* while two others, the first officer and chief engineer, owned the remaining fractional interest. The steamer made her first trip from San Francisco to Port Kenyon in twenty-six hours running time, which included a seven-hour stopover along the way.

Whitelaw traveled to Port Kenyon to make the necessary arrangements for the "rapid transportation" via the *Whitelaw* of all the produce raised in the Eel River Valley. He arranged for barges to be built that were placed along the river so that farmers could have their products ferried to the port. A smaller steamer—36 feet long and 8 feet wide—towed the barges with produce to the Port Kenyon warehouses. From there, the *Whitelaw* hauled everything to San Francisco.

During the fall of 1878, Whitelaw & Company cleared $10,000 from the steamer's services—an excellent return on his $40,000 ship investment. Captain Whitelaw, as he was now being called, had to move the *Thomas A. Whitelaw* to the Pacific Northwest on a "contractual matter." When he pulled the *Whitelaw* away, some farmers complained the replacement ship didn't make Port Kenyon, but steamed instead to another location. This delay cost them money due to deteriorating produce and the need to keep feeding their cattle and sheep. When he announced six months later that the steamer would resume its regular trips to Port Kenyon, the *Ferndale Enterprise* printed the announcement along with articles critical of the holdup problems.

Although Whitelaw was a shrewd businessman, salvaging and wrecking was still his forte. This was a rough-and-tumble business facing terrible conditions on a dangerous sea. When vessels were sailing or steaming to a wreck, storms would suddenly sweep in. The enveloping sky inevitably became cold and wet with a light-gray horizon and a deep, menacing-gray overhead ceiling. It wasn't rare for hail to suddenly clatter down on the wooden decks, especially during winter months and on the northern coastlines into Oregon. The wrecker vessel would surge high toward the sky in the rolling swells. Crashing, roaring waves pummeled the silhouetted wreck ahead with rooster-tail plumes of ocean. A carpet of violent grays, dark greens, and dirty foam swirled around the bleak rocks that imprisoned the impaled ship. Frightening winds shrilled to chill teeth and numb ears, as the low freight-car-train rumbles of crashing surf and sharp smacks echoed back from the agitated surf on a seething reef. The overpowering pungent smell of salt air gave the feeling that something very bad had happened—or would soon occur.

If the hail and rain passed, the sun might show its presence through the overcast skies and unveil enveloping layers of different hues from the ocean, sky, and cloud cover. At the horizon, a light-tinged blue-gray sky—with its dark cloud cover hanging like a shroud over the small flickers of light—could appear. The sea would be littered with foamy water from rolling waves that continually smashed with total abandon into both the stricken ship and would-be rescuer.

Captain Whitelaw's crews were hardened men who hunkered down against the elements. Seafarers were rough, their captains tough by necessity, and discipline for infractions swift. Whitelaw was as strong as steel inside. The short Scot walked determinedly around his wrecker, able to do whatever task was needed and showing his crude, uneducated men what had to be done. His men were tough and ready, but Whitelaw was forged with what a leader needed: eternal confidence, strong common sense, and the innate ability to lead others. He was one with these tough men. In his chosen trade, death and destruction existed side by side with life and renewal. As men and ships died, others lived.

Ship salvaging was not a calling for the weak of heart.

CHAPTER FOUR

THE TRAGEDY OF MERRITT'S CIRCASSIAN

I n November 1876, the iron-hulled *Circassian* set sail from Liverpool, England, bound across the wintry Atlantic for New York City. The vessel carried 1,400 tons of industrial freight with tons of bricks, caustic soda drums, and casks of soda ash that was insured for $90,000—but would be worth million of dollars today. She was a sturdy ship that was 1,538 tons, 242 feet long, with a 39-foot beam and a 22-foot draft. The *Circassian* had three iron masts and carried full sail. Including the captain and three apprentices, her crew numbered thirty-five men, and the ship's master was an able young Welshman, Captain Richard Williams.

Three weeks from port, the *Circassian* was riding a lull between gales when a crewman spotted a smaller vessel foundering in the waves. The storms had battered the *Heath Park,* an English bark, or type of three-masted sail ship, bound from Perth Amboy, New Jersey, to London with a cargo of slate. Captain Williams quickly changed his course to render aid. Seeing the massive ship approach, the bark's captain and eleven crewmen left their battered ship, rowed over in two lifeboats, and were soon safely on board.

Another bitterly cold storm with black skies swept in and caused more heavy seas with wind blasts that froze the *Circassian*'s deck and rigging in sheets of ice. While the ship labored westward toward its destination, the savage weather put the vessel behind its schedule. On Monday, December 11, Williams ordered his crew to set the sails full to make up the lost time. The ship was off the Long Island coast when evening darkness blanketed the ship and it again encountered heavy seas, freezing temperatures, gale winds, sleet, and snow. The visibility was so bad that the lookout saw less than one ship length ahead.

Shock waves and metallic yawns reverberated throughout the *Circassian* as the continuing heavy swells and breakers slammed into, rolled, and threw the ship about. Even seasoned crew members became seasick. As the ship skidded or thudded from the strike of a large wave, unsecured chairs, tables, and benches in the mess and quarters shifted back and forth in dangerous slides. Any loose items, such as personal belongings or dishes, were in constant motion, and concerns heightened over what was happening inside the holds. The captain sent seamen to investigate, but it was difficult with the ship's careening to navigate through the narrow hatches and maneuver down the steep ladders. When crewmembers were able to peer into the darkened, cavernous areas, they heard the eerie, unsettling sounds of casks and drums sliding around. The constant ocean "thumping" had forced spurts of seawater through the ship's seams, and the sloshing of water in hallways and holds was troubling, especially with the constant pounding from the outside madness.

A local pilot, Captain Sullivan, had scrambled aboard the ship before the gale's full fury howled in. Regardless of place or port, the pilot's responsibility was to guide a vessel as it sailed through unfamiliar waters and outline the best course to the port and the ship's dock. Sullivan searched unsuccessfully in the freezing gloom for known landmarks and any signs of shore. When he couldn't tell where the *Circassian* was, he went below deck to warm himself until the weather cleared with better visibility. Sullivan thought then that the ship was thirty miles from land, but Captain Williams became worried when the northeast gale worsened. The winds were blowing toward the coast.

The gale raged on with terrible power, blasting the crest of waves into shotgun sprays that splattered over the *Circassian*. The stinging sheets shattered icicles on the ship's rigging, sails, and gunnels, with others quickly forming in their place. A blind rogue wave suddenly rose up and smashed into the bridge from starboard with tons of ocean that engulfed the ship. It lurched to port, careened dangerously over, and seemingly touched another wave crest, only to pull back at the last moment and skid into a valley of blackness. Not knowing where they were in conditions like this caused crewmen to stare nervously ahead from their bunks or at closed portholes. Only the lookout stayed on deck, and replacement watches substituted much sooner than usual.

At 10:30 P.M., Sullivan returned to deck. He tried to venture outside, but the blasts of wind forced him back to the bridge, where he and Williams anxiously peered out into the darkness, the oil lamps giving off surrealistic shades of black and white. The pilot still couldn't find any identifiable landmarks. He became as worried as Williams over the gale winds now blowing them toward the dangerous Long Island shore.

Sullivan finally shouted out that they needed to quickly take soundings to see how deep the water was and where the *Circassian* was in proximity to land. Captain Williams yelled out the order, and crewmen ventured out onto the deck, "altered" the sails, and prepared to throw out a leaded line. The large ship slowly turned windward while two crew members worked the rope over to a gunnel.

But they were too late. Their worst fears suddenly became reality when the ship struck bottom and slammed abruptly to a full stop. Ice shattered down onto the deck, and the sails whipped out of control. A small sail gave way with a rending sound, and the ship listed to one side when one large wave crashed down the bow to nearly wash a man overboard.

Dressed in their oilskin coats, the crew scrambled onto the deck. Williams yelled over the screaming winds to pull down the jib (a rigged, triangular sail). Worried that the sails would twist, he ordered the men to pull the ropes tight. "Head the sails," he shouted, followed by "Brace all yards to starboard."

These attempts to wrench the ship from the bar and head back to sea didn't work. When the huge waves continued to thud into the vessel with towering, freezing sprays of seawater, the captain gave the order to throw cargo overboard in the hopes of lightening it. The crew formed a line and tried to work the casks and drums to the decks. They would need to rig block-and-tackle when the ship proved to be too unstable, the drums too heavy, and the decks slippery.

Although the seas seemed too savage to allow lifesaving attempts from land, crewmen still shot distress flares that arced into the depressing blackness. One after another, flare guns were loaded and shot upward. However, no answer was seen or heard. No one knew how long it was until one crew member shouted out that he could see a light in the sky. Turning in that direction, the seamen saw an answering red flare, its flickering light dimming before finally disappearing. Straining to see through the pelting snow and sleet, they made out the faint line of a blue flare now shooting up through the darkness. The men cheered, knowing this meant that help was at hand and close enough to see the ship's signals.

The harsh weather made it nearly impossible to jettison the cargo, and this task was soon abandoned: One hour had already elapsed before the crew was able to rig the tackle and remove one cask of soda ash with a bale of rags. Since the ship was firmly grounded, the men could only hope that the promised rescue would soon come. In the gloom of these conditions, the captain and crew couldn't know that their ship had struck the outer part of the sandbar twelve miles east of Shinnecock Light. They had no way of knowing they were stranded only 400 yards from land, two miles south of the village of Bridgehampton, west of the Mecox Life-Saving Station. The marooned men did realize with dreaded certainty that they were aground off Long Island, helpless, and at the mercy of a fierce storm. (The U.S. Life-Saving Service operated these stations for maritime rescue duties as a separate government service; it ultimately became part of the U.S. Coast Guard.)

The men on the *Circassian* anxiously awaited the coming of dawn. By daybreak, the stormy weather with its boiling gray skies had seemed to lessen and the tide had receded. When the trapped crew spotted the Mecox station men positioning their mortar (a wide-barrel, high-angle cannon), the seamen cheered and waved at them. Sharp cracks quickly echoed through the morning air as the cannon shot balls with their trailing line at the ship. The third shot thudded successfully onto the vessel's deck, and the crews on land and ship scrambled to make the shore connection with the "life car's" hawser and hauling lines.

This procedure involved a hardy sailor from the ship or land next making his "cat-like way along the line," dragging a second rope attached to a strong basket, box, hammock, or whatever was available. Anchored by block-and-tackle, the apparatus could drag people to land. Another line brought the improvised lifesaving car back to the stricken vessel for another trip. Whether the car or only the rope was utilized with this method, people were always at the mercy of the cold waves.

When the weather and seas fortunately abated during this time, the Mecox superintendent decided to bring out the surfboat. Using the life car was slow and limited in transferring personnel over the long hawser, but it could always be used if the waves were still too strong.

The land men rowed their surfboat into the crashing breakers. Despite their courageous efforts to time the lifeboat's movements with the waves rolling in, the seas nearly overturned the boat. One high roller after another cascaded into the surf, and when these waves nearly swamped the rescuing lifeboat, the crew turned back. Although the first attempts weren't successful in reaching the stricken boat, the Mecox men waited before deciding to make one more try. By "good fortune, much experience, and great labor," the rescuers finally cleared the breakers and approached the ship.

Watching out for debris, falling wreckage, and the shifting vessel's massive hull, the Mecox crew reached the ship around 11:00 A.M. Dwarfed by the huge shifting bulk of the *Circassian* that loomed overhead, the crew held the lifeboat to its close position in the choppy waters. The captain pointed toward the men who would first leave the ship, and the first six quickly scrambled down a line dropped to the bobbing surfboat.

Once everyone was in place, the lifesavers put muscle into their oars and moved the small boat back through the chop. The return trip in the overloaded surfboat was dangerous; the lifeboat seemed to surf on top of the rollers, only to crash down into boiling ocean when the breakers slammed onto the shore. Navigating skillfully, the men on the first boat finally arrived safely on the beach.

One of the *Circassian*'s seamen immediately left for town to telegraph the ship's agents in New York about what had happened. Meanwhile, the lifeboat crew made more trips into the seething ocean to bring the remaining crews of two ships safely back to shore. Seven trips were made to return forty-nine men: thirty-six seamen from the *Circassian*, the pilot, and twelve from the *Heath Park*. Many of the saved men, however, were badly frostbitten from their all-night ordeal and taken to the Mecox station house for aid—but no lives had been lost.

With the salvage contract in hand, wreckers from Merritt's Coast Wrecking Company were sailing northward along the coast to Bridgehampton. They were also quite familiar with the *Circassian*. The supervisor of the salvage operations, Captain Edward Perry, had already worked the iron-hulled ship from a sandbar at Manasquan on the New Jersey coast. Captain John Lewis, in charge of the lead wreck ship, had pulled the *Circassian* off another time at Sable Island, 100 miles southeast of Nova Scotia in the Atlantic Ocean.

One day later, the Coast Wrecking Company vessels reached the *Circassian*. Although broadside to the beach with her bow heading eastnortheast, the vessel seemed to be in good condition. The storm had nearly filled the ship's open holds with seawater, but she wasn't taking on new water and the steam-driven pumps were pumping the ship dry. The vessel lay on the sandbar's inside edge in twenty feet of water.

Ships that bottom out on sand are generally pulled off by their stern with little difficulty. These waves, however, had swept the ship over the bar but parallel to the shore, one entire side now being completely vulnerable to the waves and a storm's full force. Although still seaworthy, the *Circassian* would need to be pulled around and angled with her bow out to sea, then hauled bow first over the sand barrier.

The salvage plan was then discussed and decided. Two huge anchors with hawsers running seaward from the ship's bow would be dropped off the boat on the ocean side. The workers would wind the large cables tight around the ship's capstans and make the ropes taut against each anchor. When heavy swells or a high tide brought enough water under the ship, a donkey engine would drive the capstan bars and pull the ship toward the anchors. If the thick hawsers didn't snap or the anchors drag, these efforts could gradually inch the vessel seaward. To add greater buoyancy, most of her cargo would be off-loaded. Once the vessel was empty, the wreckers concluded that a steam-tug could pull the ship at high tide completely over the bar. As a full moon with a strong high tide was due in two weeks, the salvagers felt quite optimistic about their chances. They concluded their plan was very workable.

Merritt's most powerful steam-tug, the *Cyclops*, was now on the scene. If anything could move the beached ship, the seamen felt that this wooden side-wheel steamer could. They knew they had to free the *Circassian* by any means, however, and quickly take her out to deeper water before more serious storms developed.

Captain Perry stayed with the tug's crew, while Captain Lewis and four wrecking engineers lived on board the *Circassian*. Lewis needed more than the engineers, however, to help him on board. He needed an able crew to remove the tons of cargo. These men would live aboard the vessel and had to be strong, capable seamen with some wrecking knowledge. The Coast Wrecking Company had brought workmen for this salvage, but extra hands were needed for the cargo gang.

By December 14, Merritt's company was in full charge. Lewis hired Captain Luther D. Burnett as his ferryman. Burnett was reputed to be the best surfman available in the area. Following local recommendations, Lewis next visited the Shinnecock Indian reservation, a small settlement located seven miles from the stranded ship, to recruit the men he needed. The Shinnecock were tall, strong men who knew the sea well. Nearly all had been fishermen or whalers, and over the years they had volunteered to work on the numerous maritime emergencies that occurred along the coast.

From ancient times, the Shinnecock had been spiritually involved with the sea, and they had introduced the first white settlers to offshore whaling. In the 1830s, Sag Harbor in the Hamptons became a leading deep-sea whaling port, and the Shinnecock worked on those crews. Although Sag Harbor had no whaling activities for the past five years, whaling in New Bedford, Massachusetts—located some sixty miles south of Boston and called "The Whaling City"—was still thriving, and the Shinnecock shipped out from there. By 1876, however, ships were leaving the depleted Atlantic-based waters to seek their prey in the frigid waters of the Arctic and Antarctic.

In December, as the *Circassian* lay stranded on the Bridgehampton bar, word had just arrived on the reservation that a New Bedford ship was looking for whalers. Some had already left for that work, but other Shinnecock—glad to have a chance to earn money while staying safely near home—decided to accept a job on the stranded vessel. When these Shinnecock left to accept Lewis's offer, only women, children, and old men remained behind.

By Friday, December 15, salvage work on the grounded *Circassian* began. Steam pumps soon had pumped out "half her hold" and only four feet of water remained. Anchors ran off her bow to turn her seaward, and the removal of the cargo was underway. Engineers, wrecking men, and cargo workers swarmed over the ship to free it, and everyone's hopes were high that this would soon happen.

Spectators, including groups of families, came from afar to watch the operations on the large, stranded ship. Since the time when the *Circassian* had grounded, the weather continued its menacing ways with high tides and heavy surf. The next day, the ship rode through yet another storm, but again without incident. The continuing bad weather delayed operations, however, and the cargo gang and shuttling lighters couldn't work full-time. Aided by the storm swells, the efforts to turn the ship seaward had met more success. During the first week of salvage, the ship was moved a hundred yards on the bar. Now resting by itself on the sandbar, the bow faced the open sea. Two large bow anchors and several smaller stern anchors kept her safely pointed southeast, at an angle, to the sandbar and shore. Her position seemed secure.

Despite warnings to the contrary, Captain Lewis of the Coast Wrecking Company gave the order to remove the hauling lines and hawser from the ship's masthead. He believed these ropes would interfere with the vessel's ability to move over the bar, and with the *Circassian* no longer broadside, he felt the vessel was now out of danger. Although officials of the lifesaving district disagreed, Lewis told them the ropes were not needed and would only be a hindrance. Relying on the iron-ship's seaworthiness, he had his men cut and cast off the thick ropes from the ship's mast to shore. The breeches buoy that operated over the hawser was also discarded.

Work progressed. Filled with the *Circassian*'s freight, the first cargo schooners began arriving in New York City. By Thursday, December 28, almost 400 tons of cargo—or about one-third of her load—had been removed. With the ship resting with her bow on the bar and stern floating inside it, strong pumps had already removed the seawater from the *Circassian*. The vessel was now completely dry.

As valuable equipment and many men had been tied up for over two weeks during the company's busiest season, Lewis was anxious to get the vessel on its way. Captain Williams then stated for the record that his ship had run aground in the heavy gale due to the ship's compass malfunctioning. He argued the intense storms had probably affected the instrument during the ship's hard crossing.

On Friday, December 29, 1876, the barometer gradually fell and the raw air felt more like snow. Captain Lewis, who was on board the *Circassian*, thought the approaching storm was a good omen. With a near full moon, a storm from the east would bring even higher tides. Lewis had once before maneuvered this strong iron ship from a sandbar—and he would again. He knew the *Circassian* and his twenty years of wrecking experience gave him the confidence that this day would be the one when she would be freed.

Since early morning the crew had been busily at work removing more cargo, reducing the ship's weight and her draft—and increasing the chances of freeing her. But as the winds and seas ran high, the cargo schooners were forced to pull away and all work ceased. Surfman Burnett quickly returned to the *Circassian* to take the work crew to shore, or at least persuade Lewis to run the lifeline from the ship back to shore. With this common safety precaution, the men would be able to reach land if the storm became too severe.

Captain Lewis quickly refused this request, just as he did with the Mecox lifesavers. He believed the ship rode well through the storms that came after the grounding. Lewis had originally ordered the line unrigged so the operations on board wouldn't be hampered. Now he didn't want to take any chance that his men might panic at the wrong time and desert the ship for the shore's safety. Every member of the crew, so he reasoned, had been hired to stay on board—day and night—until the *Circassian* reached New York. And this included the Shinnecock.

Knowing the dangers from storms on this coastline, Burnett continued to urge Lewis to let him bring the men ashore. "This is your last chance," he argued. "No vessel can withstand the coming storm, and my boat will be the last to come out here." Lewis refused once again.

The Shinnecock were men of the sea and familiar with the power of these storms. They knew the signs and sensed the destructive nature of this coming gale. Yet they stayed. No one knows if it was because of the rum, said to have been passed out to warm the men against the bitter cold, or the promises of higher wages once they reached New York, or the threats that they would not be paid if they left—but they stayed.

When Luther Burnett left, the last direct communication between the *Circassian* and shore was severed. Burnett said later that Lewis's last response to him was: "We'll float tonight or we'll go to hell!" Isolated by the rising seas and near buried by heavy snow flurries, thirty-two men stayed aboard: Captains Lewis and Williams, four wrecking engineers, ten Shinnecock, one Southampton worker, and fifteen other crewmen.

The storm grew worse by noon. It became too dangerous for any boat to venture into the surf and approach the *Circassian*. Cold with sleet and wet snow, the winds increased from the southeast. The seas grew rougher than anyone had expected, and white water began to crash over the ship's high deck. In the early afternoon, Lewis ordered two stern cables be "slacked" to let the ship ride easier with the rising seas. Caught by the full force of the fierce wind and thudding waves, the ship rolled to where her stern was now positioned more to the west. Although positioned more than 300 yards from the beach, she was closer to the shore than ever before. No one on board anticipated a dark disaster; after all, this iron ship had ridden through many gales before. This storm was just another one.

At about 4 P.M., the hawsers to the large seaward anchors were also slacked to allow the ship to slip off the bar into deeper water. The shrieking winds, bitterly cold snow and sleet, and foaming waves soon put any idea of freeing the ship to rest, as the wrecking tug and three company schooners were forced to leave for the safety of open seas. Creaking and moaning while the huge waves pounded the vessel against the bar, the iron ship was alone with its men. By nightfall, the crew knew it was impossible for any surfboat to reach them—and the ship was in danger.

The winds blew fiercely and waves crashed over the decks as the vessel pounded, heavier and heavier, against the sandbar. The ship's surfboats smashed against her sides. Although laboring for several hours to keep ahead of the saltwater seeping in, the welcomed news was that the steam pumps were working well. When crewmen later discovered a leak in the ship's hull caused by the slamming waves, they were concerned but not overly alarmed because the pumps seemed to be doing their job.

The crew was eating dinner in the mess when the vessel suddenly shuddered, flooded with saltwater, and rushing water extinguished the galley fires in fits of hissing steam. With chilling ocean sweeping inside the decks, the shocked men ran pell-mell from the confusion below deck into the tumultuous world above. They knew the ocean had finally breached the safety of the ship's hull.

The men hastily sought shelter in the deckhouses or climbed into the icy forerigging to avoid being swept overboard by the angry ocean. The large waves continually washed over the decks with frightening strength and smashed the ship's wood boats into splinters. The whistling winds picked up the debris and hurtled it around with bitter, wintry blasts. The raging seas, howling winds, and stinging snow menaced the crew from every direction.

From their relative safety on board, the trapped men heard the boilers then explode with sizzling, rending sounds. Knowing that the steam pumps couldn't work, the crew now realized they were in immediate danger. One man quickly fired off a signal of distress. The *Circassian* then seemed to steady in the waves, and the trapped men felt some relief. Unfortunately, the steadying was due to the ocean filling up the vessel's holds and lower passages.

Burnett had already warned the lifesaving station about how dangerous he thought the circumstances were. A Mecox lookout was stationed on the beach and watched the ship labor in the gale and worsening seas. Brushing the heavily falling snow from his eyes, he picked up the outline of the silent distress signal arcing from the ship and rushed away to tell others. The Mecox station once again prepared for rescue. The men burned a red Coston flare in response, while horsemen quickly rode away to summon more help. Attempting to "cheer up" the *Circassian*'s men, the remaining lifesavers built a large driftwood fire that soon was ablaze in the lee of a sand dune.

Intending to fire a lifeline to the trapped men, the lifesaving crew hauled their heavy mortar out again to the beach. Flooded by the high tide and frothy surf, the first area they came to was clearly unsafe. The men searched for another place to set the apparatus. The winds suddenly veered with hurricane force screaming from the southwest and drove blinding sheets of icy rain and sand directly into their faces. The wall of wind-blown, flying particles was so heavy that looking seaward became "most difficult." Mountainous seas stormed between the shore and bar, while fear and confusion reigned on the beach.

On board the *Circassian*, the winds tore through the rigging, and the ship's pounding separated nuts from bolts, loosened deck planks, and opened gaps in the upper structure between the foremast and mainmast. When the winds shifted, the swells swept over the decks from different directions. With the waves pounding the ship literally to pieces, the captain ordered the men to lash themselves to the rigging. The powerful seas then ruptured the iron doors of the deckhouses, sweeping everything away except for the forehouse. Each huge wave lifted the ship toward the sky, only to drop her back with a bone-jarring smack.

With rain pouring down from the darkness, the lifesaving crews fought against the winds, thundering surf, and blinding sands in a desperate attempt to set their mortar close enough to reach the ship. Their final spot was "a full fifty" yards farther back, almost against the dunes and now one-quarter of a mile from the vessel. While setting up the equipment, they heard a sharp crash and cries of "My God, she's breaking in half!" The iron mainmast snapped near the mainstay, leaving only a ten-foot stump and taking with it the mizzen topmast. Three men who had been desperately holding to the rigging also disappeared.

The lifesaving crew hoped that these shot-lines would reach the ship from the new location. Although the wet conditions made it difficult for the mortar fuse to burn, the men fired time after time into the darkness in the vessel's direction. As visibility was near zero, no one knew if a ball actually managed to reach the ship. However, they doubted if one did. The winds caked the mortar too quickly with wet sands to allow any real distance, and the ocean's flooding over the sand dunes had put them a distance away.

Violent white water crested well beyond where the *Circassian* lay. Given the horrendous conditions, no surfboats could venture from land and those on board the ship had been destroyed. The ship's men were so close to shore, but so far from help, and it was estimated that over 100 people huddled on shore in groups to keep a vigil.

Although the bad winds and seas continued, the pouring rain gradually dwindled to a steady drizzle. From behind the clouds, the pale rays of the near full moon then lit the dark-gray horizon, giving off enough light so those on shore with field glasses saw a chilling sight: numbers of men had wrapped themselves inside the rigging, as if trapped by a huge spiderweb of mythological proportions.

When the high tides began to ebb around midnight, the ship steadied more and less water flooded the decks. When most of the chilled and exhausted men slowly climbed down from the rigging, those on shore watched silently in near disbelief. The crew then sought shelter inside the galley. While the ship's carpenter nailed planks against the leaks in a futile attempt to stem the watery invasion, others managed to light a warming fire in the wet shadows. If any rum was still around, the liquid potion was surely drunk. As the crew warmed up, the brief respite gave them hope again.

That hope was soon dashed when the deck they stood on began to split. It was as if a horrid earthquake had taken hold of the *Circassian* and wouldn't let up. Lewis ordered everyone to get back up the masts and lash themselves once more to the rigging. Leaving what little warmth and light they had, the seamen ran again into chilling spray and frigid winds to scramble up the masts. When the clouds broke and let through the moonlight, the chilling silhouette of men clinging to rigging was resurrected.

Holding their field glasses with clenched cold fists, those who were safely on land watched wordlessly as the sea continually broke over the ship with light-colored carpets of froth. They saw the men jump from the forerigging during wave intervals. The crew members hit the deck and fell, picked themselves up, and raced frantically over to scramble up the mizzen rigging (located near the stern and closest to shore), which they obviously hoped would be safer.

The surrealistic sounds of differently pitched singing and deep chants then echoed over the thuds of the surf and the whistling winds. Death chants, mantras, and Christian hymns mixed as the Shinnecock men led the others in a blending of cultural beliefs and prayer. When the shrill sounds of the storm abated, the strong voices of the Shinnecock carried to shore with their strains of "Nearer My God to Thee" and "Jesus, Lover of My Soul." When their moving cries were heard, some of those gathered on shore wept. It isn't known whether the *Circassian*'s men heard the emotional callings back from land, but the throngs of spectators, family members, and waiting rescuers prayed as fervently as well.

After three o'clock in that early morning, onlookers saw that the *Circassian*'s hull was clearly broken. The ocean had beaten the ship so viciously about the bar that she now listed slightly. Her forepart was off the sandbar, but her stern was scraping bottom. The vessel no longer pounded up and down.

The hull soon split in half. Bathed in moonlight, the bow portion with the stump of the mainmast drifted slowly away as it listed to port. Too much cargo apparently had been removed from the ship's center, making her too heavy near the bow and stern. The ship's dangerous position across the bar and incessant poundings had proved too much for the once-strong iron hull. With the mainmast spars already underwater, the forepart settled, bow down. It slowly sank to the sandy bottom. The aft part of the ship also settled; its mizzenmast was upright, although this thick pole began to list to one side.

The cries of those in the mizzen's rigging carried to shore. At four o'clock, the ship's stern section split down the middle and listed to port as the mizzenmast leaned closer and closer to the swollen, churning ocean. The ship's stern achingly rolled over toward the water, the mast slowly approaching the sea. The chilling swells now doused the trapped men who were clinging inside the webs. By then, onlookers believed that many of the seamen had to be near unconscious or dying from the long exposure. They silently watched the mizzen, with the tips of its spars now underwater, tragically continue its inevitable decline of torture and death.

The journey of the mast to its sea immersion took an agonizing half-hour. With the remaining men clinging to its shrouds, the mizzen finally settled into the raging seas. The ragged chorus of "Glory! Glory!" and "Hallelujah!" abruptly ended. The last words of Captain John Lewis were later said to be, "My God, twenty years I have followed wrecking and now must be drowned at last." Shortly after 4:30 A.M. on Saturday, December 30, 1876, the iron mast disappeared beneath the waves. Taking silently what men were left, the mast pointed underwater toward shore.

Staring at the chaotic scene of rigging, broken planks, and mangled parts of ship and hull, the rescuers on land felt powerless and frustrated in their inability to help. The speed of the wave sets, now running to the east, and the violent undertow and crosscurrents made any rescue attempts still impossible. No one held hope of seeing any of the thirty-two men alive again. The superintendent of the lifesaving brigade organized a patrol of twenty men, each at forty-foot intervals with lanterns, to hunt for survivors—even though he knew the odds were terrible. Volunteers and lifesavers hurried up the beach to take their positions.

When the moon broke through the turbulent overhead clouds once more, onlookers picked up the sight of a "cluster of figures" moving rapidly on the ocean with the east-sweeping current. When the crashing surf inundated one lifesaving crew, other men persevered in racing after the apparition. With only a few people in the crowd aware of what was happening, the undertow swept the small figures nearly one-half mile away before the currents angled closer to shore with the lifesavers in hot pursuit. When close enough, the rescuers waded into the maelstrom of freezing, pounding breakers and dragged limp men from the frenzied ocean.

Seeing the "concentration" of lantern lights ahead and hearing "glad" shouts, those patrolling the shoreline knew someone had been saved. When the rescuers and survivors staggered down the beach, the news spread rapidly that a few men had indeed made it to shore. Four were miraculously alive, at least for the moment, as they had floated to the beach on a boat buoy. As the rescuers helped the exhausted survivors into the Mecox station house, the rest of the lantern patrol continued searching with renewed energy.

The saved men were so overcome by fatigue and "numb from the wet and cold" that they couldn't stand. Stripped of their frozen garments, they were given warm, dry clothing. The survivors drank coffee and brandy from beds close to a warming fire. With their needs being attended to, three of the seamen revived, but the fourth stayed unconscious. He didn't revive until the "middle of the day."

Those saved were Henry Morle, the *Circassian's* first mate; Tom Rowland, second mate; Charles Campbell, a Coast Wrecking Company engineer; and Alexander Wilson, the ship's carpenter, the seaman now unconscious. When they were able to talk coherently, the men told their tale of survival.

Morle was in the ship's galley with Campbell, Rowland, Wilson, and other crew members while they tried to get warm and someway figure out how to survive. They knew help couldn't come from shore under these desperate conditions—and they were in a deadly situation.

Only a few life preservers and two canvas-covered cork fenders (cylinders slung over the side when docking to absorb the contact) were left on board. Morle gave one life preserver to the Shinnecock John Walker—a "tall, fine, strong fellow of fifty"—and cut loose a cork fender for himself. Taking it below, Morle rigged the cylindrical buoy with wooden cleats and ropes, making a life buoy that was five feet long and one foot thick. As Tom Rowland couldn't swim, he asked Morle if he would share the buoy with him. Morle, to his credit, quickly agreed. When the ship began to break up beneath them with deep rumblings and shaking, the two men hauled the buoy to the mizzen rigging. Seeing that the mast could fall, Morle studied the ocean currents by observing how the debris sailed away. He decided on the best place to clear the ship if the mast collapsed. Tying the fender to a spar, he climbed up the rigging.

Choosing not to lash themselves to the ship, the seamen watched as two others, including Charles Campbell of the wrecking company, tried the same flotation device with another fender buoy. A large hissing wave unfortunately crashed on the deck, caught them with its full fury, and ripped the lifesaving float from their frozen hands. The huge, chilling roller swept over the boat and washed several others overboard in the sil-houetted darkness into the cauldron of icy spray, currents, and wind-whipped froth.

Campbell managed to stay on board, but the wave washed him under-neath the rigging where Morle was. Painfully inching his way toward it, he edged his body into the ropes beneath the first mate, and then asked if he could share Morle's buoy. Morle agreed again.

Men began to panic. A few jumped from the deck into the surf, only to disappear quickly from sight. Two-dozen seamen meanwhile were above and below Morle in the rigging, like frozen crows in a tree caught by an ice storm. With their clothes covered with ice and freezing spray that numbed hands and face, others stayed in their precarious place to the bitter end.

The Shinnecock remained in one group inside the ropes, while they continued singing their hopeful songs of mercy and chanting tribal prayers. Others were praying. The crashing waves and biting winds soaked up the men's sounds, but between wave and wind sets, frightened high-pitched voices melded with the hopeful, deeper chants in a frozen sym-phony of pleading for forgiveness and atonement. Wrapped motionless in the rigging, swaying only with the wind, some men were silent. Their calls for help from land or the heavens had ended.

A huge, roaring wave swelled against the vessel and lifted it. As the mast fell, Morle, Rowland, and Campbell jumped down to the deck while holding onto the buoy. They then leaped together with the fender into the icy surf. Rowland and Campbell clung to the buoy "in the lee of the ship" as they hurtled down into the ocean; Morle, however, let go just before hitting the water and was separated momentarily from the group.

As Morle surfaced, saltwater and built-up ice stung his eyes. "A chaos of debris" surrounded him: riggings, spars, planks from the ship's broken lifeboats, billowing sails, hawsers, and struggling, drowning men. But for the death calls of the storm, tens of men were shocked into silence as each strug-gled to live while exposure and hypothermia shut down what was left of life.

Alexander Wilson was in the rigging above Campbell and followed the men into the ocean. Wilson panicked when he surfaced into the chilling confusion of debris and grabbed Campbell's neck for gulps of precious air above the frothing water. As the men grappled, Campbell reached with stiffened fingers to draw his knife out. Seeing this, Morle shouted at Wilson, "Carpenter, let go of that man, you're drowning him now." He let go. Campbell then helped Wilson grab and hold onto one side of the buoy.

The four men were in two pairs on opposite sides of the bobbing fender. With their arms spread through the ropes and around the cylinder, each clutched the icy lines and locked legs with the other, keeping each pair together. This maneuver also steadied the small buoy when the rolling swells smacked into the group.

Morle was clearly in charge. He yelled at the others with lessening strength to take a breath before each wave of ice struck, ordering them to rest whenever they could. Nevertheless, after only minutes in the water, their long ordeal and the chilling waters had completely weakened the men. Shivering at first from the cold elements, the crewmen were now becoming lethargic and listless. They would soon drown or die from hypothermia. As their makeshift raft sailed with the currents, the men tried to work it toward shore by paddling and leaning in that direction. The cauldron of sounds, gray darkness, and the cold were taking their toll, as the weary seamen moved less and less.

They stared numbly at the moonlight-bathed swells that crashed thunderously down in front. The men were close to the beach, but the awesome power of the surf seemed to be an impenetrable barrier. They had a gnawing feeling of doom and relief: to be so close, but to die instead.

A large roller surged under them, hurtling the buoy and the four clinging men toward the night sky and then crashing down to inundate them with choking saltwater. The crush of water flung them to the wet sands, while the seamen gripped the cork bumper and tumbled around inside the salty turbulence. One by one, however, they then felt someone or something grab them as the currents crushed back in the opposite direction, pulling them back to the open sea.

Also exhausted, frozen, and nearly at the undertow's mercy, the lifesavers hauled the survivors from the surf. Others immediately wrapped the seamen in dry clothes stripped from their own backs. Wilson suffered from severe cramps and was nearly lifeless; the others were so overcome by exposure and exhaustion that they could barely stand. All would have perished had the lifesavers not spotted them when they did.

Walking up and down the debris-filled beach, patrols continued during the ugly dawn and early morning looking for more survivors or bodies. On this Saturday morning, the rescue teams endured more frigid temperatures with gusting westerly winds. Although the glare of bright sunshine reflected from the ocean, cold stinging sand still pitted the faces of those keeping watch. Cases, chests, broken boards, spars, and bits of the wrecked vessel were strewn for miles along the beach.

The gale affected the entire Northeast, and some people considered it to be the worst storm in eighty years. The night's sleet and slush had frozen into one slippery mass in Bridgehampton. The winds and waves badly hit New England, causing much damage to the fleets and driving numerous vessels ashore or badly damaging them. Long Island's bays froze over. A heavy snow had immobilized upstate New York, New Hampshire, and Vermont.

Word of the disaster spread rapidly through the small town of Bridgehampton. Accustomed to seeing the ship's masts on the horizon, some townsfolk thought the *Circassian* had finally freed herself when they didn't see it that morning. Shocked at the loss, others disregarded the horrid weather to aid in the search. People knew each other in this small town, including those who lived on the reservation. Neighbors were dead, and the men who perished had faces.

The news spread to the surrounding areas and Shinnecock reservation. Although only a few miles away from their homes, the missing Indian seamen hadn't been off the ship for two weeks. Fathers, uncles, brothers, husbands, cousins, and friends would never again return. The survivors confirmed that the Shinnecock John Walker had tried to jump away, but that a large wave had caught and crushed him against the ship's stern. A swirling eddy carried the man down. His life preserver surfaced, but John Walker didn't.

The once-mighty ship of iron was gone. Only the small forward part of the vessel now stood above the tumbling surf, as the broken parts of hull had completely submerged. Of the three tall iron masts, only the ice-encrusted foremast remained, leaning at an angle from the bow and engulfed in the ocean's spray. Debris and wreckage were strewn for miles to the east over the ocean and shore. No bodies had yet been discovered, and people presumed that everyone else had died but for the fortunate four. They were correct: Twenty-eight of the thirty-two men were now dead.

The crew of the lifesaving service at Mecox rested in their station house after having been up all night during the calamity. They had cleared their equipment—from the mortar to life jackets—off the beach and stored them. The lifesavers moved the four survivors from the cramped station house to the recuperating warmth of a nearby farmhouse.

Captain Merritt and his officers were shocked when they received the news of ship's loss and its men. With no details at hand other than that fact, Merritt could only tell the reporters, "The ship and a large number of men have been lost." He said he was familiar with the iron ship's condition and fully confident of his men's capabilities, adding that the disaster was the last thing he would have ever expected. If he had been on the ship the day before, Merritt believed he would be as safe and secure as in the lobby of any of the city's grand hotels. If the storm had held off for just another few hours, he was sure the *Circassian* would have been freed. In addition to this loss, Merritt had more worries and anguish: The company's tug and schooners that had left Bridgehampton had disappeared. Merritt ordered another tug to steam to the scene and evaluate the damage, while other agents left by train to assist in whatever way they could.

The heart-wrenching searches continued on the Bridgehampton beach and further east. As lifesaving crews kept a watchful eye on the surf, Shinnecock women, children, and old men walked back and forth over miles of beaches while they soulfully searched for their missing. But all of those men—including important tribal leaders—had indeed perished.

The Mecox crew's search continued in the moonlight that night through another storm. On Sunday morning, December 31, the sun again rose over the ship's skeleton remains. More wreckage washed ashore east of the wreck, near Montauk, as a few old seamen had predicted. The beach patrols were now actively searching over thirty miles of coastline.

With no remains discovered so far, the searchers assumed that the bodies had been dragged out to sea and carried to the east beyond Montauk Point, or if lashed to the ten-ton iron mast, they were still tangled inside the rigging. Friends and relatives of the Shinnecock tribe came to Bridgehampton to help as the Indians continuously searched and stopped by the Mecox station house to ask softly if any new information had been heard.

Every home on the reservation was affected because so many of the lost men belonged to interrelated families. All three of the tribe's trustees had died, and all were married with the exception of one. In one house, a woman lost her husband and a brother; in another, the wife lost her husband and brother-in-law. One Shinnecock left his work on the *Circassian* a week earlier to ship out on a whaler; he now searched the beaches looking for his brother. In all, nine widows and twenty-five fatherless children were left behind. Long Islanders had never before experienced a shipwreck that was this devastating to so many closely related families.

The survivors had recovered more or less by Sunday. All four visited the station house again to silently view the scene of the wreck, and reporters from local and major newspapers descended on them for interviews. Alexander Wilson readied for his trip to New York and a long sail back home to his native England. New York newspapers gave front-page accounts and headlined the disaster.

Flags flew at half-mast at the Coast Wrecking Company. Although Merritt had lost the salvage and men on the ship, the company's wrecking tug and schooners finally reported in. Owing to the gale's reign of terror, the *Cyclops* had been forced early Saturday to steam to New London, Connecticut, for a safe harbor, and the three cargo schooners found safety at Fire Island.

As the nation rang in the New Year, the 1876 tragedy continued with the news that searchers had recovered three bodies, including two Shinnecock, four miles west of Montauk Point. When this news reached the reservation, nearly all of the remaining Indians hurried to Montauk on horseback, by wagon, or on foot to continue their search and bring their dead back home.

On that Monday morning, January 1, the ocean became relatively calm for the first time in days. Men rowed to the wreck site, but they didn't discover any bodies in the shrouds or rigging. Before nightfall on that New Year's Day, however, eleven more bodies were discovered: three Shinnecock, two of the apprentices, the cook, the sailmaker, two more seamen, and the two captains, Williams and Lewis. As other bodies were discovered, frozen bodies began to line one wall of the wheelwright shop in Bridgehampton.

One week later, eleven seamen were buried in East Hampton in the northeast part of the old South End Cemetery. Tuesday, January 9, was set for the burial of the Shinnecock. Although only six bodies had been found so far, these services were held on the reservation in the little Presbyterian church. There was a large turnout from the tribe, relatives, friends, and sympathetic townspeople from the neighboring communities. Widows, sisters, and other Shinnecock women filled the front pews, and the services were a combination of the "old Indian traditional ways" and Methodist hymns. The wailings of widows now mixed with the singing of songs.

A Coast Wrecking Company steam-tug had been at the wreck site during the entire time. Divers were recovering anchors, tackles, pumps, gear, masts, and whatever could be salvaged. Some of the company's lost equipment had also been recovered. While the search for bodies continued, the rest of those missing were found over the next few days.

The loss of the ten Shinnecock men in their prime of life was a blow to the tribe. Although 175 people lived on the reservation, the remaining men were away on whaling voyages, and at least two years would pass before they would return—if all did. The struggle against poverty had always been hard, and given the severe winter, this time would be even harder. In any independent community, small and already poor, such a loss could spell disaster.

A ship-owner at this time wasn't liable for the loss of life on his vessel, and passengers and wreckers alike were on board at their own risk. The underlying public policy then was to encourage the movement of goods and people by the vital shipping industry. There would be no rush of lawsuits, settlements, government programs, or subsidies in compensation. Knowing this, Southampton villagers took up a collection to assist in burying the dead Shinnecock. Prayers for the distressed families and appeals for help came from the pulpits of local churches. The Southampton Presbyterian Church started a drive for money, clothing, and provisions to help the stricken reservation make it through the winter. Newspapers published appeals that followed the stories of the ship's grounding and its eventual destruction.

Due to the growing resort and tourist trade, residents of Long Island and New York personally knew many of the Shinnecock. John Walker, one of the tribe's trustees, was especially popular and well known for his catered clambakes and successful hunting parties. He left behind a widow and eight children, and his brother also died with him. Contributions were received from as far away as Stamford, Connecticut, and Boston, Massachusetts, due to the tribe's industrious reputation and great sympathy for the grieving families. Though appreciated, none of the contributions were very large. For the Shinnecock, the times ahead would be difficult.

When it came time to pinpoint blame, the U.S. Life-Saving Service and its crews were completely vindicated. Although the conditions were life threatening and far too dangerous to venture out, the men kept trying to fire the lifeline to the ship; they searched for survivors, saved four men, and helped in the recovery of bodies.

Captain Williams was also vindicated of blame. Sea captains felt, however, that he should have left the vessel with his crew once the salvage operations started. During the storm, the ship grounded on the bar amidships, and this was a direct cause of the loss. The wreckers had removed too much cargo from her center, and these actions left too much extra weight on the ship's ends. When the wave sets undermined the vessel's bow and stern, the vessel sagged at those points. When the huge waves of the severe storm pounded the *Circassian* on the bar, the force snapped her in two at its weakened middle.

The strongest criticisms were left for the now-deceased Captain Lewis, who had so poorly gauged the ship's predicament. Local seamen had warned him several times about the coming storm's severity. He had refused the lifeline that the U.S. Life-Saving Service recommended on at least two occasions. In his drive to free the *Circassian*, Lewis had the men remove the cargo from the middle, thus centering the stress at that point.

Long Island juts into the ocean with no other landmass to break raging storms. Given this exposure and the shoreline's angle to incoming surf, its eastern Atlantic edge can be extremely rough in any storm and unpredictably dangerous. There was a noticeable lack of preparation in case of disaster, and sufficient life preservers weren't on board the ship. The Shinnecock were strong swimmers, by itself an attribute, and preservers could have saved some. It was rare to have such a tragedy occur, however, so close to shore and a lifesaving station.

As to blame, the U.S. Life-Saving Service report reads:

> The undue reliance of the persons in charge as to the ship's power to withstand the force of the seas (which broke her spine), and which led them, in the face of warnings about a storm with more than ordinary violence, to refuse to maintain connection with the shore, was undoubtedly the cause of the loss of life which followed. A line drawn between the vessel and the beach would have enabled the Life-Saving crews to start their rescue at any time before the breaking of the hull, which forced the hapless wreckers and mariners to mount the rigging. It is evident that from that moment no earthly power could save them.

The officer of the Coast Wrecking Company in charge of the ship, Captain Lewis, made several errors in judgment, including about the severity of the storm, the lack of life preservers, removing the lifelines to shore, and deciding that the ship could float away in such a gale. If the small boats and cargo schooners could have continually worked without the intervening bad weather, the disaster could have possibly been avoided with all cargo being off-loaded. Had the severe storm held off for several hours more, the vessel might have made it safely off the bar. In this case, Lewis would have been praised for a job well done. By today's legal standards, however, he was clearly negligent and the lawsuits and lawyers involved would be many. The high penalty was the loss of twenty-eight lives, including his own.

The tribal widows survived the winter, and the loss of their men aboard the *Circassian* did not mean the complete end of the tribe. The twenty-five Shinnecock children were left alone to carry on their traditions—and they did. However, the tribe died as a pure-blooded race on that bleak night in December 1876, when its members had to marry outside the tribe in order to survive.

CHAPTER FIVE

DYNAMITE JOHNNY
AND THE *UMATILLA*

W hen considering the challenges he faced, Captain Whitelaw observed:

The sea is a smiling witch one day—a terrible monster the next. With strength incomprehensible to the man who has not fought it, the combined force of winds, waves, currents, and tides make piles of splintered wood and steel from the best of man's sea-riding constructions. But, though we cannot hold the windjammer or the liner out of the grip of the sea, mechanical developments in the art of salvaging have brought us to the point at which, like surgeons, we are able to save life after an accident. For ships, let me say, have individuality, each leading its own life, sometimes against the will of man. Some ships survive almost incredible disasters, as do some men, while others leave their wood and steel bones on the first reef against which they are thrown.

Whitelaw's standard dress was a flat-topped derby, a dark Prince Albert coat, stovepipe-legged trousers, and brightly shined shoes—even when dealing on the docks. Over time, he grew a great, flowing white beard, and as a Scotsman, "he still betrayed the land of his birth with his richly burred R's." Although he was a small wiry man, he was also charismatic, hardworking, bright, and penurious. A friend observed, "What a rascal! I saw a longshore gang collect from him one day on considerably overdue wages. It almost broke his heart."

T. P. H. was an avid reader of the Greek classics and could remember nearly word for word what he had read and then quoted it. A self-taught philosopher, he "held strong" to the Grecian philosophy of moderation in all things. He didn't play cards, drink, or smoke, other than an occasional cigar, as these habits would keep him from doing what he loved best: taking risks, raising ships, and making money at the same time.

His determination to do all work "right" stood out: It was an intense drive so that nothing was left to be done after he was through. Captain Whitelaw's indomitable will and absolute lack of fear were among his greatest assets. He had command and confidence, which he instilled in his men, but he also had a strong concern for them. As a result, they implicitly obeyed him. If Whitelaw yelled, "Go!"—they did. If he said, "Don't go!"— no one did, even if deep inside a rocking, water-filled hulk.

When work involved high risks, he said, "No, that's not your place. I'll go." A reporter wrote:

> Whitelaw could go for forty-eight hours in wet clothes and think nothing of sleeping in them. The man did not know fear for himself, although he feared for his men. Captain Whitelaw never sent a man down to where he wouldn't go himself, and he would descend to where he wouldn't send them.

Balancing this intrepidness was his penny-pinching nature and tightness in paying his men—until they had proved themselves valuable. He was a proud Scot and stood up to the stereotype. He didn't take in equal partners—even for long-standing employees—and didn't "suffer fools well." Whitelaw was a hard taskmaster, difficult at times, and totally oriented toward getting the job done. His perfection could be fine for his clients, but it could be difficult for workers. His intuitive engineering skills stood out, however, and if a challenge couldn't be solved by his workmen, Whitelaw tried to figure out a new solution. His knack for naturally understanding how to raise ships and his straightforward nature helped in earning his men's trust.

Whitelaw was thirty-three years old in 1880. He had been married for ten years to the love of his life, Elizabeth, who was four years younger. He looked forward to his time with their two children, Thomas A. (age eight) and Daisy (age six). They still lived in San Francisco, and the U.S. Census that year listed his occupation as a ship chandler, or a retail dealer in ship parts and equipment, from sails, spars, and steering wheels to anchors and even captain's desks. Anyone who wanted to repair or build a new ship for less scoured his junkyards as they do today with cars. He had come a long way since arriving in San Francisco as a young man with a day's wages to his name.

The 1870s had been a good decade for Whitelaw. Using the cash from his successful salvaging operations, he owned several ships by the early 1880s, along with his warehouses. He had a deserved reputation in the field, ranging from his work on the steam schooner *Costa Rica* to the scuttled SS *Constitution*. He had lost his own ships and then replaced them.

Of these vessels, T. P. H. had acquired the schooner *La Ninfa* and then constructed the 176-ton steam-wrecker *Whitelaw* in 1882. It was a different vessel from the *Thomas A. Whitelaw* that he had built for Port Kenyon runs. Through his San Francisco connections, including those with the Twelfth District of the U.S. Light-House Board, Whitelaw leased the *La Ninfa* and the *Whitelaw* to the board one year later for its construction of the St. George Reef Lighthouse. The steamer *Whitelaw* towed the *La Ninfa* to North West Seal Rock at the northernmost edge of the California-Oregon border, where the schooner anchored and became the quarters for the construction crew. The *Whitelaw* meanwhile operated as the supply ship for the project. The details of these efforts are described in the book written by this author, *Sentinel of the Seas,* which tells the story of the most dangerous, remote, and expensive lighthouse built in this country.

During the 1870s and 1880s, the revolutionary developments for modern-day life continued. Alexander Graham Bell invented the telephone and Thomas Edison the electric lightbulb. A few short years later, Edison also created the first electric lighting grid system employing overhead wires, which provided service in Roselle, New Jersey. These advances would change both life in the cities and on the seven seas.

● ● ●

IN 1884, Whitelaw would face one of his most difficult challenges. John Roach & Sons in Chester, Pennsylvania, one of the most successful and skilled large-ship builders of the time, built in the early 1880s the two-masted, two-decked passenger-cargo steamer *Umatilla*. With a 310-foot length, 41-foot beam, and 22-foot depth, the large 3,069-ton ship became one of the best-known ships of the Pacific and international fleets. It could carry 2,100 tons of cargo or 400 passengers, when converted, and was a flagship of the great Pacific Coast Steamship Company fleet.

Her first voyage from San Francisco north to Puget Sound proved to be dangerous. Several hundred carboys of muriatic acid and huge railroad flatbed cars had been lashed onto the vessel's deck. This was a hefty cargo, as each carboy was a large, globular glass (or nowadays plastic) container that looked like an office watercooler bottle and was encased in a protective wood crate. Muriatic acid is highly corrosive hydrochloric acid, which causes severe irritation or burns to the skin and eyes and is deadly when inhaled. The acid was used to remove rust, wash masonry from stone, and complete different manufacturing processes.

Johnny O'Brien had joined the *Umatilla*—a virtually new iron-hulled steamer carrying fore-and-aft canvas with squares forward—in 1883 as chief mate. O'Brien would ultimately become the most colorful captain on the Pacific Coast with a history, as one author wrote, "so garish that it read like one of the florid sea novels so popular at the time." He would narrowly miss being eaten by cannibals; fight off Chinese pirates with canon fire; sup with the royal family of Hawaii; make love to a Tahitian princess; be offered a partnership by King O'Keefe, the famous white Emperor of the Island of Yap; and ship with the infamous Robert O'Malley, arguably the prototype for Jack London's Wolf Larsen in *The Sea Wolf*. A dynamic personality, O'Brien would receive his nickname of "Dynamite" on the *Umatilla*'s maiden voyage. (A second "Johnny O'Brian" was captaining ships on the East Coast during this time and became famous for his gunrunning during the Spanish-America War—but the two had no family connection.)

The *Umatilla* sailed on her maiden voyage into the teeth of a gale off Cape Blanco in southwestern Oregon, and the heavy ocean rollers swelled over her decks with seething crashes and set loose the large crates and heavy railroad cars. Conditions were perilous at best, but O'Brien led the men to the huge railroad cars. With shrieking winds in their face and slippery decks under their feet, the men lassoed the sliding steel cars with thick hawsers and tied them down to the gunnels. The floating wood containers of acid, however, were splitting open from the collisions and spilling out their corrosive contents. The captain ordered the seamen to catch and throw the carboys overboard.

As the *Umatilla* lurched from side to side, O'Brien shouted to the drenched men to line up and grab the wood cases and bottles—now sloshing around the deck—and pass them down to him. Holding tight with white knuckles to the shifting gunnels, he then grabbed each box from the closest man and heaved it overboard. "Braced against the lee deck" and inundated by the ocean's waves, he worked until the last container was over the side. Although the acid had eaten their clothing away, the men discovered later that the drenching saltwater had protected them from the acid's deadly effects.

The high winds and seas continued into the morning, and a sharp crashing suddenly sounded from below the decks. Holding his lantern high, O'Brien climbed down one hatch to investigate the dark hold. He discovered that a large safe had broken loose and was battering cases of dynamite that were stored inside. O'Brien tried to hold the safe back, but it slid with him against another box of explosives.

Calling for more men, he held on as best he could. Johnny and the others jammed mattresses in front of the safe to slow its progress and shield the explosive powder. The men finally were able to lash the safe down. From O'Brien's heroics with this situation, he earned the nickname of "Dynamite Johnny" that carried through the rest of his life.

After discharging this cargo in Seattle, the *Umatilla* steamed through Puget Sound back to California. However, in early February 1884, the ship soon sailed into a cruel northerly gale when it passed Cape Flattery.

The winds whipped the gray seas into a seething froth while the blinding snowstorm coated the plunging ship and its masts, spars, and rigging in sheets of ice and snow. The men on watch couldn't see more than a "blurry mist" ahead as Dynamite Johnny finally turned his shift over and headed below.

Snow drove furiously down with a vengeance. The sea snarled and snapped while the wind lashed the ocean into jagged peaks. Visibility was at a minimum and the ship groped blindly through the whirling murkiness. The men on deck shivered from the cold and wind-chilling blasts while Captain Frank Worth stayed on the bridge. Duty tours were shortened when hardy seamen were forced to leave early due to their uncontrolled shaking from the cold. After washing and while stepping through the snow aft to the dining saloon, O'Brien heard over the din the lookout's muffled cry, "Rocks and breakers ahead!"

An uncharted reef loomed from the gloom with ugly white-specked black rocks and shards of white spray. A jarring thud and terrifying crash rattled throughout the ship. The wrenching jolt threw everyone to the decks, and wild clanging echoed sharply from the engine room's telegraph. The ship shuddered from stem to stern, while frightened men heard the ocean pour inside from what had to be a gaping hole. Running to the bridge after hearing the lookout's cry, O'Brien was hurled by the collision's force against the hatch combing (the lip around the opening). Johnny quickly regained his footing and raced to the bridge, where he shouted at the second officer, "Why in the hell didn't you port and go inside the reef? You had plenty of room."

Since Captain Worth had ordered the engines reversed just before the grounding, the ship began slowly sliding from the reef. Her bow continued to slam hard against the rock as she slipped off, each vibration felt throughout the ship. Frozen into inaction by the collision's suddenness, Worth now stood silently by. Half-dressed, the rest of the crew raced up and milled around the deck. With most of the ship's canvas already set, O'Brien quickly ordered the seamen to lower the forestaysail, the triangular sail set on rigging that braces a mast, which was flapping heavily in the winds. Snapping out of his momentary confusion, Captain Worth ordered the engine room to start the pumps.

Checking the holds, Dynamite Johnny saw that goods were already floating in seawater and he knew the ship was in danger of sinking. The engine-room telegraph again clanged noisily when O'Brien gave the order to "push her nose" back onto the reef. After the gears reversed, the propeller's thumping momentarily stopped, but then quickly started up, and the *Umatilla* bounced back onto the reef. The wind gusts whipped the ship's overhead sails out of control, "straining the rigging with a fury." Once the ship's new position caught the winds, the sails swung tautly over and pulled the ship over into a noticeable list.

With the ocean rushing into the torn hull faster than pumps could handle, the ship angled farther toward the sea. Captain Worth ordered the *Umatilla* abandoned, and the crew quickly filled the lifeboats. Sailors passed the ship's direction-finding chronometer and other navigation equipment to the captain's boat, while others lowered the boats from their davits into the ocean. Those remaining shimmied down a rope into the tossing lifeboats—all except Dynamite Johnny O'Brien.

He thought the ship could possibly stay afloat, since the pumps continued to suck water out of the boat nearly as fast as it came in. Staying on board seemed to be a better decision, since it was close to "zero weather" out on the ocean: The snow was still falling severely, and Johnny thought it made more sense to stay there until they could see if the ship couldn't make it. To directly countermand a captain's order was a serious offense, however, so he untied a raft from the deck. An engineer who had scrambled back to retrieve money left behind then helped O'Brien get the ten-foot-long, six-foot-wide raft into the seething waters.

Held upright by two airtight cylinders, the flat structure bobbed beside the waiting boats. "The ship is sinking! Get into the boat!" demanded the captain. O'Brien silently lowered himself on a rope into the raft. He sprawled lengthwise inside it, clutching to its wooden frame with both hands. Captain Worth demanded that he get into one of his boats, yelling, "The ship's going down, O'Brien. If you stand on that raft, you'll be sucked down when it goes down."

Dynamite Johnny kept to his feeling that the looming vessel above just might not sink and it was safer to stay by it. He told that to Worth. The captain ordered two seamen to row over and pull O'Brien into their lifeboat. When the men reached out to grab him, he stood up, seized them instead, and pulled the two surprised men into his raft. Telling them they were better off with him than in the sea, O'Brien shoved the lifeboat away. The unidentified seamen stayed, not having much of a choice either way. Shaking his head, Captain Worth ordered the boats to row away and leave the "damn fool where he was."

Once the surfboats left, it was an easy choice to climb back on board the warm ship. If the ship started sinking, they would have scant minutes to get onto the raft and pole away, but O'Brien and the men had made their choice. Climbing to the rail, the three men gingerly walked over the snow and ice-covered steel deck to the galley, where they ate sandwiches of thick meat with generous swabs of butter. They took pairs of blankets from the cabins and cut one into wide strips that they wrapped around their feet and legs to prevent frostbite.

Staying on the wobbling ship now appeared dangerous, as the men wouldn't be able to get to the raft if it suddenly rolled over. They climbed down the heavy line that held the raft to the ship's railing. Riding easily on top of the long swells, the men huddled together for warmth while waiting to see what the ship's fate, and theirs, would be. Flurries of thick snow swirled around them, and the huge hulk of the *Umatilla* swayed above, still pinned to the hissing rock. When the vessel rolled, a loose iron door banged above and equipment shifted noisily about. With the cold seeping through clothing into their very bones, the men were as near frozen as statues.

❦   ❦   ❦

TIME PASSED by slowly while they silently waited. Then the ship seemed to move. A metallic sound rang through the snowstorm, and as they stared upward, the vessel slid off the reef with a sharper list. Worried about the angle, O'Brien watched closely and then quickly decided that the wind-whipped sails were causing the ship's problem.

The bow was low in the water, since the collision had neatly shaved its front completely away, and her propeller shaft broke the sea. However, the *Umatilla* seemed to have stabilized in the ocean. Dynamite Johnny instinctively felt the ship was still seaworthy. He ordered the two men to pull hard in tightening the dripping line that still connected the raft to the ship. When O'Brien's frozen hands couldn't pull him up this rope, one of the men handed him a small flask of whiskey found on board. He took deep draughts of the sharp liquid, rubbed some on his stiffened hands, and tossed the empty container into the sea.

When O'Brien grabbed the thick line, a large roller picked the raft up and slammed him hard against the ship's hull. He felt momentary pain. Coated now with ice, he began to move his hands tortuously up the rope. His clothing was soaked; the heavy weight and icy conditions sent a shiver of fear through him that he just might not make it. The anxiety and booze worked, however, and O'Brien finally pulled himself up, climbed over the railing, and lay exhausted on the icy deck. He walked slowly to a storeroom, grabbed a Jacob's ladder, and threw it down to the other two.

Once everyone was on board, they started the most important business at hand: mastering the whipping sails. The ship was veering out of control and back toward the reef. They hoisted the fore-topsail and sheeted her to windward; they let the main sheet swing out to the wind. Although the large, iced sail pounded and slatted with crackling sounds, it was finally able to take hold. O'Brien and his crew shifted the steering gear from its inoperable steam control so they could work it by hand; they jibed the sails so that the wind came from over the *Umatilla*'s starboard quarter.

The vessel slowly started to move away from the reef. The winds and strong northerly current pushed the steamer away broadside, and it drifted toward the graveyard coast of Vancouver Island. As the ship worked itself away, the men saw their once-safe-haven raft falling behind. Its connecting rope had somehow been severed. With the lifeboats gone, they were now marooned on the *Umatilla*—to live or die.

Although the ship was riding low in the frothy seas, the pumps seemed to be keeping the ship afloat. When the ocean surging inside doused the boilers in near-explosive clouds of steam, the dangerous winds became the *Umatilla*'s sole source of power. With the important sails reset, the ship picked up speed on a direct course. O'Brien estimated the vessel was moving about three knots, or a little over three miles per hour. The winds still shrieked, the snow still whirled about, and the waves were frothy, but the crippled vessel sailed erratically through those gale conditions into the late afternoon.

The water continued to pour into the *Umatilla*, and the vessel rode lower in the ocean while the waves crashed over her gunnels. As she sank lower, the situation worsened and their prospects seemed dim. For three men to sail a 3,000-ton steamer is foolhardy at best, but O'Brien had already earned the reputation of trying to do what most men never dared.

Shivering with cold and greatly tired, the men tended to the sails that they could, while the ship slowly smacked through the waves. When the seamen finally picked up the outline of the first oncoming ship, they lowered the vessel's flag to half-mast and brought down the Union Jack, a signal requesting immediate help. A small sealing schooner came by, and a voice yelled out through the din asking what they needed.

O'Brien shouted back, "All the men you can spare and one or two dories." The waves continued to crash into the large gaps in the bow and drained away in hissing waterfalls. When the schooner's crew hesitated to answer, he added, "And fifty dollars a day to whomever will come over and help." Three men rowed over the white-capped sea to O'Brien's much larger vessel. With six men now working on board, they were able to set the square sail forward and the ship gained another half knot. When night finally came, the exhausted men hunched down and alternated watch. The deck was "frigid cold" and the small crew shivered in the lee of the after deckhouse.

Around midnight, the faint lights of another ship were visible on the horizon. The lights became larger as the vessel approached and its silhouette stood out. This was a large ship and it identified itself as the steamer *Wellington*. The San Francisco-bound vessel had sighted the distress signals and came to render aid. The ship anchored by the *Umatilla* in the storm, and the captain sent a small boat over to investigate. The lantern's light on the dory dance with the swells as the surfboat approached. When a man asked what was happening, O'Brien told him and then asked, "Can you give us a tow?"

The seaman expectedly answered, "How much will you pay?" Under the laws of the sea, any ship that came to the rescue of another in "immediate peril" was entitled to be paid a handsome fee for that assistance. The men haggled over the price but couldn't agree. Dynamite Johnny concluded the matter by shrugging his shoulders and saying, "The ship and its crew will be well paid for your efforts." He knew that they would take this offer, since towing a ship as large as this one would be a well-paid trip, indeed.

The ship's "sluggish helm was put hard over" and the bow-heavy ship came around into the wind with flapping sails. Because steam wasn't available to run the crippled ship's winches, *Wellington's* men had to take the *Umatilla's* hawser, row it over to the steamer, and then attach it to the tow ship. The *Wellington* altered her course, came about, and headed for the sheltered waters of the Juan de Fuca strait. Within an hour, the steamer was towing the crippled vessel through rough northeast seas.

Their goal was Esquimalt, British Columbia, and the swirling snow, winds, and seas continued to beat against both vessels. The *Umatilla* was down by its head and sinking lower by the hour. The seamen on board the Wellington kept a wary eye on the hawser and planned to cut it immediately if the *Umatilla* started to sink faster. Bucking bad winds and tide, the towing team battled on.

There were no guarantees that the stricken vessel would last long enough to be towed into safer waters. The winds howled and seas gnashed their white teeth, seemingly waiting for one final moment to put the ship and its crew out of misery. The low bow of the *Umatilla* slowed the efforts to move through the ocean. Its crushed prow lowered deeper into the seas, like a snowplow, drowning by the strength of its efforts. The ships slowly inched their way through the raging waters.

As O'Brien watched closely, another surfboat rowed back through tossing seas from the *Wellington* and a seaman hailed him from below. O'Brien yelled down that he didn't need any more help, knowing that having more men on board would simply increase the rescue fee that would be demanded later. Although Dynamite Johnny argued he only needed a tow, he agreed that *Wellington's* chief mate could come aboard as his guest— but not as a rescuer.

The sails over this ghost crew finally began to shred. The whistling winds tore up the remaining canvas as if they had been made of crepe paper. But by this time, O'Brien didn't care, because his ship was under tow and heading to the safe waters of Esquimalt. Intensely keeping watch over the effort, Johnny waited out the night until the dim grays of the dawn filtered over the horizon.

By now, the ships were by Cape Flattery and had left the open sea. The totally exhausted first mate felt the pains of his efforts. A sharp throbbing came from the side that absorbed the beating when O'Brien was slammed against the deserted ship—but he kept working through his pain.

By that afternoon, the two ships were inside the harbor breakwater. After many anxious, hectic hours, the safe and protecting docks were near. Despite O'Brien's yells to haul his ship along a wharf, however, the *Wellington's* captain decided not to take the risk. The men on the lead ship dropped the towline and anchored away from the docks. Due to the towed ship's tight turn in the anchoring and an engineer's mistake, the *Umatilla* started to take on more water. During the night, the ship sank, and the seamen onboard were just able to get off in time. O'Brien waited until the last minute before diving from the sinking vessel's bridge into the approaching ocean.

A lighter picked up Dynamite Johnny from the harbor's waters and took him to shore. Once there, he borrowed dry clothing and paid a livery stable owner fifteen dollars to drive him to Victoria. Once there, he forwarded a message to the owners in Seattle about what had happened to their ship. After returning to Esquimalt, he collapsed and awoke in a small hospital. He was forced to stay there for two days while doctors tended to his hypothermia and internal injuries.

Although the owners were understandably dismayed at the news, when they understood the *Umatilla* had made the harbor, they changed their attitude. However, even in the nineteenth century, lawyers and the courts were used to resolving differences. The owners of the *Wellington* pressed their claims for a $50,000 rescue fee. The insurance company, Lloyd's, brought its own suit arguing that the captain of the *Umatilla* had been responsible for causing the wreck. Dynamite Johnny O'Brien received wide publicity—although no money—and returned to San Francisco for another venture.

Any salvage operations would have been near impossible in the deep, forbidding waters near *Umatilla* Reef—the name given to the rock after the ship struck it. Although the ship lay peacefully inside calmer harbor waters, the gales, storms, and cold weather that blew through delayed any salvage work until late spring.

●   ●   ●

THE STEAMER was the property of the Oregon Improvement Company, and it valued the ship prior to the loss at $350,000. English experts traveled to Esquimalt to decide on how to refloat the wreck, but they decided that they couldn't get the necessary equipment there without great delay and expense. Captain Whitelaw then came forward and agreed to raise the vessel for $60,000, if he was successful. If he wasn't, then he wouldn't receive any money for his time, equipment, men, and out-of-pocket expenses. The owners quickly awarded him the bid.

This was a daring project. The sunken ship was a large, massive ship, as long as a football field, with extensive damage to the bow. She sank in nearly sixty feet of water and listed badly on the bottom, settling so that her starboard side was thirty-two feet from its rail to the surface and her port side twenty-one feet. With the business and salvage successes that he had to date, Whitelaw wanted the challenge—and the large fee (equivalent to millions in today's dollars).

His approach was to first determine a sunken vessel's capacity (or volume), its cargo type and amount, and the weight distribution of the water inside the ship. He dove down to determine the extent of the damage. Whitelaw and his divers next broke bottles of limewater inside the wreck to help locate the holes and hull damage. The milky currents caused by the limewater traced the damage, just like "a muddy river shows up some distance out in the sea or the bay into which it empties."

Captain Whitelaw related:

What I did in this case—after my divers had gone down and patched her holes with boards—was to build a cofferdam completely around the hull, rising from the sides of the deck to two feet above the water surface. This cofferdam not only had to be watertight, but so braced from within, with a system of crossbeams and braces to withstand the external pressure when the water was removed, or the water's outside pressure would have crumpled the cofferdam like so much cardboard. All of this was to be completed before we could pump the water out.

What Whitelaw failed to say in his usual downplaying of challenges was that his men encased the vessel in a strong enclosure that was 321 feet long by 35 feet across, 23 feet high on one side and 34 feet on the listing side. Whitelaw's crews used 400,000 board feet of lumber and 40 tons of iron in his construction of the immense corral. The number of workers ranged at any one time from 90 to 200 men, and he employed ten divers alone for the underwater work. Designing, engineering, and constructing such an immense cofferdam was a building project in itself: The dam had to wrap around the immense ship's silhouette at the bottom of the sea with a strong list to one side.

The needed patching was much more than covering holes with boards. The *Umatilla* struck the reef with such force that her prow was twisted back and upward until it almost touched the "'tween decks hatch" near the first steerage quarters. As Whitelaw observed, "In other words, her nose was 'busted in.'" The divers needed to build another nose inside the sunken vessel. They bolted "carefully cut" timbers across the gaping hole and constructed an artificial bow from concrete.

All of this work had to be watertight. Meanwhile, storms raged in, waves rose, and winds howled during the work. Obtaining and transporting these huge amounts of material to the construction site wasn't easy. The men had to be supported with equipment, and working in the ocean is always risky.

Another large problem was that these ships weren't built with the strong, watertight bulkheads that confined damage to one compartment—a later development during Whitelaw's time. In the older ships, divers needed to descend down into dark, dangerous holds and passageways to construct walls of planks, two to four inches thick and one foot wide, set on end, to wall the ocean out. Strong pumps next had to suck out the huge quantities of ocean "that the ship had swallowed" inside the vessel and behind the newly constructed shields of planking. "With her buoyancy restored, she then floats," Whitelaw succinctly said.

Once the walls of planks had been built around the *Umatilla*, Whitelaw's men then sank large tanks on both sides of the ship. The tanks were filled with water and had huge rocks set on top. Divers laboriously worked chains underneath the hull and pontoons and lashed the tanks to the ship; once the water and rocks were removed, the air-filled tanks would give a strong buoyant push to the surface.

When all of these tasks were completed, the ocean could be removed. Three large steam engines started to pump, throwing out seawater at the rate of forty tons per minute—an awesome display, similar to the powering water channels at a rain-filled dam. Whitelaw's steam-wreckers anchored close by with large groups of men and massive steam boilers, engines, and pumps—all in all, a massive undertaking.

The pumps strained to suck the water from the cofferdam, hull, and pontoons, as levers forced off the large holding rocks. These actions made the ship lighter and caused the pontoons to lift up powerfully. The successful refloating didn't take long. "As soon as the water was all pumped out," Whitelaw observed, "she bobbed to the surface like a cork. It took us five months and ten days, or 160 days, to prepare for raising this ship, and twenty minutes to get her to the surface, once everything was ready."

Although predators, from sharks to barracuda, were always a danger to salvagers and divers, Whitelaw was concerned with octopuses. He once observed:

> Inanimate enemies such as the tides, winds, currents, rocks, reefs, hard sands, and quicksand are more dangerous to the divers than all of the supposedly threatening life beneath the waters. It has been my experience, and that of my divers, that sharks are afraid of a man in a diving suit, whatever they may do to the undressed swimmer. The octopus, however, is a real menace, although fortunately for the ship-salvaging business, these great devilfish seldom appear near a vessel unless it has been in the water for months.

During the time the *Umatilla* was on the bottom, these denizens of the deep took residence inside the hull. One time, his men lowered a pontoon to the bottom and a diver descended to begin his work. He was moving across the rocks when a "long, gray, powerful, snaky arm" suddenly reached out and grabbed him around the leg, almost knocking him down. At once realizing his danger, the diver jerked out a knife from his holder. The octopus countered the movement by seizing the arm that wielded the knife. Moving as swiftly as his heavy suit allowed, the diver twisted his pinned arm behind his back and transferred the knife to his left hand. More tentacles reached over him. The man began to frantically slash away at the large feelers that encircled his body.

Whitelaw told what happened next:

With one slice, he severed the tentacle that was freezing his leg. With another, he freed his right hand. Now he was slashing in all directions! Did he signal to come up? He did not! He was mad! He signaled for the harpoon. Guessing that something important was going on below, we quickly sent down the harpoon.

The water surged and boiled, and in a few minutes the diver signaled to be hauled back up. He came up with the octopus hooked onto the harpoon! Stretched out on the deck, the monster was a fearsome sight—great beak, ugly domish head, and terrible arms. It measured fourteen feet across.

The diver involved in the fight was Martin Lund, who became known later as a champion deep-sea diver. He also put together expeditions to try and locate the *Brother Jonathan,* a long-lost gold-bearing steamer that went down off Northern California in 1865 (written about by this author in *Treasure Ship: The Life and Legend of the S.S. Brother Jonathan*). Lund was a "diver of renown," and Whitelaw had recognized his abilities from the very beginning.

As usual, Captain Whitelaw paid accolades to his workmen:

But without the divers, the ship salvor would be almost powerless. And the diver in this work is a highly specialized man. He must be not only a competent diver, thoroughly familiar with all underwater work, but he must also be a carpenter, a steelworker, a riveter, and, to some extent, a shipwright. He also must have at least an elementary knowledge of hydrostatics, and be able to estimate the strength he must build into bulkheads, patches, and cofferdams, while working in the complete dark.

Although no newspapers or interviews mentioned the deaths or injuries of workmen during the long, hard salvage, the memoirs of Dynamite Johnny O'Brien indicated that two died. Being directly involved with the ship as its chief mate, O'Brien watched the salvage and wrote about two fatal occurrences.

A diver, one named McLaughlin, was an alcoholic. Whitelaw told the man, "One drink and you're fired!" When McLaughlin was working beneath the ship, O'Brien saw the diver's alarm signal line "being frantically pulled." When men on board the cofferdam tried to haul the diver up by his rope, they found that the line was snagged. Another diver quickly headed down to "clear things below." When both divers were brought up, however, O'Brien saw that "poor McLaughlin's eyepiece in his helmet was broken and his face almost as black as ink." There was no indication the man had been drinking.

The next fatality was when a heavy cofferdam plank fell twenty feet and struck a workman on his skull. O'Brien wrote: "I was close by in a skiff. His brains were oozing out through his skull. To this day, I can see the poor fellow's lips and body quivering; the doctor gave one look and he quickly said, 'The man is dead.'" There is little reason to doubt O'Brien's accounts, because this work was dangerous and many workers were involved.

It isn't known if these men were temporary contractors or longer-term employees of Whitelaw. In one instance on a later salvage, a German diver by the name of Dolph became trapped under a log. He was underneath a deep sea for four long hours before another diver finally freed him with a hacksaw. Once brought up, it was apparent that Dolph had been underwater too long at a bad depth. Whitelaw's grandson relayed, "Dolph went nuts from being under too much water pressure. However, Cappie kept him afterward on the payroll picking up nails." Workers compensation wasn't in existence back then, so an injured worker relied on family or his employer's generosity—in this case, it was Whitelaw.

⚜ ⚜ ⚜

ANY RAISED ship needs to undergo permanent repairs and refurbishment. "After a vessel is patched, she may float a little lopsided," said Whitelaw. "All we try to do, of course, is just to fix her enough so she can make it to the dry dock for permanent repairs." During this expedition, the weather was at times "extraordinarily wet, cold, snowy, and wild." The tides and currents swept in, changing intensities and directions, and complicating the entire project. Five months of hard work were consumed in raising the vessel, and more than a year went by before the *Umatilla* was completely refitted and returned to duty. The immersion in the sea causes erosion, rust, and rot, not to mention the need of repairing equipment, re-carpeting and painting rooms, and replacing canvas sails—all of which Whitelaw could provide with his "junkyard of ships and things."

Meanwhile, legal battles erupted over the responsibility for the accident, the salvor awards, and rights to insurance proceeds. An inquiry was held in Seattle to determine fault, and this investigation exonerated Captain Worth from all blame. The testimony indicated that a very strong northerly current prevailed during the snowstorm, and the board concluded the vessel would have crashed on the rocks despite any precautions that could have been taken. Although held to be innocent of all charges, Worth felt very uncomfortable admitting that it was his first officer, Dynamite Johnny O'Brien, who had brought his command into port.

The inspectors highly commended O'Brien for his acts of bravery, which did little to quell the frustrations of Captain Worth. "Sizable hunks" of salvage money were paid to those involved in the saving of the *Umatilla*, and the Whitelaw men took home a generous sum of greenbacks—although they had assumed much risk in the process. Although the *Umatilla* was well insured, her owners and the insurers took Whitelaw's bet.

This was a "win, win" for them, as they came out ahead either way: If Whitelaw wasn't successful, he simply went broke and the owner received the insurance proceeds; when Whitelaw was victorious, the insurers paid the $60,000 for his efforts and the owners had their ship back. The insurers paid out the salvage money, but they didn't have to pay the full insured value in this case.

For being able to "refloat the impossible," Whitelaw saw accolades pour in from around the world. The British Admiralty congratulated Captain Whitelaw and said his effort was the "most scientific piece of work most masterly handled that they had ever known." Maritime experts still view both Johnny O'Brien's and Captain Whitelaw's exploits as being rare in the history. The "famous" Whitelaw Salvage Company of San Francisco—as author Jim Gibbs called it—performed a "marvelous salvage feat in raising the ship from the harbor floor." Whitelaw himself said years later: "I consider the raising of the *Umatilla* one of my greatest accomplishments, because it was done under such difficulties, and at a time when ship salvaging methods were not as advanced as they are today."

O'Brien and the *Umatilla* went on to enjoy long and colorful careers, both carving niches for themselves in maritime history. Dynamite Johnny was a seaman for sixty-five years and an American master mariner for fifty-three of them. His shipmates and friends called him the "Nestor of the Pacific," one who feared God but defied everything and everyone else with hard fists and spirit. He captained different ships on Pacific Northwest routes, including carrying thousands of would-be miners toward the gold fields during the Alaskan gold rushes. Back in San Francisco, a motion-picture studio chartered a ship to film Buster Keaton's *The Navigator,* and this picture brought in Dynamite Johnny's experiences and observations.

After the repairs, the *Umatilla* continued operating on the West Coast. As with all ships on the sea, she had more misadventures during her long career. In September 1896, she hit another uncharted reef, this time in a thick pea-soup fog while crossing the Juan de Fuca from Victoria to Port Townsend, Washington. Two nearby lighthouses hadn't run their foghorns, as they didn't have freshwater for their foghorn boilers due to an exceptionally dry summer. No one remembered that the *Umatilla* was then equipped with watertight doors, so these closures weren't activated; the water poured in through a thirty-foot hole through her bottom. The ship beached within a stone's throw of one of the lighthouses and its silent foghorn. However, the ship was again repaired and brought back into service.

On July 25, 1897, and bitten by gold fever, novelist Jack London boarded the *Umatilla* in San Francisco Bay. Prospectors loaded down with heavy clothing and camping gear crowded the decks and rooms. The *Umatilla* took the author to Port Townsend on the Puget Sound, where he boarded another steamer bound for Juneau, Alaska. From there, he made the rough passage through the mountains to the Klondike gold-fields, and Jack London's experiences in these wilds became the subject of his most famous works.

The *Umatilla* steamed into Seattle Harbor in 1902 and approached her docking place. Owing to pilot error, the mighty ship continued on without slowing. The vessel sailed "majestically" through piers and decking, finally stopping with her strong iron nose embedded in the street, as waterfront traffic now detoured around the huge ship on land. Tugs pulled her away with little damage.

Later that year, an insane passenger became convinced he was the skipper of the *Umatilla* and the only man aboard who could save her from certain disaster. Mounting the bridge, he issued orders to the crew, much to the amazement of one Captain Nopander, who was the steamer's real master. Eventually the captain decided to humor his deluded guest, who remained on the bridge as the ship steamed down the coast, periodically bellowing out orders that he felt were essential for the ship's safe passage. At San Francisco Harbor, upon Captain Nopander's request and as agreed, the passenger politely turned the ship's operations back. Several men in white coats then took him ashore.

Three years later, while heading to the coal bunkers in Tacoma, the vessel steamed into a lumber schooner during a heavy fog and smashed in a large section of the schooner's hull. The *Umatilla* was relatively undamaged. Another time, Captain Nopander was navigating the ship through more dense fog. With the ship's whistle blasting away every minute, he soon heard an answering whistle that seemed to be very close. Slowing down and listening intently for the sounds of another nearby large ship, anxious passengers crowded the railings and prepared for the inevitable collision. A huge whale suddenly swam alongside, however, and blew water over the people with a large gush from its blowhole. This "ship" then disappeared back into the sea.

For years, the *Umatilla* sailed on different Pacific routes. While on a transpacific voyage, the old vessel in 1918 was stranded off the coast of

Japan. Although the passengers on board were saved, the veteran steamship was considered to be a hopeless loss and abandoned. However, she still wouldn't die. A sandbar gradually built up over the months between the wreck and shore. The Japanese took advantage of the natural occurrence to dismantle the *Umatilla*—plate by plate and section by section. They later reassembled the vessel from plans received from the original builders, and this remarkable and virtually indestructible craft subsequently operated for many years as a Japanese steamship. Finally sold for scrap after World War II, the *Umatilla* had outlived the men who built her six decades before.

CHAPTER SIX

MIDWEST AND COASTAL OPERATIONS

A
s more guarding lighthouses were built on the coasts and inland waters, wreckers weren't as necessary as they once were. Once navigation charts became better, iron-hulled ships were constructed, and laws were enforced, the unsavory aspects of the salvage business, where wreckers cruised the waterways in search of shipwrecks, became blunted. The business became civilized.

Salvaging on the West Coast was quite limited at first, which was in contrast to the East Coast, with its long history of trade, commerce, and shipping. Until Californians turned their attention from mining gold to building cities, they didn't focus on what to do with the increasing shipwrecks. The years following the Civil War became a turning point. In 1868, the lighthouses guarding U.S. waters numbered nearly 500, and the great majority were on the East Coast and sweeping around Florida toward Texas. By the 1900s, this number had more than doubled to more than 1,000 warning lights concentrated along the entire U.S. coastline and inland lakes.

The rule of law was now trying to govern wreckers and their activities, especially when a competitive contract didn't exist. With the courts working to apply uniform maritime law, the principles were clear: If a wrecker went to the aid of a ship in distress, he was entitled to compensation for what was rescued. No award was given for saving lives, since every mariner had a duty to save lives in peril without expecting payment. Although this principle sounds good, a few salvors extracted higher-than-normal agreements for saving goods when people needed to be saved as well.

The amount awarded by the admiralty courts depended on the circumstances: first, the degree of danger to the lives of the salvor and his men; second, the risk to the salvor's ships and wrecking gear; third, the assessed value of property that was saved, including if the distressed ship was refloated; fourth, the skill displayed by the salvor; and fifth, the complexity of the save, including how much time and effort was required. Awards were substantially increased for "high order" situations. Examples of high-order salvage were boarding a sinking ship in gales, working on a vessel that was on fire, or raising one that had sunk. Low-order salvage would include towing or working on another vessel in calm seas, simply supplying a ship with fuel, or pulling one from a sandbar.

The compensation awarded to salvors on saved goods averaged about one-third of the salvaged value; the rest went to the owners, underwriters, and even insurance agents. When the underwriters took contract bids, the amounts earned were much lower. When circumstances permitted formal, bid agreements, these salvage contracts controlled and over time became the dominant form of fixing a salvor's "reward."

No claim for salvage could be established under maritime law unless proof was made that the captain abandoned the wreck, or the master requested assistance by his signal or acceptance of the offered help. Depending on the circumstances, the captain could refuse any offer or agree to what he could to save people and cargo. Unscrupulous mariners still existed, however, who would try to convince an upset skipper—who didn't know the local coast, sands, or tides—to abandon his vessel. Taking advantage of their knowledge, these wreckers then freed the ship and claimed it as salvage.

Although the steamship companies and insurers were setting the standard of paying a set, negotiated fee, disputes at sea still occurred—such as when the frightened captain simply yelled, "Go ahead, please, and save us," or words to that effect. When the shipowner wouldn't pay an exor-bitant bill, the matter ended up in court, as did the disputes over contract language and "gratuitous" efforts, such as Captain Scott with the Hoboken Ferry in Chapter Two, "The Wrecker Chronicles."

The payments demanded were high, since the wreckers needed to maintain expensive equipment and had to be paid well for their assumed risks. When the luxurious Atlantic liner *New York*—the sister ship of the *Paris*—ran aground off Sandy Hook, the owners paid nearly $100,000 to float her again. She was the largest ship at the time, carrying up to 1,300 passengers, and this sum would be in the multimillions of dollars today.

Different wrecking companies combined to work on the great American Line steamer *St. Paul* off New Jersey, and divided $160,000 in the process. When their New York offices first received the telegraphed news that the big ocean liner had "run her nose into the sand," rival enti-ties made a "lively race" down the bay. The wreck was too thoroughly embedded in the sand and its salvage value too great for one company to handle alone, even the salvager who first arrived. This operation is more fully described in Chapter Nine, "Wrecks—and a Ghost Ship."

The controversies were not just over the amount of money due to the wreckers. The owners of the ships and goods ended in arguments over who owed them compensation for their losses. To the extent insurance policies were in effect, these payments were made—but not without legal skirmishes over the language and amounts owed. Attorneys then did argue cases over who was at fault and who should pay. For example, if a captain's error caused a loss, then lawyers made claims or filed lawsuits brought on behalf of their clients—but there were major limitations.

Maritime law at this time severely restricted what could be awarded as damages. In an 1886 case named *The Harrisburg* (119 U.S. 199), the U.S. Supreme Court held that maritime common law did not create a cause of action for wrongful death—despite all of the deaths occurring on the seas. A federal statute in 1920 then conferred legal action for wrongful deaths, although a growing number of state statutes already provided remedies for negligently caused loss of life on navigable waters within their coastal limits. If no statutory cause of action was available, then the rule in *The Harrisburg* controlled, and it did for over eighty years until the U.S. Supreme Court overruled the case in 1970.

Although passengers and shippers could freely sue for the goods and possessions lost due to another's fault—whether pilot error or lookout neglect—this right was also very limited. For years, a unique aspect of maritime law was that the total damage liability for negligently causing loss of life, personal injury, ship loss, and cargo damage was limited to the wrecked ship's value after the destruction, or its salvage value. Regardless of loss or degree of fault, if the ship was old and near valueless, this amount was all that could be generally awarded for damages.

These limitations, however, don't exist in today's world where high damages are frequently awarded. The number of lawsuits filed, moreover, wasn't even close to the multitude of actions filed nowadays over just one event. If rocks sheared off a ship's propeller, then plaintiffs sometimes filed lawsuits alleging that defects in the propellers caused the ensuing damage. Back then, however, judges weren't sympathetic as a rule to such claims.

Shipping contracts also contained language that limited liability; unless the shipper or insurer could negotiate the removal of this wording, these boilerplate provisions usually exempted shipowners from liability for nonperformance caused by "accidents or damage from machinery, boilers, and steam, or from accidents of peril of the sea, land, rivers, navigation, or of whatever kind or nature." Negligent claims based on failure to exercise due care—whether steaming into fierce storms, being slammed by rogue waves, or people becoming sick from the food—were virtually nonexistent. In those days, waivers or exclusions from liability were upheld as a general principle. The bottom line: Whether loss of life or possessions, the families of passengers and seamen basically assumed their losses until more modern times.

The United States had a population of more than 30 million in 1868, and only 4,000 Americans were said to be in the wrecking business. The great "mass" of wreckers lived on the most dangerous parts of the American coastline, with the "large majority" on the Atlantic side. They favored the coasts of Maine and Massachusetts, Nantucket Island, the numerous inlets of New Jersey, Florida's Key West, and the basic "pocket" formed by Long Island, New York, and New Jersey. Wreckers lived with their families in the same village while they waited for the "big score" and earned their living by fishing, piloting boats, or repairing craft. Ship salvagers also lived on the U.S. West Coast in settlements, but they were much fewer in number.

Most wreckers were fishermen or boat operators who worked alone and only around their home port. The few with larger operations, such as T. A. Scott, Israel J. Merritt, and T. P. H. Whitelaw, owned or leased different wrecking tugs, cargo schooners, lighters, and gear. In addition to salvaging vessels, the larger operations on the East Coast also were engaged in lightering (freighting goods from ship to port), dredging, pile driving, and building wharves. Most wreckers didn't pay wages to their workers, as each man received a proportionate share of the earnings from each salvage after a certain amount was set aside for the "flag" vessel. This arrangement motivated the men to rip everything away that they could, once the operation was underway.

By the 1880s, wrecking contracts were usually let by fixed bid, whereby the salvor bid a certain amount to save the ship, or for the ship and its contents if the vessel wasn't refloated. Whitelaw on one coast, Merritt and Scott on the other, finally brought class and order to this industry. They were interested in running a business, doing the best job, and gaining long-term relationships with the shippers and insurers.

One writer in the 1890s observed:

By nature, they are brave and daring to a point bordering on recklessness; careless of the present and indifferent to the future; too easy of conscience and too free of hand; their interests make them enjoy "a strong wind with a nasty swell and a hazy day"; and they look forward with keen zest and eager expectations for the wrecks which the swell and fog will bring; yet they are not wholly hardened as to their feelings. They will spring to rescue life without a reward—not only due to the love of adventure and its excitements, but also the provisions of the law that makes it their duty to "save life before property."

❦ ❦ ❦

WHEN SHIPS were in trouble, not being able to communicate their predicament added an extra degree of danger. Edward Very patented what became the modern flare-gun in 1877 for ships in peril. However, as seen with the *Circassian,* vessels had to be close enough to shore for people to see the signals—and that didn't always make a difference. It wouldn't be until 1910 that ship-to-shore wireless communication would become generally available. Until then, crews during the day could only invert their flag as a distress signal; at night they lit a barrel of pitch on the deck or shot flares, hoping some passing vessel would see these lights. If close to shore, they prayed that a nearby lighthouse or lifesaving crew—or a nearby farmer—would somehow learn of their danger. And everything depended on how bad the weather conditions were.

If ships were far at sea, days could pass before they were sighted, especially if the winds blew them away from shipping lanes. As the crew took to their long boats, messages were stuffed in bottles—after the contents had been drained—but not as much to summon help as to make a final record of what had happened to them. Men of the sea were truly at the mercy of the elements.

When a ship wrecked close to shore, a frequent way of moving passengers and crew to land was by stretching a rope or cable hawser from the ship to the beach. Lifesavers shot their lines from mortars and attached the saving ropes. If the vessel wasn't close to a lifesaving station, the crew threw a cask with a line overboard into the swells heading to shore. The waves carried the cask onto the beach and the crew, wreckers, or residents on shore then pulled the line tight. Once in place, this approach could save people, but its limitations—from slowness to difficulties in getting the line aboard during high waves—made surfboats the first choice.

If the ship and its passengers were fortunate enough to encounter favorable surf and weather conditions, the vessel's lifeboats shuttled people to shore. If the vessel was close enough to a lifesaving station, then its rescue teams came with their lifeboats, mortars, or equipment. Once lives were out of danger, then the work of saving property began. If the sea was too heavy for a large schooner to approach, the salvagers scrambled on the bucking, sloshing wreck from a smaller lighter or surfboat.

If the current and winds were sweeping to the beach, the men threw into the sea all of the cargo that saltwater wouldn't ruin. Men on shore grabbed the goods from the breakers for the underwriter's appraisal, if one was there. If the winds and waves were bad, nothing happened until these conditions abated.

The law now mandated that wreckers had to guard the goods from loss. However, it was said that "occasionally a basket or two of wine suffered" or a bale of cotton goods or a case of clothing was "confiscated for immediate wants." The risk of being discovered, however, and the admiralty court or an underwriter deciding on the penalties began to check this behavior. As the industry matured in the mid- to late-nineteenth century, fixed-price contracts removed this motivation from the salvors—although they needed to employ honest men who wouldn't steal from them.

When calmer weather allowed a wrecker tug and lighter to operate, the contracted salvagers would begin stripping the wreck in earnest, provided the derelict was in one piece. One owner observed:

> The sloops descended like carrion birds upon a carcass, and gathered about it, taking on board their vessel all of the available cargo, and such of the rigging and appointment of the ship that was worth taking. When only the bare and empty carcass was left, the ship was abandoned to the winds and waves, and to time which then rotted it, if the other elements didn't scatter the remains far and near.

At the time of Whitelaw's operations, large wrecking companies were working on the East Coast, and warning sentinels, better charts, and insurer networks had reduced the numbers of easy pickings for lone-wolf independents. These larger salvagers employed tugs and steamers of different sizes, specifically outfitted with strong pumps, fire equipment, cranes, and gear ranging from old-style casks to pontoons for raising a ship. These companies had offices or a friendly telegraph agent in Boston, New York, Norfolk, and even New Orleans. The West Coast salvors were small independents without this presence, as T. P. H. Whitelaw quickly ascertained.

Other East Coast companies also had a regional presence or "supervision." For example, the Boston Company was quick to respond to wrecks off the coast of New England; the Submarine Company of New York worked from Montauk Point, Long Island, to the Virginia Capes; and the Norfolk companies watched the coast off the Hatteras. They and other smaller firms quickly called in a Merritt or Scott if the problem was beyond their capabilities.

A network of paid informants existed to support the salvagers. Every morning a particular company's or insurer's agents—who were generally farmers or fishermen living along the coast—rode down the beach trails or sailed away with their glasses trained to the sea. If they discovered any vessel ashore or in distress, they hastily rode to the nearest telegraph station and sent off a dispatch with the information.

No matter where located, tugboat captains and boat owners were salvaging wrecks around their ports of call. It was natural that those in the shipping or towing business would gravitate to wrecking. For example, captains George Flavel and Daniel Kern operated from Astoria, Oregon, ten miles inland on the mighty Columbia River, where large ships sailed into Portland and other inland cities. With a one-half mile width at the Pacific, this huge river flows 1,200 miles from its headwaters in the Canadian Rockies, draining an area of more than 250,000 square miles, and is the largest waterway in volume flowing into the Pacific Ocean from the North American continent.

In the late-nineteenth century, Kern had heard about the loss of the French bark *Henrietta*, which sank off Astoria. He repaired the leaks, half-floated the ship onto the surface, and then towed the vessel to the port. After Kern pumped the seawater out, he brought it to dry dock. Workmen cut the ship in half there and constructed a long middle inside. The men sawed off the masts, installed a steam engine, and attached a propeller. Captain Kern then used this vessel as his steam-wrecker that operated on the river, just as Captain Whitelaw had renovated some of his salvage ships.

In December 1851, Captain George Flavel earned a pilot's license and came to dominate Columbia River pilotage from Astoria for the next twenty-five years. Flavel became the city's first millionaire, amassing a fortune through his Columbia River Bar piloting monopoly and later expanding his empire into shipping, banking, and real estate. Although these were his prime operations, Captain Flavel salvaged his own ships that ran into problems, as well as others that were in range when he had an available vessel and crew.

Between 1884 and 1886, Captain Flavel constructed a magnificent home in Astoria's center that overlooked the Columbia River, and from its fourth-story cupola, he watched the comings and goings of his fleet. Taking up almost a full city block, the splendidly extravagant Queen Anne mansion reflected the rich style and elegance of the late-Victorian era. The Flavel House is now a museum and listed in the National Register of Historic Places. Scant miles away, the Columbia River Maritime Museum was built in 1962, with its impressive facilities now totaling 45,000 square feet of exhibit space.

San Francisco also had its share of salvage operators, including one Captain Henry J. Rogers, who advertised his wrecking service availability in the San Francisco City directory in the late-nineteenth century. He owned the steam-wrecker *San Pedro* and was a dealer in "secondhand engines, boilers, and machinery of every kind." Despite these local salvagers, there is no question that the Whitelaw operation became the largest, most venturesome, and best-known.

● ● ●

THE GREAT LAKES was another center for shipping and salvaging. Five large lakes in North America are grouped near or on the Canadian border: Lake Superior (the largest, which is larger than Scotland), Lake Michigan (the second largest), Lake Huron, Lake Erie, and Lake Ontario. These bodies of water comprise the largest group of freshwater lakes on earth, and the Great Lakes-Saint Lawrence Seaway is the world's largest freshwater system, which is why the lakes are sometimes referred to as inland seas.

Entering on the Atlantic Ocean side of Canada, a large ship can steam through the Saint Lawrence River, through locks, and then dock in Chicago by way of Lake Ontario, Erie, Huron, and finally Lake Michigan. The

shipping of grain, iron ore, coal, lumber, wheat, corn, and different manufactured goods was a big business during Whitelaw's era—and still is.

The Chicago River was a very busy freight and passenger portage. The
river is not particularly long, but is notable for the engineering feats that
directed its flow south through the city, away from Lake Michigan (into
which it had previously emptied), and toward the Mississippi River Basin
for sanitation purposes.

Captain James S. Dunham and his Dunham Towing and Wrecking
Company of Chicago became one of the best-known wrecking outfits on
the Great Lakes. Born in 1837, he began marine life at age fourteen as a
cook on a vessel that plied the Hudson River, and his wages were three
dollars a month. Three years later, he came west to Chicago and worked
in the towing business.

In 1857, he brought two tugs from Chicago to New Orleans through
the Illinois and Michigan Canal, and then down the Mississippi River—
these being the first ships that made the entire trip. During the Civil
War, the Confederates seized the vessels. Dunham eventually wound up
in Philadelphia, where during the winter of 1861, he built another tugboat. He brought this vessel to Chicago via the New York and Erie Canal
(that runs from the Hudson River to Lake Erie) and then made this city
his permanent home.

With that one tug, Captain Dunham grew his towing and salvage
business until he had the contracts for most of the heavy towing work
on the Chicago River. Like Whitelaw, he acquired steam pumps, divers,
hawsers, lighters, a wreck-tug, schooners, and different tugs for towing.
Dunham ended up with what he categorized as the only complete wrecking outfit on Lake Michigan.

He also owned various tugs used just for towing. These smaller boats
were necessary to move larger vessels from close docks, narrow passageways, and ice-filled water to the channels. Dunham built up other ventures, such as the Chicago Steamship Company and the Chicago Transit
Company. He was an alderman, president of the Chicago River
Improvement Association, and an officer of different organizations.

On the Great Lakes, the elements truly conspired against shippers.
Fully one-half of all wrecks occurred during the late autumn and winter

months when ice jammed the waters and winds and waves wrecked vessels. A ship crashed or sank nearly every day on the lakes.

Among the ships owned by Captain Dunham was the three-masted schooner *Wells Burt*. Built in 1873 at Detroit, she was a full-rigged, 201-foot-long ship. After ten years of service, Dunham bought the ship, but his ownership unfortunately didn't last very long. The vessel was carrying coal from Buffalo to Chicago when the fierce gale of May 20, 1883, caught it and many other vessels on the waters. Terrible winds whipped the lakes into a frenzy of white-capped water, and this storm lasted for three days. On Lake Michigan alone, the storm damaged 100 vessels and destroyed four. One of the vessels lost was the *Wells Burt*. She wrecked off Evanston, Illinois, and her crew of ten perished. The wreck is today considered to be a prime dive site, and the ship rests upright in forty feet of water.

Other wreckers joined Dunham in the region. Diver Peter Falcon, Jim Reid and his son, Tom, of the Reid Wrecking Company, and Captain J. B. Green were other notables. The Reids were salvors of the early 1900s who started out in the log rafting business on Lake Huron. Tom Reid and his son, Jim, became well known later because of numerous ship salvages on the Great Lakes.

Peter Falcon stood out with his salvage work by working at depths greater than 100 feet. In the mid-nineteenth century, only a few men operated at these dangerous depths due to the crushing pressures, zero-visibility, and the risk of decompression sickness (known then as "diver's blackout" and nowadays as the bends). In 1866, Falcon had become famous after raising the schooner *Ocean Wave* from 113 feet of water and the steamer *City of Boston* from a depth of 100 feet, both in Lake Michigan.

Wherever underwater work was attempted, diving during these days was very risky. The equipment was crude, and as a diver descended deeper, the "pumpers" had to work harder to operate the rotary hand pumps used in maintaining the necessary air supply. Salvors didn't know much about the body-crushing damage from deep-level water pressures, nor the deadly effects of the bends, and their work in unknown waters with limited- or zero-visibility created more dangers.

Divers routinely suffered injuries throughout the country, and death was not uncommon.

In 1859, the propeller-driven *Milwaukee* collided with the schooner *J. H. Tiffany* and sank near the Straits of Mackinac connecting Lake Michigan with Lake Huron. Both vessels sank. Falcon found the *Tiffany* in some 100 feet of water and saved its cargo of railroad iron. He later salvaged the boiler and machinery from the steamer *Milwaukee,* using a number of "inflatable wooden casks," which he patented. The equipment basically was a forerunner of the "salvage drum" that's used today. Unfortunately, these successes also cost the life of one of his divers, who died from the fatal bends.

Father-and-son salvors Tom and James Reid ran into similar dangers when they tried to raise the sunken steamer *Cayuga* in 1897. The ship settled in 105 feet of water, and Tom Reid decided to sink giant pontoons with water, attach them to the hull, and pump in air for the needed buoyancy. His attempts weren't successful, and son James took over, nearly bankrupting the firm with his obsession to float the ship even as different underwater tragedies occurred. By descending too deep or falling into a deep crevice, one diver was crushed to death so badly that workers couldn't at first remove his helmet. Others were viciously stricken by the bends, including Tom Reid. When the *Cayuga* finally rose to the surface, it ripped away from its chains and sank again, dragging the barge down to the bottom and apparently another worker to his death. Divers can view the wreck remains today, even with four of Reid's pontoons still attached to the *Cayuga* and the barge—100 feet away—littered with different hoists, pumps, tools, and tackle.

The Great Lakes shipping operations exemplified how ships could work in tandem with railroads. Train ferries developed around the industrialized Midwest in transporting ore and iron products. Railroad tracks were fitted on a vessel's deck with a door at the bow and stern for access to the dock's railroad. A floating ramp that moved with the tides connected the land tracks to the vessel. A train pulled on, or backed its cars on board, to be quickly taken off when the ship reached its destination. Before the distant, span bridges were constructed, these train ferries operated on runs from Oakland to San Francisco,

Whittier (Alaska) to Seattle, and New York City to Norfolk/Cape Charles (Virginia), among others.

● ● ●

WRECKING HAS two distinct approaches: pulling stranded craft from beaches or rocks and raising sunken ships from the sea. When a ship grounded, rocks and debris could punch holes in the hull or strain planking or plates with seawater rushing inside. If the captain was lucky and the vessel remained structurally sound, divers didn't need to patch or plug the hull and pump seawater out; however, the wreckers might have to use steam-tugs and hawsers, anchors with capstans, and the tides. Interestingly enough, sometimes a tug couldn't drag a heavy boat off with an iron chain—but a heavy rope worked instead. A thick hawser stores a "strong momentum of mass" inside the rope as the tug stretches it. Continuing to pull on the hawser after the stretching stops, the line can spring away with considerable force and jerk the vessel free.

If a heavy steamer ran high on a beach and embedded in the sand, using tugs and towlines might not be enough to pull it off. In this case, the wreckers dropped large anchors offshore that were attached to thick, fifteen-inch hawsers. Capstans and winches tightened the long ropes as the steam-tugs pulled on their lines, and these actions with the ropes' elasticity might be enough to do the job. Care had to be taken, however, so that the pulled hawsers didn't rip out the ship's sides.

The salvagers also waited for more "favorable" ocean conditions. If the ship grounded at low tide, moderate waves and a high tide might be enough to lift her. If the vessel grounded at high tide, it usually took a storm nearly as severe as what drove her ashore, along with tugs and sea anchors. The salvors sometimes had a long wait for a different season, since the higher tides might only occur during the spring.

Quicksand at beaches trapped vessels, when the unstable sand collapsed and sucked the ship down until it finally hit bedrock. As this level could be stories down, the wreckers needed to construct deep "route" trenches for the craft to be pulled out. Seas that might lift a stranded vessel from a sandbar could break over her and create more problems. At times, one long pull wasn't enough to bring the vessel off and a series of heaves had to be used. After each jump seaward, the cables were tightened again, and little by little the ship "hitched" toward deep water before finally floating away.

Even when pulled from a smooth beach, a ship needed to be closely inspected. These collision and salvage operations were hard on vessels. As one salvager observed, "When at last she quivered and went to the cables, she received a shock that seemed to jolt every spike and bolt in her frame." Running aground on a beach could age a vessel more than a "score of storms at sea." The winds, seas, and rocks twisted planks and frames, loosened bolts and spikes, and sheared away hull rivets.

The depth, of course, to which a ship sank was quite important. Up to the early 1900s, diving operations were usually limited to 100 feet or less, since most divers couldn't dive or work long at greater depths. Within this limit, a tug could lift a small vessel with its crane—cargo and all—until her deck openings were out of the water. Divers then patched her, nailed or bolted planks over openings, and pumped out the seawater. Even if a ship was half-submerged, a tug could tow the stricken vessel to a dry dock for repairs, its pumps keeping the leaks under control.

Salvors preferred to use large derricks to lift smaller vessels (generally no more than 750 tons gross) that sank in shallow bays and harbor berths because this was considered to be the quickest and cheapest way to save a ship. Divers secured a hawser or strong cables underneath the ship, and the salvor's derrick barge or wreck-tug (with an "A" frame hoist) lifted the small boat by a steam-driven engine. Two barges positioned on either side or in a line by the boat could be used with greater lifting power on larger vessels. The Chapman Wrecking Company in New York was best known for its use of these large derricks.

When decks were able to be sealed, wreckers could pump compressed air into air bags stuffed inside the sunken ship. This technique forced the seawater out while the air bags added buoyancy, and it could be used when cranes couldn't initially lift the ship. The use of inflatable air bags didn't work as well, however, with heavy steamers, vessels loaded with cargo, or when beams were splintered.

When cranes or air bags didn't work, more expensive pontoons were used and attached. Depending on the ship's position, these flotation devices were attached at the boat's bottom, midway, or even on the surface. After workers fitted them on the vessel's sides, divers placed heavy chains under the boat's keel and fastened the ends around the pontoons. At the same time, others were busily patching and sealing the wreck. Steam pumps next filled the pontoons with water until they sank by the vessel's sides. When the chains were tightened, steam engines pumped air into the pontoons to replace the water, and this additional buoyancy helped to bring the wreck up. The process might need to be repeated several times, as men tightened the chains each time to keep the ship at its higher float position. Provided the wind, tides, and sea conditions were favorable, the ship finally could float to the surface. Care had to be taken, however, when the craft rose through the waters. At times, sunken vessels became erratic in their upward movement, even turning over or rising at an angle to slam into the hovering salvage craft and cause damage.

In shallower waters with less water pressure on decks, divers could work quickly in shoring up the ship to withstand the pressure change when the seawater was pumped out. The workmen covered the necessary hatch and deck openings with strong canvas and planking, then opened up holes large enough for the suction and air hoses to pass through. When all was ready, steam pumps on nearby wreck barges or tugs sucked out the water with buoyant air being forced into the holds. Cranes could also be used.

When the depth was great and water pressure too strong, then more arduous and expensive salvaging efforts were required. Divers at those depths expended great time in bolting or nailing large planks over all of the ship's openings, such as the passageways, doors, ports, and holes. They fastened thick timbers to the vessel with large sections of canvas and oakum as seals. (Oakum was loose hemp or jute fiber—treated with tar, creosote, or asphalt—that divers used to caulk the seams.) Underwater beams were constructed to hold the sides when the water pressures changed. The steam pumps were then put in use.

No matter how simple any job first looked, complications always seemed to take place. In 1887, the steamer *Wells City* sank in New York

Harbor. After patching holes, closing the openings, and attaching large pontoons, the salvagers started their steam pumps. As the steamer moved close to the surface, however, her sharp keel cut the pontoon chains in two. The entire chaining, patching, and floating operations had to be started all over again. When the *Oregon* sank off Fire Island on the East Coast, the divers labored long and hard for weeks, but nothing seemed to work. Although the salvors were able to retrieve the cargo, the wreckers finally had to give up their efforts due to the ocean's depth, turbulence, and lack of visibility. These failures were commonplace.

Once the ship was on the surface, a tug towed the wreck into shallower water or a dry dock for permanent repairs. A successful salvager had to know the local tides, weather conditions, storm fronts, and geology in his operations. For example, tides were high off England and Canada, but not as dominant comparatively on the East Coast and near New York. Given the unpredictability of storms, the changing currents, and human error, deadly situations occurred regularly.

The elements seemed to conspire against salvors, as storms raged in and destroyed the work completed or tore more of the vessel apart. Pumps broke down, anchors dragged, pontoons leaked, chains snapped, and the vessel drifted out of control with the tides. Although a wrecker's life was always full of danger and life-threatening risks, the emotional rush from beating the storms, tasting salt on their lips, and feeling the winds against their faces seemed to motivate these men into trusting their lives to swaying ropes and worn windlasses. They were adventurers who felt they were masters of the sea.

● ● ●

WRECKERS NEEDED to show ingenuity along with perseverance. The *Milwaukee* was a large vessel, 483 feet long and 56 feet wide, that grounded on a huge rock in September 1898 near Aberdeen, Scotland. The collision ripped open the hold for thirty feet to a height of "eight feet above the tank top." When the salvage operators agreed that it would be impossible to save the entire vessel, they decided on a different plan. To save her, the wreckers decided to blast the ship in two.

The salvagers exploded successive charges of dynamite around the severing point, each charge used for a four- to six-foot section of ship. Although more than 520 pounds of explosives were used, none of the surrounding structural sheets of steel were damaged. When finished, a 180-foot section of the ripped fore-end was left on the rocks.

The saved portion extended from the forward end of the bridge to the stern, including the *Milwaukee*'s engines and boilers. With the ship's own engines helping to move it, a tug towed the 300-foot section to Tyre, the port in England where the ship was first constructed. The saved section was moored in the river until a new bow was built, launched, and later connected to the stern remnant. The new addition was so successfully placed that it was impossible to pinpoint the line of connection.

Fourteen years later, the tanker *Jose* lay at her dock in the East River of New York City, taking on a cargo of case oil and gasoline bound for Central American ports, when a bad fire broke out. A tug towed the flaming vessel away to prevent the fire from spreading to other ships. Fireboats raced over and finally extinguished the flames, but they pumped so much water into the *Jose* that the ship sank.

The owners later hired salvors to save the ship, even though the wreck sank in an "unfortunate place." The ship was thirty-eight feet down on a bottom covered with huge boulders that formed an eight-foot-deep pocket. The *Jose* lay right in the path of shipping, moreover, and the tides were so strong that work could only be done during the "slack water" between high and low tides.

The Merritt & Chapman Derrick & Wrecking Company (the entity formed after Merritt merged with its chief competitor) agreed to raise the steamer. The wrecking plan was simple: Six underwater pontoons, three placed on a side, would be attached to the hull, and two barges would run the steam pumps to refloat it. The pontoons had triangular chain wells, or openings, that flared out on their bottoms for the connecting chains.

Since the wreck squatted over huge rocks, divers first had to blast channels through the boulders, pass a small line in and out of the wells, and then haul the heavier, stronger chains in. The underwater crew painstakingly maneuvered the heavy chains through the wells on one side, underneath the hull, and then to the pontoon openings on the other—each pontoon with four wells to work. As the chains were brought through an opening, divers worked them through supporting planks, and hydraulic jacks pulled them tight.

Bringing the chains under the *Jose* was a long, tedious, difficult task. Workers had to regulate the tension on each one to carry the required weight. When the tide was running, divers couldn't work because the underwater currents were so strong that they swept men away. The rushing currents shifted the sunken ship, and this movement by itself crushed the chains. Since divers could only work during slack water, their efforts dragged on for months. The swells from approaching ships rocked the pontoons, causing more delays when the attaching chains snapped.

Due to the angle of the connections, the wreck's pull on the shackles dragged the salvage barges perilously close together. To remedy this situation, workmen constructed beams, or "spreaders," between the barges that kept the salvage craft apart. To hold the pontoons level, laborers ran timbers from one boat to another with more chains passed around the sunken hull.

To raise the wreck, pumps filled the pontoons with water and sank them as deep as possible. At low tide, jacks tightened the shackles while workmen adjusted their tension. When the tide rose, the pontoons were pumped dry, and their combined lift and the increased ocean volumes raised the vessel from the deep pocket where she had rested.

Once the ship settled on higher ground, the wreckers left it on the bottom. When the tide was low, pumps filled the pontoons full again and the chains tightened. Once more, pumps removed the pontoon water at high tide until the *Jose* finally left the bottom; the chains were pulled tight to hold the ship toward the surface in that position. This process was repeated until the decks were clear of water and divers could descend to cover the ports and openings. Now watertight, the steam pumps cleared the trapped water out. The *Jose* finally floated to the surface, and waiting tugs quickly towed her away for repairs and further service. Despite the long, complex operations, the salvage cost was less than the expense of constructing a new tanker and a navigational hazard had been removed.

❋   ❋   ❋

AS SEEN WITH the *Milwaukee*, salvage operations were conducted around the world. A Hamburg salvage company refloated the American liner *Paris* that stranded on rocks in 1899 near the entrance to the English Channel. This ship was a large steamer with three stacks, triple-expansion engines, and three masts rigged for sail. Ten years later, the same ship ran aground on one of the most dreaded hazards to navigation that ran along England's south coast and rightly named "The Manacles."

Stranded 150 yards from shore, the *Paris* stayed fast on the rocks for six weeks. British salvors left when they couldn't pull the vessel away with a combination of steam-tugs and the ship's engines. Although an alternate plan called for the use of pontoons and air bags placed underneath the bow, one problem first had to be solved: A thick granite pinnacle had penetrated high through the vessel's bottom and held the *Paris* tight to the reef. Thick seaweed further impeded the new divers. These obstacles had to be removed before work could proceed.

The thick granite spike that impaled the ship next had to be removed, and the ensuing underwater explosions blasted away more than 15,000 cubic feet of rock. As rapidly as the boulders were separated, underwater divers attached thick hawsers to them and wreck steamers dragged them away.

The salvors then temporarily patched the bow "aft to the midship section." Loading granite rubble in the stern and filling her back compartments with water, the wreckers managed to lift the bow out of the ocean and free her. However, the workers had filled the steamer inside with water to the ship's depth of fifty feet. When the ship's pumps couldn't cope with this extra water, the salvors needed to quickly cut holes into her decks and sides to insert hoses. Nearby wreck-schooners then powered up their steam engines and sucked out the heavy water ballast.

As the vessel righted itself, a rush of water tore out compartments and inundated the engine rooms and furnaces. After the wreckers pumped out the engine rooms and the *Paris* righted once more, a strong gale suddenly roared into the channel. Its crashing waves opened the stricken ship's seams and filled her once more with saltwater. When these winds and waves subsided, the boat had to be pumped out again. The divers needed to complete "considerable" additional patching, and they made these patches of wood shields, padded first with canvas and rubber, before fitting them over the breaks. The *Paris* was finally raised, taken to a dry dock, fully repaired, and placed back in service. The costs of the salvage proved to be a fraction of the cost needed to build a new ship in the manner of this grand vessel.

Another talked-about salvage attempt came from a furious gale that drove one boat so hard onto the shore, it rolled over "all but upside down" with her smokestack sticking in the mud. This was the *Silurus,* which was a dredger built for use in the Port of Bombay.

The wreckers first constructed a huge, strong framework of logs to the hull so that the pull of the tow cables wouldn't rip the vessel apart. Divers used hacksaws to cut holes into the steel hull to pull the cables through. As the wreck was lying on a submerged hill, workers removed a thousand yards of the seabed to create a flat table for the vessel to move over. Although rust and mud made work and visibility difficult, the laboring men finally completed these tasks.

As 2,000 tons of ship would power away with the attached hawsers, the salvagers had to find something that could withstand the harsh tug-of-war pulls. The salvors solved this problem by sinking four old boilers into pits that were dug into the rock and then filling them with concrete. As such, they had created four bollards (the thick posts on ships or docks for tying hawsers) that were as solid as the rock they were set in. The men cut a twelve-inch propeller shaft into lengths, placed them at different intervals into the shore opposite the wreck, and set them in concrete as more bollards. The workmen next wrapped "some ten miles" of six-inch-thick steel cable around everything.

They lashed giant wire ropes around the "top gear" to prevent it from breaking away when the ship rolled over. The laborers next dug a wide, long trench to the boat, so the steam-tugs could get a direct pull. When the time was ready and high tide drew near, they filled the ship's compartments with compressed air, emptied the water from the pontoons on the ship's tower, and started the steam engines to pull on the giant steel cables.

The *Silurus* slowly came up as her funnel tugged up from beneath ten feet of mud. The hauling went on until the pontoons cleared the water.

When these floats hindered their efforts, the salvors cut through the wire lashings with their "blowpipes" and freed the ship from their constraints. Adjustments were made and the next haul set the *Silurus* on a fairly even keel. She was towed out, repaired, and put back into service.

● ● ●

EACH SHIP presented a different problem. One might have caught fire and left a burned-out, red-hot shell. The salvors might sail next to where a gale had thrown the vessel onto the beach. Ships collided, smashed into rocks, grounded onto sandbars, overturned in gales, and in any number of ways created danger for crews and rescuers alike.

Head wreckers had to be skilled sailors, carpenters, boilermakers, electricians, and shipwrights. They needed to know marine, civil, and hydraulic engineering, as well as the tides, seasons, and weather. These men had to quickly give first aid to the severely injured and save them, as well as preside over funerals. If they couldn't (or wouldn't) toil strenuously for fifty hours straight with little food or sleep, then they soon retired or were out of business.

The author C. J. Cutcliffe Hyne wrote in the 1924 British monthly *Discovery*:

> The expert diver descends to make an accurate survey, re-ascends, and is then unhelmed. He is rather blue in the lips, being middle-aged, having stayed down at eighteen fathoms [108 feet] too long, and too quick in his ascent. He has a good deal to say about the viscosity and other qualities of the mud, but between profanities is distinctly cheerful. He tells about the hot place where the number-two hold's forward bulkhead has gone to, and the man rubs his water-puckered hands when he reports that the collision wound is on top-side.
>
> Being a practical engineer, the expert who brought the intimate survey inside his head, then scratches on a slate what's needed to make the full working drawings of the steamer's wounds and how to temporarily repair them. A patch is in hand soon afterwards and

with everything else needed for this job, he is in a small matter of hours being taken back across the ocean to the scene.

The men then wriggle into their diving suits and head down to patch the gash. They trim jagged edges and fit on C-shaped clamps. The patch is lowered to them, and they see it dimly, if at all, in the muddy water as it sways and struggles in the tideway. They get it canted against the ruin and make it fast. They bolt where they can. They caulk generously, and then they or the other divers make fast or caulk or patch all scuttles, companions, hatches, and ventilators, leaving only apertures large enough for the air hoses and water to exit.

Then the salvage ship starts up her air compressors, or opens her air-bottle valves, and eighteen fathoms below, the ocean, mud, and possibly the rags of men are blown from the wreck, and with jerks she comes to her normal vertical position. Then in a pother of bubbles, and mud, and stink, the ruin shoulders herself sullenly to the surface.

Salvaging was an art and not a science. Whether employing deflated air bags inside or attaching water-filled pontoons outside, wreckers had to decide on what lift—including from hovering wreck derricks or barge cranes—would be equivalent to the derelict's water-swamped weight. If the ship lay on the bottom, they had to decide on how best to attach the pontoons. If grounded, salvagers needed to find the way to the open sea.

Deep-sea diving was obviously grueling, dangerous work. Aside from the risk of encountering predators of the deep and being trapped on the bottom, divers found themselves coated with mud and iron rust. In addition to the sweat and aching muscles, abrasions and broken limbs were not uncommon. The lower temperatures at deeper depths forced them to don warm woolen socks, sweaters, and pants, sometimes layering on two or even three combinations. Their bodies endured pressure five times or more than atmospheric pressure, and much greater than what the human body was designed for. A man's exertions used so much oxygen that his heart had to pump at an ever-increased speed just to replace the depleted oxygen supply. As the air pressure within the body worked to equalize the water pressure outside, the salvor toiled under a water mass that would squash an unprotected worker. Divers had to know the terrain, for if they fell into an unknown abyss, the increased water pressure alone could crush them.

Then there was the matter of the ascent. When the outside water pressure suddenly became less, air pressure inside the body caused excess nitrogen to bubble, as the gas seeks to escape, just as the bubbles do in soft drinks. To avoid the sickness, paralysis, and death from the dreaded "bends," divers had to ascend very slowly. A worker could slide a hundred feet down a rope in seconds, but he couldn't come up for at least two hours. The longer a person worked at deeper depths, the more time was needed when surfacing. Tables exist showing the precise relationship between the ocean's depths, the time spent working underwater, and the time required for an ascent—but these guidelines weren't developed until the 1910s.

Despite the risks, even the uninitiated tried salvaging. Due to the potentially high rewards from aiding a disabled ship, some captains undertook an irregular wrecking business. Ever on the alert for a stranded ship, they would veer away from their route to render assistance. A tramp steamer that located and towed a disabled transatlantic liner back to port realized much more money than the owner and crew could ever make by hauling its cargo. Since harbor jobs were easier than the remote, deeper locations, they paid less, and so professional salvagers such as Whitelaw sought the open-sea work. In fact, he seemed to prefer these challenges.

SUCCESS, SEALING, AND THE ARCTIC

Regardless of which coast they sailed, those working on the sea were hearing about Captain Whitelaw and his exploits. With his luxuriant white beard, homburg hat, and dark three-piece suit, Whitelaw was likely to appear wherever a West Coast vessel went down or plowed into a reef. His network of friends and agents, not to mention the crews on his ships and wreck-tugs, tipped him off about ships in distress. Owners and captains of ships that just wrecked took to their longboat, docked on the San Francisco waterfront, and appeared in his office to ask for help.

He had a simple way of looking at complex problems. Whitelaw demonstrated each year his "uncanny cleverness," as reporters commented, in finding the ways to raise sunken ships. His philosophy was:

> Every job presents a different puzzle. The underlying principle, however, is to create an artificial buoyancy—to make the ship lighter than the water it displaces. Divers first patch up sunken ships; they are then closed as near watertight as possible, and then are pumped out. These actions make the vessel behave like a "bubble." And a bubble can't stay under water. Powerful forces

are at hand for the ship salvor to use; for example, there is the buoying power of the ocean. Tides and winds also help in moving vessels from the rocks—although they can sometimes be a hindrance too."

T. Kenneth (Ken) Whitelaw was a grandson of Captain Whitelaw. Having worked directly for Cappie, as close friends and family called him, Ken pointed out that his grandfather "got things done because he worked with his crew." Even after he had hired a tough, burly crew to work a wreck, T. P. H. in his "older days" still grabbed a sledgehammer and told everyone, "I can still sling that sledge." Dressed in his standard frock coat and derby hat, Whitelaw slammed the sledgehammer down with sharp cracks on a chain being attached or a boiler being taken apart. He used wit in encouraging his men: While a man swung a heavy mallet, he would say, "Hit harder. It doesn't have any brains." Or he'd shout, "Hit it even harder! This sledge doesn't have friends."

Another time, T. P. H. was on one of his salvage ships, but the vessel was steaming too slowly toward the wreck's location. He investigated and decided that the ship's bilge keel had somehow become turned at an angle. Much like having the rudder set in the wrong way, this slowed his vessel down. Ordering his men to bring the steamer to a complete halt, Captain Whitelaw jumped overboard. He spent four hours under the water with a hacksaw while he cut away the interfering metal.

Salvage efforts were, of course, hard and dangerous work. Before acetylene torches were invented, divers used hacksaws to cut anchors and chains away. Using tools underwater such as axes, hammers, and saws required great effort when working against the ocean's force and pressure. Days were long. "We would work and work until you couldn't work anymore," said Ken Whitelaw. "We worked at least twelve-hour days. The men didn't have coffee breaks then, and there was no concept of overtime."

During the first decades of Whitelaw's career, men unloaded wrecked cargo by hand or with steam-driven donkey engines, as electric-motor-driven cranes to handle containers had not been invented. They didn't have the benefit of electronic, sophisticated navigation, or storm-warning techniques and equipment. Men washed ships down with canvas bags filled with water, becoming creative when doing this. One crew filled a few canvas bags with whiskey and now and then took "nips" from the bags. It isn't known if someone saw the men taking odd swigs from their water bags or whether their tipsy behavior gave them away, but they were fined for their acts.

Grandson Ken said the Captain spoke with "a little" Scottish accent. To others, it was more than "a little," and closer to a full-blown brogue. He was a Scotsman, after all, and quite proud of his heritage. The family attended every Scottish picnic, outing, sporting event, or occasion, and his grandson remembered the family crossing the bay to attend Scottish picnics and festivals.

T. P. H. brought several members of the Whitelaw clan from their North Ayrshire hometown in Irvine, Scotland, to the United States. At the time, according to his grandson, Captain Whitelaw was "a very wealthy man." Cappie had four brothers and brought over their sons to work in his business. Nephew Jack (Uncle Jack to Ken) was a diver with the salvage company—and a "great one," according to the grandson. Nephew Jim delivered the salvage yard's maritime equipment by horse and wagon to the docks and shipyards. Nephew Tom (or Thomas) was a mechanic.

"The grand old man of the waterfront" called his sons and grandkids by their middle names, since the family practice was to name all of the boys "Thomas" as their first name. To distinguish him from all of the other Thomases, grandson Thomas Kenneth was called Kenneth or Ken. His father and Captain Whitelaw's son was first named Thomas Andrew, so he was called Andrew. Although the "old man" was "Thomas Patrick," he was called the usual dad, granddad, or even Captain. Otherwise, his name would have been Patrick.

The businesses under Whitelaw's watchful eye prospered. His reputation was now widespread for taking on any type of salvage project. For example, when the steamer *Ajax* wrecked off Eureka, in northern California, in 1890, the insurance companies sent their representatives to investigate. When the underwriters two weeks later abandoned all hope of saving anything from the *Ajax*, they immediately sent a telegram to Captain Whitelaw and asked if he would buy her. He did. The parts ended up in his overflowing scrap yard.

The *Elizabeth* also wound up in his salvage yard. This tall sail ship was a 1,866-ton wooden vessel built at Newcastle, Maine, and it was launched in 1882. Searsport, Maine, sea captains—"active and retired, along with their relatives"—owned the vessel. Based on the East Coast in New York City, the ship hauled "general" cargo to San Francisco. The ship was loaded with California grain on one trip to Liverpool, England, and then returned with products to New York City. In all, the *Elizabeth* made six round-trip voyages, only to be lost on its seventh.

Arriving at the Golden Gate on February 21, 1891, the *Elizabeth* carried a varied cargo of iron rails, pipe, ink, whiskey, burlap, and other consigned general merchandise. Despite the rapidly deteriorating weather conditions, Captain J. Herbert Colcord thought he could work his ship through the channel. He refused the offer of a tow from a tug to save the towage cost of fifty dollars.

Colcord was a famous New England seagoing name, and the captain had his share of confidence in his navigating skills. His ship sailed partway into the harbor when the winds suddenly shifted and combined with a "strong eddy and the heave of the sea" to drive the *Elizabeth* backward. Just before the ship went onto the rocks, Colcord hailed two tugs, but his haggling over the tow price delayed taking a line aboard, even as "the ship was fast driving toward the shore."

The price was finally agreed and the tow taken. However, when the towing hawser parted, the ebb tide and southwest current drove the *Elizabeth* past Point Bonita, which is across the bay on the tip of the Marin Headlands. The ship grounded on the banks, and with heavy seas breaking over the decks, saltwater flowed into the holds through broken hatches.

The hissing breakers swept Captain Colcord and his son off the aft deck to the lower main deck, injuring the captain in the fall. The tugs approached cautiously in the shallow water, threw across another tow rope, and finally took off Colcord's wife and family. This operation was accomplished at risk to boats and crew; the waves crashed also over the tugs as they held their positions on the ocean side of the bobbing vessel.

When the tugs steamed away with their tow, the *Elizabeth* pulled off the bank and continued northward, as the injured Colcord stayed aboard with the rest of his crew. The heavy poundings opened up the ship's hull, and water levels rose inside when the pumps couldn't keep up. When the weather worsened, the men on the tugs were forced to cut their lines and flee for the safety of calmer water.

John Silovich was the captain of one tug, the *Alert*. He recalled:

> It was blowing a hurricane, the sea was sharp and choppy, and little headway could be made. With hawsers breaking, lifeboats tossing, and seas flooding every deck, this was a scene that no one would forget. No ship could have survived beyond the Heads [above the Golden Gate]. When an enormous sea threw one lifeboat across the tug's bow from the ship, the mate shouted, "Cut the tow line!" [And the tug did.]

Without any assistance, the *Elizabeth* seemed doomed. Striking once more on the north shore, the ship drifted off again, before finally grounding ashore seven miles north of Point Bonita. Pinned on a gauntlet of sharp rocks, the raging seas slammed the ship over the white-specked boulders and it began to disintegrate. Crews from the lifesaving stations at Golden Gate Park and Fort Point Lighthouse (both located on the San Francisco Bay side) responded to the distress calls. Just as another tug towed a surfboat from Fort Point with would-be rescuers, a large crashing wave swept over the small boat. The roller washed the men overboard and the station head drowned.

The Golden Gate Park keeper then picked up the Fort Point crew, and the men crossed the bay by ferry to Sausalito on the Marin side. Unable to obtain horses from the local liveries, he told the men to harness themselves to a heavy wagon. Although the load weighed nearly a ton and a half, the men began pulling the cart to the disaster scene. The muddy road led them over high hills and through deep ravines of adobe mud and soft slippery clay, but the tired surfmen trudged on until five o'clock in the morning. They stopped when they reached a point some eight miles from Sausalito.

The men finally were able to obtain horses there, and the party quickly reached the ocean where the *Elizabeth* had last grounded. Upon arriving there, the exhausted lifesavers discovered that the ship had pulled free once again to drift even farther north. Continuing their trek along the rugged Marin coast, they finally arrived at the wreck—but too late to help. Eighteen of the twenty-six-man crew died, and among the dead was Captain Colcord.

The vessel was ground to splinters. Onlookers later said:

Scattered, mashed, and pulverized, the ship lined the shore—a breakwater of matchwood a third of a mile long. Here and there, on some jagged rock near the bar, a larger lump of wreckage than any in the pulpy breakwater could be seen. Almost flattened by the battering it received, a part of the stern lay by the surf. The raging seas had lifted it bodily over a twenty-foot crag and flung it fifteen yards beyond.

The ocean tossed some of the remlains ashore in distinct pieces. The port side of the bow lay in deeper water, however, weighed down by the anchor chain.

After helping to save eight crew members who washed ashore, the local residents worked with the lifesavers in their search for the dead. Most of the badly pounded bodies were recovered, among the last being the captain, whose body was discovered two days later. People carefully picked over the flotsam in the surf, but little was seen floating in the water.

The ship was carrying a large amount of heavy freight, and Captain T. P. H. Whitelaw consequently bought the wreck and cargo rights. Using the wreck-schooner *Sampson* as a working platform, Whitelaw sent his divers down to salvage what they could from "the heterogeneous mass of stuff" that had once been the *Elizabeth*. The disaster that befell this vessel was a tragedy for the Pacific Coast maritime community. The horrible strength of the gale that blew the *Elizabeth* to its doom, the heroic rescue of Captain Colcord's wife and family, the efforts of the lifesavers, and the loss of the men and ship made this wreck stand out.

❧ ❧ ❧

DESPITE THE advent of warning lighthouses, lifesaving stations, stronger-built vessels, and better equipment, the risks of sea travel were many. Ships continually wrecked due to unexpected storms, uncharted reefs, engine malfunctions, and collisions—not to mention pilot error. As an example of how one mistake resulted in tragedy is the story of the *Escambia*.

The iron-hulled, 1,401-ton screw steamer *Escambia* was built in England in 1879 and sailed to the Orient, exchanging its cargo to take on wheat bound for the United States. After that voyage, the ship was leaving the Golden Gate in June 1882 with 2,450 tons of general goods, coal, and wheat bound for Portugal.

Eighty tons of coal had been heaped high on the deck and reached to the bridge. Noting that the Plimsoll mark—the line marking the depth to which goods could be legally loaded—was now underwater, Captain Purvis ordered the engineer to pump the ballast tanks free of water and raise the ship above the mark. To save on pilot fees, he dismissed his pilot while the *Escambia* still sailed inside San Francisco Bay. The pilot left but warned that the ship was unmanageable due to its cargo imbalance and lack of steadying ballast.

The top-heavy vessel soon capsized. Rushing to abandon ship, a panicked sailor overturned one lifeboat. The smallest boat aboard was the only one that managed to pull free of the sinking steamer. Captain Purvis, the engineer, steward, cook, and three seamen pulled on the oars for the beach, but the heavy surf capsized the boat as they approached the shore. The three sailors drowned, while the captain and three others survived. Twenty-five crewmen died.

An onlooker watched in disbelief as the disaster took place and quickly ran away to spread the alarm. Due to a fire then raging at the docks, the search for survivors didn't start until the next day. A tug was dispatched to search for survivors, but its penny-pinching captain delayed until he received a call from an outbound ship that requested a tow. After completing this paying assignment, he circled around the area. He finally discovered the mast of the *Escambia* rising above the water as she rested in five and a half fathoms (thirty-three feet) of ocean.

Wreckers later blasted the hulk to clear the channel. Despite the reports of faulty loading, a court of inquiry exonerated the captain. The British Consul ruled that her engines had eased off at a dangerous moment, the vessel fell broadside into the waves, and the opposing pressures of wind and strong ebb tide had tipped the *Escambia* over.

The *City of Chester* was another ship lost in San Francisco Bay. This iron steamship was built in 1875 and had a typical succession of owners. On August 22, 1888, the Oregon Railroad Company owned her, but the ship was under charter to the Pacific Coast Steamship Company. When a second steamer, the *Oceanic,* collided and cut the ship cleanly in two, the *City of Chester's* boilers exploded and she went down minutes after the collision. Thirty-four people died without a chance.

No attempts were made to raise that ship, since no diver could descend to the assumed thirty-one fathoms (or about 185 feet) where she rested. Two years later, Whitelaw and his wrecker *Whitelaw* sounded the wreck. The salvagers discovered that the ship lay on a sloping ledge with her bow in forty fathoms (240 feet) of water and her stern another thirty-five feet deeper. The depth, strong underwater currents, and limitations of existing technology prohibited any salvage attempts.

The Pacific Coast Steamship Company filed a claim against the owners of the *Oceanic* for the value of the *City of Chester.* (For years, any damages for the negligent loss of a ship, its passengers, and cargo were limited generally to its salvaged or after-disaster valuation.) The case was an unusual one, as the court actually held its proceedings at the scene of the disaster while a U.S. District Court judge presided. The judge, jury, witnesses, and everyone connected with the case were taken aboard the tug *Vigilant,* and while the "courtroom" vessel tossed to and fro during a heaving running tide and sea, the facts of the case were heard. The jury returned their verdict against the *Oceanic's* owners for the damages caused by its vessel, which was limited to the *Oceanic's* value just before the collision. The *City of Chester* charterer was also successful in the litigation involving the deceased passengers. Although held to be mutually responsible for the tragedy, the total damages it could be held responsible for was limited to $75, the appraised value of a small lifeboat saved from the lost vessel.

Divers again located the wreck in 1901 while searching for another sunken vessel near Fort Point. Within a distance of a hundred feet of this ship, but separated only by time, were the wrecks of a passenger steamer, a schooner, and a second steamer—all wrecked on the Fort Point reef.

● ● ●

IN THE 1880S, Whitelaw became friends with Robert Louis Stevenson, the famous Scottish novelist, poet, and travel writer. Stevenson was born in Edinburgh in 1850. His father (Thomas Stevenson), grandfather (Robert Stevenson), and great grandfather were famous Scottish lighthouse designers and engineers—and the family was nicknamed the "Lighthouse Stevensons." Cursed with ill health and suffering from tuberculosis, Stevenson traveled throughout France, his native Scotland, England, and even the United States (San Francisco in 1879 and the Napa Valley in 1880) in search of the best place to live for his health and writing.

When Stevenson was in the San Francisco area, he and Whitelaw met at a Scottish function. The two men shared a strong interest in books, being Scots, and an abiding love of the sea. However, Stevenson spent the great majority of his time afterward in Europe. In 1888, Stevenson chartered the schooner-yacht *Casco* and set sail with his family from San Francisco for the Pacific. By then, he had written books such as *Treasure Island* (1883), his first widely popular book; *Kidnapped* (1886); and *The Strange Case of Dr. Jekyll and Mr. Hyde* (1886), which brought him wider recognition. He also had published numerous short stories, articles, poetry, and volumes of verses.

The *Casco* was a ninety-five-foot-long, fore-and-aft topsail schooner of seventy tons, and Whitelaw had been a crewmember when that craft took her trial trip in the early 1870s. In fact, years later in 1924, T. P. H. was noted as being the "last surviving member of the famous Robert Louis Stevenson schooner, when that craft went on her trial trip more than fifty years ago.

The salt air and thrill of adventure restored Stevenson's health for a time, and the Scottish writer wandered the Pacific Ocean for two years with his wife, mother (his father had passed away), and a maid. He finally came upon Samoa and stayed after buying land and building a home there. Although Stevenson traveled back and forth from his island paradise, he continued to write during the entire time, but eventually died in Samoa in 1894.

Whitelaw meanwhile continued on with his wrecking and maritime operations. In 1889, the British ship *Clan Mackenzie* was anchored near the appropriately named Coffin Rock in the Columbia River on a wintry night. A few hours earlier, the stern-wheeler *Ocklahama*—the actual name of the ship—had been towing the *Mackenzie* upriver to Portland. While on this job, the steamer ran low on fuel, unhitched its tow, and left to take on more cords of wood. The anchored *Mackenzie* was a sitting duck.

Moving at a good speed and heavily laden, the steamship *Oregon* knifed into the *Mackenzie's* side. The heavy steamer struck the ship near midship, cut the *Clan Mackenzie* cleanly down to its keel, and ran thirty feet inside her victim. The lookout had not picked up the stationary vessel's outline until the collision was imminent.

When the *Ocklahama* came clanking along later to pick up the tow, her master and crew were horrified to find that the *Mackenzie* was now sunk where they had left her. The *Oregon* had already picked up the crew, and a search was underway for two men that were still missing. Their bodies were never found. It was said these seamen had probably taken advantage of the situation and deserted the ship. Discontented sailors were known to sometimes secure berths easily on other ships with few questions asked. If so, their whereabouts still remain a mystery, and it is therefore more likely that their bodies washed away in the currents.

The sunken wreck, however, was a barrier to river traffic and had to be removed. Captain Whitelaw bid for the job and received the contract to refloat the ship. He took his near-mystical approach to wrecking, commenting:

The underlying principle of all victories won over the sea is to compel the wrecked vessel to float. Their hulls usually cannot be lifted from the sands or rocks, because the wreck ships can't get sufficient "purchase" on the ocean's surface to give their cranes the leverage to raise several thousand tons of a water-filled hulk. The ship salvager therefore must do what the shipbuilder does: He must see how to create an artificial buoyancy within the hull that makes the vessel lighter than the water displaced; but he must do this under conditions far more difficult than those confronting the shipbuilder. In accomplishing this result, the salvager is constantly confronted by new conditions, as no two wrecks are alike.

This task was particularly difficult due to the freezing wintry conditions. Large pieces of ice continually slammed against the vessel with harsh scrapes and thuds, jarring tugs, knocking away equipment, and damaging tools. While steaming back and forth, the salvage ships had to dodge the ice flows, and workers needed to continually set explosives to blast away the ice that blocked their efforts. Another problem was the freezing cold water that limited the divers' time to a fraction of what they could do under warmer conditions. When ordinarily they worked underwater for four hours at shallow depths, they now could only stay fifteen minutes in the ice-cold water.

The job was still completed in a short three weeks. From Whitelaw's plans, his men closed openings, sealed passageways, and "made sufficient" sections of the ripped-out, V-shaped gash watertight so that water could be pumped out and the ship brought to the surface at its gunnels. After more plugging and patching, Whitelaw raised the 260-foot square-rigger to where it "wobbled" on the surface. His steam-tugs then towed her to nearby Portland for "urgent" repairs. The owners gave the repair job top priority, and she was completely repaired in four months to carry a full load of grain to Liverpool. The *Clan Mackenzie* was later renamed and sank off Scotland, another one of the countless ships saved only to ultimately die later.

Although ships were forever being saved, wrecks were increasing at such a rate that derelict vessels became a hazard to shipping lanes, especially during storm seasons when crews were forced to abandon those vessels. As a result, the mission of the U.S. Revenue Cutter Service was expanded to include pursuing, finding, and destroying abandoned vessels. One crew deserted the three-masted schooner *Alma Cummings,* for example, in the Atlantic Ocean off Virginia in February 1895. One year later, the vessel was still afloat 800 miles away with her decks awash, but now off the coast of West Africa by the Cape Verdes Islands. More than three years after being abandoned off the United States, the ship finally washed ashore near Panama.

Another notable derelict was the 120-foot schooner *Fannie E. Wolston,* whose crew deserted the ship in 1891 off Cape Hatteras. The unmanned vessel began a long, meandering voyage in the Gulf Stream, and nine months later, she was halfway across the Atlantic. Fifteen months after being abandoned, the ship had turned around and headed southwardly in the mid-Atlantic. The last sighting of the *Wolston* was off the coast of Georgia after covering a distance of over 1,000 miles.

The number of deserted ships declined, however, as more iron and steel ships were built and replaced the wooden vessels. When iron steamers were abandoned, they usually sank to the bottom. After wireless radio was installed upon ships, the Revenue Cutter Service's task of locating and destroying the derelicts became quite easier with faster reporting times.

●　　●　　●

BY 1890, Whitelaw's businesses were well established. He owned the salvage tug *Greenwood,* three large steam wreckers, and two good-size freighters. With more ships under construction or chartered, Whitelaw was an extensive builder and operator of vessels. He was under contract with the federal government to provide a number of its West Coast maritime operations. He owned four large, resale warehouses filled with his marine salvage. Extensively engaged in mining speculation and real estate, Whitelaw owned a huge stock ranch in Arizona and had large land holdings in different California regions.

The Bay of San Francisco, an 1892 publication of noteworthy people, published Whitelaw's biography. Among other facts, it stated:

> In Captain Whitelaw's twenty-three years of experience he has raised ninety-seven wrecks, and his work has been phenomenally successful. He has employed upwards of 10,000 men, and keeps a force of six divers on steady pay, so that he is prepared for service at a given moment. He is also one of the largest shipowners on the coast, and numbers among his vessels the *Whitelaw,* a wrecker; the *Sampson,* a very large wrecking vessel, capable of lifting sixty tons dead weight; the *Catalina,* also a wrecking vessel; and two large

schooners freighting between San Francisco, Mexico, and Central America. He has also been an extensive builder of vessels. He does all the coast work for the government in removing maritime obstructions, the preliminary work of building new lighthouses, and is now at work on the government breakwater at Port Harford [San Luis Obispo].

The Captain has been a large purchaser of wrecks, and has four large storage houses well filled with everything pertaining to shipping outfits. He has also been extensively engaged in mining speculations and in real estate transactions. He now owns a stock ranch of 43,000 acres in Arizona; 1,300 acres in Plumas county; 360 acres in Butte county; 53 acres in Placer county, upon which are two valuable granite quarries, and 200 lots in the city of San Francisco, improved and unimproved, with his handsome residence at No. 631 Harrison street.

With his business successes, it was natural that Captain Whitelaw would enter the lucrative sealing and whaling markets off the Pacific Northwest, British Columbia, and Alaska. His long voyage through the Bering Strait as a young man had showed him this work firsthand. San Francisco had become a center for these operations, and Whitelaw's yards supplied the parts for their repairs. He already owned vessels that could be easily converted.

Seals were primarily hunted for their skins, which were prized for their beauty and warmth. Seal oil was often used as lamp fuel, lubricating and cooking oil, and an ingredient of soap. Cooked down from the blubber, whale oil was used for many decades as the lamp oil to light homes and offices on land as well as lighthouses and ships at sea. The oil moreover had usefulness as a lubricant, candle wax, and wood preservative, while the baleen or whalebone was made into buggy whips, parasol ribs, women's stays, and corsets. From the Arctic to the Atlantic, whale and seal meat was eaten in large quantities.

Whaling and sealing were important economically from this country's very beginnings into the early-twentieth century. The discovery of petroleum in 1859 would eventually push down the price of whale oil over the next several decades. By the end of the century, low oil prices and declining whale populations began bringing these operations to an end. As substitutes were developed for the seal by-products and seal populations dramatically decreased, this U.S. industry also came to a close in the twentieth century. (Other countries around the world didn't have this experience and these industries are still operating there.)

As early as 1800, East Coast ships sailed from the Bering Sea down the West Coast. With the services of hired Russian hunters, they went as far south as the Farallon Islands off San Francisco in their search for whales and seals. As four-fifths of the fleet was then based in Victoria, British Columbia, each year nearly a hundred small schooners set sail and farmed the waters of the Pacific Northwest. Over time the West Coast industry developed, and with their wooden steam whalers bringing back profitable cargoes of oil and whalebone from the Arctic Ocean, even Yankee whalers built on the East Coast shifted their registry to San Francisco. Its portage became the principal anchoring, supply, and repair facility for whaling ships by the early 1880s and well into the early 1900s, until the price of whale oil and whalebone collapsed.

T. P. H. Whitelaw was not only ambitious, but he was a maritime entrepreneur who was willing to undertake risks. He built a steamer of forty-four tons, the *Daisy Whitelaw*, and outfitted it to hunt finback whales near the Farallon Islands. He owned ships in partnership with others, such as the *Matinee*, which were also used in this work. In 1890, Whitelaw applied for permission to hunt whales in Canadian provincial waters with his salvage vessel *Whitelaw*, which had been converted into a whaler.

Nearly 100 feet long, the *Whitelaw* was twenty-five feet wide and had a gross weight of 127 tons. Built in San Francisco in 1882, the ship was constructed as a sturdy wrecker. The *Whitelaw* had been used for salvage jobs and to bring supplies, tow quartering ships, and carry materials for the construction of the St. George Reef Lighthouse off the Northern California coast.

Whitelaw's application for whaling bounced from the Minister of Customs to the Minister of Marine and Fisheries, who turned it down on the grounds that Whitelaw proposed to use an American-registered vessel, "rather than employ a British hull." T. P. H. planned to refit his

steamer with steam-launches and the "latest patent guns." He also proposed to outfit the old *Alexander* as a floating refinery to serve in lieu
of a shore station. This vessel was 180 feet long, had a 27-foot beam,
and "cost a fortune to build," but Whitelaw had bought her at his usual
bargain price. T. P. H. thus anticipated the twentieth-century factory
ships by more than a decade and was trying to introduce modern whaling techniques.

With the growing demand on the West Coast for whale and seal products, and the centering of the fleet in San Francisco, sealing and whaling
became even more lucrative in Whitelaw's time. As there were more
ships with even higher catches, the Alaska Commercial Company—
which had a twenty-year lease of the seal-breeding islands—resented this
interference with its operations. The company's protests caused the U.S.
government to send the cutter *Corwin* to the Bering Sea with orders to
seize any vessel found sealing in those "protected" waters. *Lewis and
Dryden's Marine History of the Pacific Northwest* called this act, "The
beginning of one of the most disgraceful and unjust policies to which the
United States has ever been a party." The cutter seized ships on the high
seas, "a territory universally recognized in international law as a free
highway for the commerce of all countries."

The first seizure was made in 1884 of the schooner *Thornton*, and
then each year U.S. government cutters grabbed progressively more
ships discovered in the disputed waters. Based on faulty reasoning, the
judge in the federal district court lawsuit over the seizure of the *Thornton*
ruled in favor of the government. When it later turned out that the
United States had itself argued, years before, for the Russians to release
a comparably seized schooner—and won that case—the Americans realized any enforcement of restrictive laws beyond the traditional three-
mile limit was unreasonable. Men who had been long confined in squalid
prisons and schooners that were rotting on Alaskan beaches were
ordered released.

The monopolies continued to protest, however, so the United States
began seizing ships again, this time claiming that it wished to protect the
diminishing seal population. The problem was that sealers and whalers
were sailing all of the waters from the Bering Sea to California's Pacific

coastline and taking these animals wherever they could be found. To be consistent, the federal government should have banned the taking of all seals, no matter where they were.

In the late 1880s, the cutters searched to seize such ships, sail them south, and dock them at Port Townsend, Washington. Some of the impounded ships were released and others sold—politics and being on the right side decided what happened to one's vessel. The Russians, Americans, and British seized different ships seemingly at will, while capriciously letting others go on their way. By 1891, the British and American governments entered into a modus vivendi (an accommodation between disputing parties) that set a jurisdictional line, dating back to the Treaty of 1867 between the parties, that each agreed to respect. An international arbitration panel would rule on disputed seizures, and both countries issued proclamations that legally enforced their accord. They did such a good job that within two years, one-half of the international fleet sailed to Japanese waters to hunt seals.

Before England and the United States signed their agreement, Captain Whitelaw decided to sail his *La Ninfa* into the disputed and dangerous waters. Constructed in 1877, the squat, wooden schooner was eighty-six-feet long with a twenty-five-foot beam and still in good seaworthy shape. The two-masted, 127-ton schooner *La Ninfa* had first been chartered to the U.S. Light-House Board for use in the early 1880s as the crew's quarters in the building of the St. George Reef Lighthouse. From there, it was used in activities ranging from fishing to wrecking.

Whether due to deadly explosions of the harpoon-cannons, huge chilling waves washing men overboard, collisions at sea, or ships wrecked on reefs, numbers of sailors died each year while hunting in the dangerous waters off Alaska. Wearing worn dungarees, broad-brimmed hats, vests, and sealskin or oilskin coats, these were mustached, stern, tough men—and they had to be. At the same time, more U.S. warships sailed to join the *Corwin* to enforce the proclamation that prevented any further catching of seals during the season.

Regardless of East Coast or West Coast origination, ships were seized; U.S. owners then registered some of the vessels to sail under British colors, since their own government wouldn't protect them. T. P. H. out-fitted *La Ninfa* in San Francisco for "whaling, walrusing, hunting, and fishing" voyages to the North Pacific and Arctic Oceans, choosing not to include the word "sealing." The Captain sailed her northbound from San Francisco on April 1, 1891. Although Whitelaw was in charge of *La Ninfa* when she sailed toward Alaska, he probably left her once the ship sailed from California waters. Three months later, the ship passed into the Bering Sea, and the crew soon lowered their boats. They brought back fourteen sealskins.

On July 7, men from the U.S. *Thetis* boarded the schooner. The officer in charge told the captain that the sea was closed for sealing. He was acting under orders that required his cutter to board all vessels in the Bering Sea and, if they were engaged in sealing, to give them a copy of the June 15, 1891 proclamation with a letter that warned them to leave at once.

La Ninfa's captain informed the officer that the ship had nineteen skins on board, some of which had been killed in the Bering Sea. The officer testified later at the trial over the seizure and forfeiture of *La Ninfa*:

> As near as I can remember, I asked him if he had killed any seal in the sea, and if he had been warned before, and, learning that he had not, I gave him a copy of the warning, asked for the ship's papers, and endorsed them. Captain Worth [of *La Ninfa*] said he was fitted out for whaling, and asked me if he could whale in the Bering Sea. I replied that some arrangements might be made to that effect, but that I had no authority to make them; that I had warned him by serving these papers; and that, if he remained, it was at his own risk of being seized.

La Ninfa's captain and officers testified they didn't hunt any seals after they received the warning, but they did search for whales, and the ship was on "good" whaling grounds when next stopped. On July 14, the officer of the cutter *Corwin* boarded *La Ninfa* and seized her for violating the proclamation. At the time, the schooner was eight miles from the closest island or landmass with nineteen sealskins on board, of which Captain Worth said five hadn't been killed in the Bering Sea. The cutter towed the schooner to Sitka, Alaska, for condemnation.

There was no evidence that any seals had been killed within one marine league (or three miles) from Alaska, whether from the mainland or any islands. The facts showed that the entire seal killing had taken place ten miles from the closest shoreline and what was presumed to be outside U.S. territorial limits. This had been Whitelaw's assumption when he first sent his schooner northward.

In a quick proceeding and short opinion, the U.S. District Court for the District of Alaska handed down its decision (49 F. 575; 1891 U.S. Dist. Lexis 202) two and one-half months later. The judge held the government had legally impounded *La Ninfa,* the ship was forfeited, and Whitelaw's ownership terminated.

In retrospect, the decision was curious. The judge dismissed Whitelaw's contention that the ship had the right to remain in the sea with one paragraph:

> It is very plain the law was violated when fur seals were killed within the domain of the United States in the waters of the Bering Sea, that is, on July 6th, as shown by the logbook. The *La Ninfa* had an American register and an American owner. Whatever jurisdiction the United States may have over foreign vessels sealing in the Bering Sea, American bottoms are governed by the act of Congress above cited [that provided for the seizures].

The judge didn't consider any of the prior treaty agreements involving Russia, England, and the United States, or the arbitration tribunals with the United States and England that held the jurisdiction was to be "one cannon" shot, or three miles, from the Alaskan territory—not ten miles. The court relied on an act of Congress that allowed the seizure and didn't consider previous international treaties and decisions. The judgment upheld the sealing limitations and jurisdiction of the U.S. government, but it was not based on international law.

Although contesting the decision would be expensive and an uphill fight at best, T. P. H. decided to keep contesting the seizure and appealed the decision to a higher court. Whether this court would reach a different decision or Whitelaw would ever see his ship again wasn't known, but he would fight on, even if this meant going against a government with unlimited funds.

⚫ ⚫ ⚫

TEN YEARS after gold was discovered in the California Sierras, wealth again poured into San Francisco from the Comstock Lode beneath Virginia City, Nevada, and further accelerated the port's growth. Seeing more expansion potential, the harbor commissioners in 1881 decided to construct the San Francisco seawall. This project would eliminate the patchwork of jagged waterfront lines by wrapping and backfilling the waterfront at a city line where the Embarcadero now lies. From barges and scows, workers dredged a sixty-foot-wide channel in the mudflats to twenty feet below low tide and dumped in huge loads of rock to make an evenly graded ridge. After pouring thick slabs of concrete over the rocks and constructing a strong masonry wall, the area inside was pumped out and filled to city grade. The construction would take fifty years before its last sections were completed.

Travelers from the east arrived at Oakland, which was the western terminus of the Central Pacific Railroad. The trains stopped at the docks where passengers then boarded the San Francisco–bound ferry, a large riverboat steamer with huge paddle-wheels. Before the construction of the great bridges like the Golden Gate Bridge in 1937, these boats— with engines chugging and trailing dark plumes of smoke behind— crisscrossed the bay from San Francisco to Alameda, Oakland, Vallejo, Sausalito, and other points. With the ringing sounds of cable cars echoing down from the hills at night, the fog bells guided the ferry captains to their slips. The pilots knew the distinctive sounds of each as they navigated their vessels to the dock. In time, the hand-struck bells gave way to electrically driven ones that rang with a metallic dryness.

These side-wheel ferryboats were low-hulled, four-stories high (not including the bridge), painted white over a dark hull, and with pilothouses on both ends. Depending on which direction the ship sailed, thick dense smoke furled away from the tall smokestack, creating the optical illusion of the smoke spreading in the wrong direction from one bridge. When living in Oakland, Whitelaw took the ferries to the San Francisco waterfront. These boats mixed in the harbor with the large, full-sailed, and smokestacked freighters of the Orient, clipper ships and side-wheelers heading up the coast, and small scow-schooners plying their trades.

From the San Francisco Ferry House at the foot of Market Street, horse-drawn carriages, wagons, and buggies carried passengers into the city along with the sleek, long cable cars. Rincon Hill—now the abutment for the sweeping Oakland Bay Bridge—was the home of multiple-storied palatial mansions and considered to be what Beacon Hill, Rittenhouse Square, and Gramercy Park were in older cities back east.

The infamous Black Bart was captured in the city during the early 1880s. Black Bart was a notorious Wells Fargo stagecoach robber who held up its coaches for eight years, never fired a shot, but always left a poem behind with some humor and occasionally a vulgar line. With criminals being on land and sea, San Francisco police patrolled the bay in rowboats, searching for opium smugglers in the Chinatown trade, "pier muggers," and other rule-breakers.

The heart of the city was the intersection of Market and Geary with its cobblestoned streets and Lotta's Fountain, a gift from the volatile actress, Lotta Crabtree. The renowned Palace Hotel stood two blocks away. Food stands were in abundance from which vendors sold fresh fruit, vegetables, and cut meat. Eight- and ten-storied rectangular buildings, built of brick or white stucco, now lined the streets.

Although bearded, baggy-trousered, capped workmen worked on the docks, businessmen strolled down the streets wearing their formal attire of high-necked collars, white shirts, and three-piece dark suits. The women wore long dresses with tight bodices, snug in the waist, and hoop skirts. Women also donned flowering or large hats on almost every occasion, which caused the city fathers to enact a law forbidding the ladies from wearing hats at the opera.

Fires were a constant threat, as horse-drawn pumpers careened around street corners to race to fires. Horse-drawn buggies, cable cars, iron-rimmed bicycles, and formally dressed pedestrians coexisted on streets. Clanging cable cars carried people up the steep hills from the ferry building, while horse-drawn wagons hauled kegs of beer, heaps of vegetables, and stacks of clothing. Cooking was done on iron stoves, and wealthier people, of course, had more elaborate and larger wood-fueled stoves.

The Barbary Coast was the name of an actual neighborhood. Originating during the California Gold Rush, the area was known for gambling and prostitution and became a popular hangout for the rich. The parlor houses of the Barbary Coast were the upper-class resorts of San Francisco's golden age of prostitution. These establishments had from five to twenty-five young ladies on the premises, and the price for their services varied with the "class" of each place. Parlor-house women took home several times more money than what the average law-abiding citizen could earn.

The Cliff House overlooking Seal Rocks became a favorite place for Sunday drivers and their stylish horse-drawn rigs along with taking a boat ride around San Francisco Bay. On these occasions, men and women dressed in their finest. The Cliff House burned down three times and once exploded. After one such fire, Adolph Sutro rebuilt the Cliff House in 1896 below his estate on the bluffs of Sutro Heights. Layered into apartments with spires and a towering pinnacle in the middle, the magnificent white-stucco, eight-story Victorian chateau seemed to soar over the very ocean and was called by some "the Gingerbread Palace."

In that same year, the extremely wealthy Sutro started work on his famous Sutro Baths, an elaborate and beautiful glass-enclosed entertainment center. Located below the Cliff House, this complex included six of the largest indoor swimming pools, a museum, and even a skating rink. These Roman-like baths were heated saltwater and springwater pools, and they were very popular despite the remote location across open dunes to the west of the city's populated areas. To see these sights, great crowds of San Franciscans arrived by train, bicycle, cart, and horse-drawn wagon on their Sunday excursions. (The baths now lie in ruins just below the Cliff House, which is part of the Golden Gate National Recreation Area.)

The magnificent Palace Hotel was completed in 1875. It was eight-stories high, covered one complete city block, and had a glass-domed rotunda. Inside, Roman columns stretched upward, lining a courtyard that opened to the outside to allow horse-drawn carriages to clip-clop inside. With jutting edifices, abutments, and apartments, the structure was the home to kings, queens, the rich, and the famous. This impressive building dominated the city's skyline until the great 1906 earthquake and fire completely destroyed it.

Although this era was later referred to as the Gay Nineties due to the perceived fun and merriment of the period, in fact these times were ones of large economic fluctuations. A financial panic in the mid-1880s severely depressed the overall economy before finally improving. The 1890s were then characterized by another terrible financial panic, which was followed by the Spanish-American War of 1898.

Despite the economic disruptions, the West Coast's maritime industries continued their growth. From San Francisco to Seattle, shipbuilding, marine repairing, lumber milling, and agriculture concentrated and grew. Hawaiian sugar and coconut oil were shipped to the West Coast, while their products (coconut oil was used for cooking and in cosmetics and shampoos) headed in return to faraway ports. Ships, fishermen, cannery workers, and equipment sailed in the spring from San Francisco to Alaska, and all returned back with the salmon catch at summer's end.

Sailing craft plied the rivers and bay like taxis do today. While steamers carried large cargoes on the major runs, locally built sloops, scow-schooners, and even barges worked their way into the inland towns on out-of-the-way sloughs, creeks, and rivers. Dairy products from Oregon joined wheat, coconut oil, refined sugar, and other exports being shipped out.

San Francisco in the mid-1890s became home to the large masterful "Sugar Ships," which were known for their brilliant-white, sleek hulls and sails. This unusual fleet of tall, full-sailed ships was built in West Coast shipyards. Attractive and fast, the Sugar Ship fleet helped establish the California & Hawaii Sugar Company, as these vessels brought raw sugar from Hawaii for the C&H refineries that were located near San Francisco.

A West Coast triangular trade developed. For example, ships left San Francisco to load lumber at Tacoma, Washington, that was bound for

Sydney. From Australia, the tall-masted vessels took on boatloads of coal for Hawaii and then brought the raw sugarcane from Honolulu to San Francisco for processing. At times, the ships even raced one another over these routes. Leaving twenty-four hours after the first vessel did, a second ship sailed away on the same course. The losing captain had to pay for a very expensive champagne dinner for the shipping company's employees and the winning ship's crew.

As seen with major East Coast cities, different ports developed around San Francisco's preeminence. Across the bay, Oakland not only served as the ferry landing, but also as a site for loading goods brought by trains for outbound shipping. Martinez, Port Costa, and South Vallejo shared with San Francisco the great movement of wheat and barley from the coast's riverboats, barges, and railroad cars to the square-riggers that carried these precious cargoes to Europe and Asia. From San Diego and Los Angeles to Portland and Seattle, extensive ports, maritime facilities, and support industries developed, as they followed San Francisco's lead. Shipbuilding and repairing ships became a big business, and as shipping increased, so did the need for more firefighting tugs, police launches, dredges, and pilot boats—an experience that San Francisco now shared with its Eastern counterparts.

West Coast shipyards concentrated first on building smaller bay and coast vessels, as this business was easier to establish, requiring relatively little capital. Around 1880, an ingenious mariner hitched a steam engine to a small Mendocino windjammer, and this act revolutionized small coastwise hauling. No longer did coastal sailing vessels have to be idle and wait for the prevailing winds; small rivers and shallow harbors were now accessible.

Change also occurred in the outward appearance of the converted steam schooners. An unorthodox, box-like cabin was built on the after deck, and a slim stack rose from this cabin structure just forward of the main mast. As the first steam engines were unreliable, the ships retained modified sails—and this design continued for thirty years. Compound engines with 100-horsepower drove a single propeller.

Soon lumber vessels were built with steam engines and no sails. The design of these vessels later grew in size, and the triple-expansion engine replaced the less powerful compound ones. Made possible by advances in metallurgy, the triple-expansion engine was powered by running the same steam three times through a series of cylinders.

The West Coast shipyards also built large vessels. In 1885, Captain Whitelaw watched as the Union Iron Works in San Francisco built the first steel ship on the Pacific Coast, a coal carrier named the *Arago*. San Francisco yards built naval ships, even for foreign countries, such as the 4,700-ton light cruiser *Chitose* for the Imperial Japanese Navy.

In the early 1900s, steel quickly became the primary building material for ships and the use of wood quickly declined. As the triple-expansion engine replaced the simple compounds, the new steel ships were faster. They could transport large cargos of sugar, salt, and cement that wooden ships couldn't due to the risk of leaking beams and seams. Using steel ended the maintenance problems from marine borers and rot, and these ships had a greater cargo capacity. With far less internal space taken up by thick frames, ceilings, keelsons, and other massive woodwork, there was more room for cargo and profit.

Transoceanic steamship lines operated from both coasts, as eastern port cities were likewise supporting extensive fishing, exporting and importing, shipbuilding, and other maritime industries. While East Coast ships were plying the European ports from London to Lisbon, on the West Coast ships were steaming back and forth from ports such as Honolulu, Hong Kong, Yokohama, and Sydney.

The changeover to using oil as fuel was underway as well. When a Los Angeles oil company converted a small steam schooner from burning coal to oil in the 1890s, the use of oil was then introduced into its coastwise fleet. The more efficient technology of pressure-oil feed, however, soon made burning coal obsolete, and by 1911, less than a dozen coal-burning steam schooners were operating on the West Coast. The switch to oil burning also altered the ships; the square schooner stern gave way to a rounded stern, which made maneuvering alongside wharves easier.

While ships were undergoing change and increase, the railroads, too, were experiencing strong growth. More and more towns and cities were being linked together, and trains now carried the great majority of people traveling between cities.

Although railroads were spreading, maritime shipping was still an important means of transportation due to its lower cost, international trade expansion, flexibility in changing routes (tracks couldn't be moved), and ability to quickly change destination points. The continuing maritime dominance also meant an increased need for the services of salvors such as Captain T. P. H. Whitelaw.

Vallejo Street Wharf in San Francisco in 1864 with moored full-sail vessels. *San Francisco Maritime National Historical Park.*

Broadway or Green Wharf, San Francisco, mid-1860s with steam-driven-donkey engine used to lift heavy goods. *San Francisco Maritime National Historical Park.*

Due to the great numbers of horses used to pull trolleys and drays, scow schooners carried huge amounts of bales to the Hay Wharf. *San Francisco Maritime National Historical Park.*

With whalebones drying in the sun, a waiting ship stands by to load. In the 1880's, San Francisco became a center for the whaling fleets. *San Francisco Maritime National Historical Park.*

A later picture of Captain Whitelaw (far left), Elizabeth (far right), grandchildren, and grown family in early 1900's. *San Francisco Maritime National Historical Park.*

This early picture of Captain Whitelaw and Elizabeth shows them holding their two babies, Andrew and Margaret Elizabeth (Daisy). *San Francisco Maritime National Historical Park.*

The grand full-sail ships like the *E. B. Hutton* in this picture were prevalent into the 1900's. *San Francisco Maritime National Historical Park.*

Whitelaw's salvage of the *Umatilla* in 1884 was complex, distant in British Columbia, and expensive—but successful. A long cofferdam needed to be erected (top), and T.P.H. used different wreck ships in this salvage (bottom). *Royal British Columbia Museum.*

Once Whitelaw raised the ship, the *Umatilla* was refitted and had a long maritime history that continued past World War II. *Royal British Columbia Museum.*

A later inquiry exonerated the *Umatilla's* Captain Frank Worth of blame (left), as the inspectors highly commended first officer Dynamite Johnny O'Brien (above) for his heroics in saving the ship (picture taken later). *Royal British Columbia Museum (left).*

Captain Whitelaw and his long, flowing white beard became a fixture at docks and harbors. *San Francisco Maritime National Historical Park.*

In 1896, Captain Whitelaw created a unique way to raise the ghost-ship *Blairmore*—a large square rigger—that had completely keeled over at its dock. *San Francisco Maritime National Historical Park.*

The U.S. Government seized *La Ninfa* when sealing in the Bering Sea; years passed before Whitelaw and other owners received any compensation for these illegal acts. *San Francisco Maritime National Historical Park.*

The Reid Wrecking Company on the Great Lakes spent six years with the *William C. Moreland* before the ship's long stern was attached to a new bow. *Michigan Tech University.*

The Merritt companies had worked to save the *St. Paul* on more than one occasion, including this time when the ship capsized on its side in New York Harbor. *Mystic Seaport Collection, Mystic, CT.*

Merritt & Chapman Derrick and Wrecking raised this tugboat with its *Monarch* wreck barge. Shipwrecks in New York Waters, *Paul C. Morris & William P. Quinn.*

Different salvagers tried over time to raise the steamer *San Pedro* from a reef by Victoria, British Columbia. No one could and Whitelaw received the final contract to strip the ship. *Royal British Columbia Museum*

The strange, overland odyssey of Lightship Station No. 50 through Oregon forests in 1901 saved this vessel after it had grounded on a beach. *Columbia River Maritime Museum.*

Some twenty-five years later, the tides and winds worked the *North Bend II* one-half mile over a sandy inlet to the same protected bay and inclusion in *Ripley's Believe It Or Not.* *Columbia River Maritime Museum.*

Ferryboats brought people and their cars across bays until the bridges were built starting in the 1930s; the winds blowing from right to left and twin pilothouses help to create an optical illusion as to the direction of the vessels. *San Francisco Maritime National Historical Park.*

On one of his wreck barges, Whitelaw outlines a salvage plan. He continued the same exacting schedule in his later years as when he first began. *San Francisco Maritime National Historical Park.*

At one of Captain Whitelaw's docking areas, the salvaged ship *Unimak* is beached and the wrecker *Greenwood* rises in the background. *San Francisco Maritime National Historical Park.*

The *City of New York* salvage effort in 1895 turned out to be Whitelaw's worst tragedy. *San Francisco History Center, San Francisco Public Library.*

The *Progresso* was being converted into an oil-tank carrier in 1903 when her tanks exploded; the Fort Point Lifesaving Station crew is pictured in front of the burning hulk. *San Francisco Maritime National Historical Park.*

The once four-masted, 190-foot long *Polaris* ran aground on a reef in 1914 near Bolinas when sailing toward San Francisco Bay. It was a total loss. Salvagers began removing items including the donkey engine (center with workman bending over). *San Francisco Maritime National Historical Park.*

The oil tanker *Rosecrans* in 1913 gave Whitelaw "one of his thrills," when the runaway vessel just missed his wrecker and needed to be "roped like a steer." The wave is over twelve-stories high. *San Francisco Maritime National Historical Park.*

The Oakland Long Wharf, circa 1905. Note the railroad tracks that run from the dock to carry goods to and from the port. *San Francisco Maritime National Historical Park.*

This classic picture shows the sinking steam-schooner *Riverside* that wrecked on Blunt's Reef off Cape Mendocino (1913). *San Francisco Maritime National Historical Park.*

The *Eastland* tragically overturned when leaving its Chicago dock in 1915, and the Dunham Towing and Wrecking Company succeeded in righting the vessel in a complex salvage operation. *Chicago Historical Society.*

Seven U.S. destroyers crashed north of Santa Barbara, California, in 1923 in the U.S. Navy's worst peacetime loss. The broken *USS Delphy* is in the foreground, her forward section capsized to port (left); behind the rocky outcropping to the far left is the stern of the *USS Chauncey;* the capsized *USS Young* is upper center; in the distance, the *USS Woodbury* lies by its namesake rock with the *USS Fuller* beyond her. *U.S.* Naval Historical Center Photograph.

While working on the four-masted, sail ship *Drumburton* in 1904, Captain Whitelaw had to quickly get off when the vessel began to disintegrate. *San Francisco Maritime National Historical Park.*

Nearly twenty-five years later, his grandson, Ken, was serving on the "super passenger ship" *Malalo,* when a large steamer slammed into its bow. Built of steel with safety changes enacted after the *Titanic* disaster, the 582-foot-long *Malalo* was safely repaired in port. *U. S. Naval Historical Center Photograph.*

CHAPTER EIGHT

FAILURES FOLLOW ACCOMPLISHMENT

W hether approaching a vessel with decks awashed on the ocean or impaled on a reef, the first sight greeting wreckers was one of chaos. Only a few hours before, the ship was alive with people; conversations and laughter filled the air, and the vessel was neat and tidy. If this was a passenger ship, travelers would have been dressed in dark three-piece suits or flowing sequined dresses, while uniformed stewards graciously served them dry martinis and liver-pâté hors d'oeuvres at their deck chairs. Attendants swept the decks, polished the brass, and changed the linens. If it was a cargo ship, the crew and officers ate, slept, lived, and worked on a boat that had been their home for weeks. Then, in an instant, everything changed.

An 1893 article in *Outlook Magazine,* entitled "Wrecking," described what it was like to board a wrecked ship, this time the steamer *Cherokee* off the East Coast:

Decks, cabins, staterooms, and the gallery show sad confusion. The ten-inch hawser from the wrecking tug lies in a huge coil on the forward deck as a silent witness to the prompt, unavailing efforts to foil the greed of the sands. A hoist of signal flags trail on the deck from their slack halyard; miscellaneous ropes—usually coiled away, shipshape, on handspikes, or in lockers—lie scattered about promiscuously; a barrel of hardtack stands open in the saloon; a china plate on the bridge bears fragments of icing from a cake; in the staterooms, the little accompaniments of travel, such as toothbrushes, combs, magazines, and razors lie scattered, dropped, or forgotten in the haste of departure. Confusion had even penetrated to the pilothouse—the inner sanctuary of seamanship and orderliness—as the mute engine-room telegraph points to the words "full speed astern" and tells of the moment when the touch of the shoal was felt. The leaded hand-lines hang in useless coils, which for some mysterious reason had failed to warn the mariners, then bewildered by the fog, of the dangerous shallows that were so near.

A trip down one hallway ends abruptly in a deep expanse of cold saltwater covered with floating debris, tabletops rising above in the dim light like shadowy islands. The ten feet of water in the hold has doubled, and the ocean throughout the ship was at that same level, but rising and falling as did the tides. Until the sea can be gotten out, this good ship will stay where she is, nestled slowly but inevitably in the coaxing, cruel sands. Meanwhile, there was plenty of work for the wreckers to do. All of the ship's fittings that can be carried away must be collected and transferred with as much of her cargo as can be reached at ebb tide.

Once on the ship, the wreckers began their hustle. That afternoon, the men were ripping up carpets, unscrewing lamps, taking candleholders, mirrors, and washbasins, coiling up ropes, stripping the pilothouse and bridge of the chronometer, compass, binnacle lamps, and charts. The tide was at ebb, and in the next few hours, they must get out as much cargo as they could.

A fishing-smack tied alongside amidships, and a miscellaneous collection of merchandise was poured into her. Bags of raw sugar, soaked in saltwater until half their contents dissolved, were slimy, slippery masses of stickiness; great square logs of satinwood; misshapen chunks of fustic [or yellowwood]; round logs of lignum vitae destined to become bowling balls, ship's blocks, and rulers; bales of sisal hemp, the best fiber for making cordage [rope or string], next to manila hemp. Not only cargo is taken, but also a dozen hand trucks, used for loading and unloading in port; great coils of hawsers and mooring lines; and heavy chains for hoisting cargo from the hold were dragged out and stowed away on the smack.

Overhead, at the ship's rail, stood the jovial little custom-house officer, carefully noting every log of wood, every bale of hemp, and every piece of good or equipment that left the ship, for nothing must pass Uncle Sam's protective wall, even in case of disaster, without his knowledge and consent. Beside him a young member of the wrecking crew kept equal tally of the cargo. A list of everything that went ashore was for the insurers to know what was saved against the insurance they had to pay out.

Below in the 'tween-decks, a gang of wreckers—rubber-booted to the hips and armed with iron hooks—waded through the dirty flood and dragged the cargo to the open port. The pale wintry light from the outside mingled with the smoky gleam of the ship's lanterns, half revealing a scene that was weird and unnatural. The incongruity of this expanse of water inside the ship, the tide rising and falling, the swells sweeping regularly through her in unison, emphasized the pathos of her plight. On deck, the work of dismantling was going on: All the metal fittings, stateroom and cabin furnishings; everything, in fact, that was movable and detachable, went over the side into the rapidly filling smack.

The steamer tug with her big attendant lighter lay out at sea, as close as the water depth would permit. Toward noon, a surfboat left the wreck bringing the free end of a hawser from the coil on the deck, the thick rope attached to a bollard. The end was taken to the lighter, made fast to her steam-winch, and the broad-beamed craft began to pull itself in, hand over hand, toward the motionless wreck. The lighter came alongside, and men made her fast to the wreck's bow and stern. One of her big derricks picked up from the deck, like a toy, a twenty-foot boiler and swung it around. It was lowered lightly into position on the lighter's deck, followed by a centrifugal pump, looking like a great snail mounted on a pedestal for mounting purposes.

The engineer and his assistants followed and began with work-manlike dispatch to fit up the pump and boiler with the proper steam pipes and valves. They cut a hold into the deck and dropped a six-inch inlet pipe far down into the water in the hold. The cap-tain of the wrecker looked over the vessel with the eye of experi-ence, and said, "If this wind shifts, though, we're likely to lose the pump and boiler too. It wouldn't take many seas breaking over her the way they did the other night to pick them clean off the deck. Well, let them go; they don't owe us anything. They've done some good bits of work in their time."

As we left the wrecked steamer that afternoon, the pump was ready to start its task in the morning—a task that had as much promise of practical results as trying "to spit to windward."

Back in the city a few days later, an item tucked away in the corner of the morning paper was discovered: "Atlantic City, N.J., Jan. 27—The stranded steamer *Cherokee* was entirely cleared of water by pump last night, and was promptly freed from the shoal by the wrecking tug *North America*. She is proceeding this morning to New York in tow of the tug."

❧ ❧ ❧

BROTCHIE LEDGE is a submerged reef in the Strait of Juan de Fuca, one-half mile south of the entrance to Victoria Harbor in British Columbia. This reef is a major hazard for ships, as it is entirely hidden at low tide. When Captain William Brotchie ran his bark *Albion* into it in 1849, the Hudson Bay Company, the owner of the vessel, renamed the reef Brotchie Ledge "in honor" of the hapless captain.

On Sunday evening, November 22, 1891, the *San Pedro* ran onto Brotchie Ledge. Owned by the Southern Pacific Steamship Company, a division of Southern Pacific Railroad, the *San Pedro* was a large iron steamship built nine years before. It was valued at $400,000, registered 3,119 tons, was 331 feet long, and had a 42-foot beam with a 19-foot "depth of hold."

One of the "finest" colliers (coalers) on the Pacific Coast, the ship carried 4,000 tons of coal and was steaming to San Francisco on a calm night. The captain and pilot were on the bridge at the time looking for the Brotchie Ledge buoy, and they planned to stop at the Victoria harbor's mouth to drop off the pilot.

At 8:30 P.M. the *San Pedro* struck the ledge, glanced off it, struck again, and then stopped dead in its tracks. Even with the engines running full astern, the vessel stayed stuck and the tide was falling fast. With her steam whistle blasting distress calls, the ship was reached by two tugs about 11 P.M. Her stern by then was low in the water and the bow hard on the sharp rocks.

In an effort to refloat the ship, the crew and twenty longshoremen, who came on board to help, tossed 300 tons of coal over the side, but the ship remained grounded. By 3:30 A.M. that Monday, the ship was at a steep forty-five-degree angle, and the incoming tide didn't raise her. When divers examined the hull at daylight, they discovered holes in the hull that were thirty-feet long. Sightseers crowded on the shore that Monday to see the ship, while others sailed by her in small boats to see the sight close-up.

On Tuesday morning, the *San Pedro* gave a sudden lurch, filled up with the ocean, and settled into the sea, "leaving only the wheelhouse and foredeck above water." Men working then on the ship shouted warnings to one another and jumped into the cold water. The current carried some of the men away, as surfboats chased after to save them, while the boat settled to the bottom with only the bow, smokestack, and masts being visible. The steamer sank in eight and one-half fathoms (fifty-one feet) at its stern with nearly thirty feet of ocean abreast (its middle).

An ensuing commission of inquiry concluded that the pilot was grossly negligent by not taking proper bearings by the nearby warning light or keeping the ship on a proper course, and that these inactions had led to the ship's loss. The pilot later filed an affidavit agreeing with the captain's account that the destruction was due to pilot error and not the captain's negligence.

The Southern Pacific Company hired Captain Whitelaw to salvage the vessel. Whitelaw, a "well-known wrecker" and of *Umatilla* fame, according to newspaper accounts, immediately left San Francisco for Victoria. His plan was to use multiple pontoons to raise the vessel. Whitelaw had the pontoons constructed at Victoria by year's end. In January 1892, the *Victoria Daily Colonist* reported his progress:

> The pontoons built at the outer wharf have been placed in position. The full number will be put down before they are inflated, and it is hoped that the *San Pedro* will be brought to the surface. For several days a large gang of men have been clearing the holds to lighten the vessel. They have removed several hundred tons of coal, and from the examination of the machinery, it appears that it has suffered little, except from the water.

Captain Whitelaw was confident of success when he talked with a reporter on January 25:

> Within ten days, you will see the *San Pedro* above water again, just as good, barring the damage she sustained in striking, as when she went down. I haven't the slightest doubt of the success of my line of action. The *San Pedro* lies right on top of the ledge, with one rock penetrating her bottom for a distance of five feet, and another that is three feet in. Some days ago, we put in a series of wooden cribs under her keel at distances of twelve feet from one another. We are placing twelve pontoons on each side of the vessel.

Whitelaw explained that each pair of pontoons worked separately, so extra air pressure could be injected as needed to different wreck sections. After the ship was floated, which he estimated would take four hours, he felt that a half-hour would be needed to tow the ship to the beach. The wages paid out each week by Whitelaw in this operation were $3,000—a very high total at the time.

The pontoons had still not been deployed by April, and the *San Pedro* remained on Brotchie Ledge. Although eight "large" storms had passed since the ship sank, the vessel still remained in salvageable condition. On June 23, spectators lined the shoreline road to view the long-awaited raising. However, they were disappointed when the ship didn't budge, despite the "heroic efforts" of the gangs of workmen on the four ships that Whitelaw had leased for this project. Although few people doubted the ability of the "genial captain from San Francisco" to accomplish the work, the effort was turning out to be much more difficult than first thought.

Captain Whitelaw decided to arrange the huge pontoons, tenders, and steam-tugs so that their lifting power would be greater than the steamer's "dead-water" weight. Despite the ship's donkey engines being stoked to maximum power and sending "heavy clouds of black smoke heavenward" in their efforts, the results again proved unsuccessful.

Despite the lack of success, people felt that Whitelaw's cribbing (timbers used to support a ship's bottom) and pontoons were quite workable, but that extra buoyancy needed to be added somehow to the ship before she would float. The next year, Captain J. M. Lachlan, who was an officer in the marine department of the Southern Pacific Company, then inspected the wreck. He concluded that the only way to succeed was to put in a false deck with air bags for more space to achieve the needed buoyancy. When Whitelaw's efforts over the next weeks again weren't successful, he left the job and Victoria.

Another wrecker came in to work on the ship, and Captain Whitelaw said he had lost "a bundle" on the unsuccessful salvage attempts. He had lost this time—or so it seemed—and turned to other projects.

❖ ❖ ❖

THE DECADES after the Civil War were a period of neglect for the American merchant marine. In the early 1870s, only three shipyards in the country could build modern iron-hulled steamers "of large size," or more than 2,000 tons. One was the Chester, Pennsylvania, shipyard of John Roach, where he built and launched in 1875 the huge 3,019-ton

City of New York, which was 339 feet long with a 40-foot beam and 20-foot depth. She had a single screw, compound engine, with three masts, a single smokestack, and an iron hull.

Roach was a controversial figure and a well-known builder of ships for steamship lines and the U.S. government. Among his clients were the Pacific Mail Steamship Company, for whom he constructed the largest vessels built or owned in America at the time—the *City of New York* and the sister liners *City of Tokyo* and *City of Peking.* Also constructed in this yard were two other vessels that met tragic ends in the waters of the Golden Gate, the *City of Chester* and *City of Rio de Janeiro.*

The *City of New York* and its sister ships were built to make American vessels competitive again in world trade and to replace the earlier generation of wooden-hulled side-wheel steamers that dated back to gold rush days. Spurred by the success of the transcontinental railroad, Pacific Mail began to supplement its Panama-to-California route with trade to Australia and the Orient.

The cargo carried for the Asian markets consisted of manufactured goods, flour, canned goods, and a variety of "other foodstuffs." These items were off-loaded in exchange for spice, bamboo, indigo, rice, silk, rubber goods, and curios considered to be exotic in the West. For almost two decades, the *City of New York* had earned her reputation as a "solid" ship while it plied the sea between San Francisco and China, Panama, and Australia.

On October 26, 1893, the huge *City of New York* left the Pacific Mail dock and steamed through the Golden Gate bound for Asia. The vessel had 104 crewmen and 133 passengers on board; its cargo consisted of 20,000 barrels of flour, 15,000 pounds of beans, and countless barrels of dried shrimp, all destined for China and Japan. The fog was dense, tides at their highest, and the foghorns at Point Bonita Lighthouse were inoperative. When the ship was a short way outside the Golden Gate, the vessel was already off course to the north without anyone's knowledge.

She struck on submerged rocks about a hundred yards offshore, to the southeast of Point Bonita, and ground to a screeching stop. A large roller suddenly picked up the vessel like it was a toy and dropped the *New York* on the jagged rock tops, bursting the bottom plates and flooding the hold with eight feet of water. When her masts sprang up three inches from the deck plate, those on board knew the ship's spine was broken.

Panic gripped the passengers, many of whom were Chinese sailing back to their homeland and berthed in steerage quarters below the waterline. As soon as the ship struck, the crew sent off distress signals. Luckily, "the cannon booming could be heard and the signal rockets seen as they burst above the fog." When the Point Lobos lookout sent the distress message "at once to town, every tug in the bay was racing [for the salvage reward] for Point Bonita." When they arrived on the scene, however, the would-be wreckers found the steamer wedged fast on the rocks.

One reporter wrote:

> The *City of New York* met with disaster by a hair. So close was she from the cliff on which the lighthouse stands, it was possible to look down on the steamer's decks. The lights of the vessel reflected in the stretch of water between the ship and the point of land. It didn't look to be more than five-hundred feet to where she was lying, and it could hardly be more than that distance from the rocks, as those which fringe the North Heads do not reach out for more than three-hundred yards. Beyond that is deep water. Indeed, the lighthouse keeper said that if the steamer had passed fifty feet farther out from shore, she would have entirely cleared the rocks.

With help there and the *New York* in no immediate danger of sinking—despite a heavy sea running—the passengers calmed down. Due to the nearby rocks, however, the tugs couldn't approach the stranded ship. The lifesaving crew from Fort Point courageously took all of the passengers off and transferred them to waiting rescue craft. The crew of the Golden Gate Lifesaving Station arrived and helped to remove the mail and $241,000 "in specie, articles of value, and crew effects." Four boats were recovered the next day that had broken loose and drifted out to sea with some of the Chinese passengers aboard.

The Pacific Mail Steamship Company hired wreckers in vain attempts to tow the ship free from the reef. Salvage efforts from the ship *Fearless* (not one of Whitelaw's vessels) started immediately, and the workmen began removing the cargo of flour, shrimp, beans, and other general goods, in addition to taking off $44,000 in silver bars and $111,000 in pesos. These salvagers also threw overboard a number of Orient-bound camphor-wood coffins. The grim sight of the gaily bobbing caskets in San Francisco's bay quickly brought forth an "outraged hue and cry from the local citizenry."

For several weeks, the men of the *Fearless* worked to lighten her by removing cargo. Although they were able to haul off most of the goods, strong storms rolled in and continually swept against the wreck's exposed position until her hull became battered beyond any hope of salvage. The owners realized the *City of New York* was now a total loss.

They decided to sell the wreck for scrap to Captain Whitelaw. Reporters followed the story, calling Whitelaw "the best-known operator of his time." He used the wreck-schooner *Sampson,* which was built in 1890 and constructed strongly with a shallow draft. This design allowed the vessel to anchor close to shore and be a platform for any dismantling operations. The *Sampson* carried a small steam engine for its hoisting, but the schooner-barge depended entirely on steam-tugs to move it.

Captain Whitelaw put his best men on the *Sampson* and *City of New York* to strip away all of her metal fittings, anchors, chains, davits, doors, ventilator ports, plumbing, and anything else that was salvageable. Using explosives, they began cutting up the ship for its scrap iron. When stormy weather began in November 1893, the crew was forced to abandon the site. The big wreck lay there for months, "dismantled and dreary, like the decaying carcass of some vast black monster of the sea, sinking inch by inch into the surrounding depths." Then a great storm arose in March 1894. The winds and waves shook the large hulk free from the rocks and deposited the derelict in deep water between the reef and shore. When the strong blow finally ended, *Sampson's* divers continued their work to cut up and take away the sunken ship piece by piece.

Whitelaw had assigned his best men, including the "well known" divers James Dolan and George Baker, for the underwater demolition. The workers toiled for months on the long, grueling salvage. It was chancy just being aboard the 109-foot, 217-ton *Sampson,* because the bottom was rocky, the reef close, and near-perpendicular cliffs rose directly on the other side. Although anchored perilously close to the wreck, the ship and men managed to work safely into the winter.

Whitelaw traveled back to Scotland that year to learn the "latest tricks" on salvaging ships from those he believed to be the masters. Even though he was considered to be the foremost salvager and best engineer on the Pacific Coast, T .P. H. wanted to learn all he could about the latest developments. Once back, Whitelaw juggled his workforce and wreckers on other projects while the salvage efforts on the *New York* continued off and on during a second winter.

On January 1, 1895, a southeast storm blew in to welcome the New Year. By the next day, the fierce gale had whipped up cutting winds and white-capped waves. The conditions worsened on January 3 with waves breaking over the sides and forcing the *Sampson* around. The ship's captain knew his vessel had to face the winds. To allow the *Sampson* to swing freely at anchor, the stern moorings were first cast off, and the bow came around into the steadily increasing gale. When the winds continued to increase, a second anchor was let go, but by mid-morning the vessel had begun to drag its bow anchor.

The pitching was so bad by noon that a second bow-anchor was set, but within half an hour, both anchors were dragging along the bottom. The winds and waves were so strong by now that they drove the salvage vessel and anchors—even with her engines on full speed ahead—back toward the close, jagged fangs of rock.

The *Sampson* and her crew were in deadly peril. The men broke out signal flags and blankets to run up the halyards as distress signals, but the "scud" was so thick that no one at either Point Lobos or Fort Point saw them. By 3:00 P.M. the men "stoked up" the donkey engine and blew a loud steam whistle to signal that they needed help. The howling storm drowned out sound and obliterated sight. Due to the thick weather, no one on land even saw the puffs of steam as the whistle shrilled out its unanswered message into the storm.

The crew launched a surfboat, and men rowed through the turbulent seas to the nearby lighthouse wharf to plead that its foghorn be blown to summon aid. Growing to "unprecedented ferocity," however, the storm drowned out even that loud noise. The seamen continually burned torches to request help, but they didn't follow the example of the earlier surfboat and leave the *Sampson* while they still could. By nightfall, the waves were too tumultuous for anyone to leave the ship. Those who went to the lighthouse stayed there.

Early in the morning, a surfman from the Fort Point Lifesaving Station spotted the distress lights, and at 3:00 A.M. the lifesaver sent word out that he needed a tug. He burned a Coston flare to show the ship's crew that someone had finally picked up their distress signals. Under the command of Captain Silovich, the tug *Reliance* immediately steamed from its San Francisco dock to aid the *Sampson*. No one on board the barge could know help was on its way. Consequently, at 3:30 A.M. the two divers, Dolan and Baker, launched the *Sampson's* yawl (a small, two-masted sailboat). The turbulent seas and waves quickly engulfed the tiny boat and capsized it. The two men disappeared in the darkness and were never seen again.

With lives at risk, the *Reliance* did its best to steam to the rescue, but the storm was so severe that the captain decided "prudence forbade" continuing on until daylight. Before dawn, the waves were still driving the *Sampson* without fail toward the cliffs. At 4:00 a.m., the wrecker touched bottom for the first time and the crew had to abandon ship. They lowered another small yawl overboard, but after two men had boarded, the waves snapped the lines holding it to the ship. Drifting rapidly away, the boat and its men disappeared never to be seen again. One tiny surfboat was left, and eight men crammed into it. Using all of their strength, they managed to pull away from the *Sampson*. They barely were able to keep offshore in the crashing waves and avoid being dashed to pieces on the frothing rocks.

At dawn, the *Reliance* and the Fort Point lifesaving crew came to the violent scene. The tug's crew spotted the manned lifeboat tossing in the ocean. At "great peril to the boat," Captain Silovich ran his tug almost onto the rocks, coolly came about, and ordered a few men to take a lifeboat out. The small boat drifted down the line of waves and, in a lull between sets, the seamen were able to rescue the eight men. Once they were on board, the seamen told Silovich that four others were still on the *Sampson*. They had stayed behind because the lifeboat would have swamped if anyone else had tried to get on.

Silovich ran the *Reliance* to within sixty yards of the *Sampson* and dropped anchor. Seeing the men on the ship, he decided to run a cable to the stricken vessel and bring them back on that lifeline. Hearing a loud hissing to one side, he watched an enormous breaker approach. It crashed over both boats and swept them toward the cliffs. Seized by the towering wave, the wrecker smashed against the rocks with splintering sounds.

The *Reliance* nearly capsized and the currents began dragging the tug and its anchor toward the bleak rocks. There was nothing that anyone could do. But then its anchor miraculously held. The captain turned his attention to the *Sampson*, but he couldn't see any men in the wreckage that the waves were tossing about. The four men aboard her were lost. The *Sampson's* hulk caught fire from shattered oil lamps, and the flames rose to quickly consume the vessel. Little trace of the wreck-schooner and tragic incident was left.

Six men had died. Whitelaw was near heartbroken over the loss of "good men" with whom he had worked for some time. He could always replace the ship and equipment, but this was a tragic loss of personnel.

● ● ●

HIS PRIZED workhorse for operations was the steamer *Whitelaw.* Although he employed or chartered the vessel out in a variety of ways, its prime use was in wrecking. Seeing the potential of the Klondike gold rush, however, he leased the *Whitelaw* to another carrier and put his wreck-tug *Greenwood* in place of the *Whitelaw* for salvaging.

In 1898, the British Steamship & Yukon Gold Dredging Company took his charter for the *Whitelaw* to haul miners and their supplies during the gold rush. Most prospectors landed at Skagway, Alaska, or the adjacent town of Dyea, and then made the long, tough trek to cross the infamous Chilkoot Pass into the Yukon and eventually find the gold fields. As the need existed to use anything that could float to move the masses of gold-struck prospectors, T. P. H. received a very good fee for the ship's services.

Neither the captain nor the pilot on the *Whitelaw's* last voyage had been in Alaskan waters before. On March 4, 1898, the ship was steaming through the Lynn Canal, an inlet of the Pacific Ocean in southeast Alaska that connected Skagway with Juneau, a major route to the goldfields. On that day, an Arctic gale stormed into the Lynn Canal and blew the ship onto the shore. The fierce winds hit the *Whitelaw* with such force that the ship's oil lamps overturned and shattered in flames. The vessel burned into a smoldering hulk. Although all of the passengers were saved, they lost everything in the ensuing fire. The *Whitelaw* was a total loss, but with its owner being a wrecker, Whitelaw sailed to the Lynn Canal and salvaged the ship's machinery, fittings, railings, and metal.

When the schooner *Augusta* was rebuilt as a tug in Seattle, it was fitted with the engine from the wrecked steamer *Whitelaw.* The tug had a useful life, but when the *Augusta* was scrapped, so ended the career of what was virtually a floating marine museum. Her engine was from one wreck, the pilothouse from another, and large steering wheel from a third vessel.

Whitelaw had also been fighting during this time for the return of *La Ninfa,* which the government had impounded in 1891. It was hard enough to acquire ships, let alone lose them the way Whitelaw and others did when sealing in the Bering Sea. After nearly five long years, the Ninth Circuit Court of Appeals, which heard appeals taken from the District Court of Alaska, finally began its deliberations on the case.

Because the ship was more than one league (three miles) from the Alaskan shore, the basic question was whether the Bering Sea was subject to U.S. regulation. The pertinent U.S. statutes (Section 1956) provided that:

> No person shall kill any otter, mink, marten or fur-seal, or other fur-bearing animal, within the limits of Alaska territory, or in the waters thereof; and all vessels, their tackle, apparel, furniture, and cargo, found engaged in violation of this section shall be forfeited.

The statute unfortunately didn't specify what distance was specifically "within the limits of Alaska territory." If its jurisdiction covered the Bering Sea, then *La Ninfa* was U.S. government property under this act. By a prior treaty between the United States and England, however, any issues concerning these jurisdictional rights in the Bering Sea and preservation of the "fur-seal" were to be submitted to arbitration. This tribunal had made its decision before the seizing of the ships, including Whitelaw's *La Ninfa*. The arbitrators' decision held that a prior treaty between the United States and Russia in the sale of the Alaskan territory had restricted U.S. rights to "the reach of cannon shot from the shore"— or three miles.

A majority of the arbitrators had agreed the United States did not have any rights of protection in the fur-seals that frequented the islands of the Bering Sea, as they were outside the three-mile limit. The Circuit Court of Appeals found the tribunal ruling in the Bering Sea controversy to be valid, despite the fact that the earlier U.S. statute suggested a different result. This was especially true since the tribunal's decision was agreed to later in a treaty, and Congress then accepted that agreement in 1894. The statute therefore could only apply to within three miles from the shores of Alaska, and *La Ninfa's* captain was not in violation of the antisealing law or any decree enforcing that law. England and the United States were confirmed as having a common right for men to hunt for seals outside of the three-mile limit from Alaska into the Bering Sea.

The decision of the Ninth Circuit Court of Appeals in *La Ninfa; Whitelaw v. United States* (75 F. 513) reversed the district court's decision, which had forfeited Whitelaw's schooner to the United States for unlawfully killing seals in the Bering Sea. The appellate court handed down its decision on June 29, 1896, and on that date *La Ninfa* was set free.

Captain Whitelaw sent *La Ninfa* that year to fish for cod, another business that seemed profitable. The cod-fishing industry based in San Francisco, which had at one time nearly monopolized the work, was the home port for five schooners—including *La Ninfa*—and their crews landed over 600,000 fish that year. Although his ship was back in business, Whitelaw still wanted to be compensated for the repairs needed and the loss of income for five years. He was not alone in this desire; other owners and captains whose vessels had been illegally confiscated wanted to collect, too.

Whitelaw couldn't sue the government under the existing law of sovereign immunity, otherwise known as the "king can do no wrong." However, he doggedly lobbied with others and Congress for legislation that would allow him and the rest to collect for their losses. The odds were against T. P. H. and it would take more time and effort—but that hadn't stopped him before.

CHAPTER NINE

WRECKS—AND A GHOST SHIP

Over these years, Israel J. Merritt, William E. Chapman, and Thomas A. Scott's salvage operations would be the most visible on the East Coast. After Merritt bought total control of the Coast Wrecking Company in 1880, he renamed it the Merritt Wrecking Company and brought in his son, Israel Jr., as a partner. Merritt's competition with the Chapman Derrick & Wrecking Company was obvious, as Chapman's maritime hoisting and salvage business also centered in the large, flourishing port of New York City, where both businesses had offices.

With seven years of work on Race Rock Lighthouse ending in 1878, Thomas Scott was a little over fifty, but still strong, muscular, and motivated. Deciding to concentrate on salvage work, he soon enlarged the docks in front of his home on Pequot Avenue in New London, Connecticut. Scott then constructed sheds and bought or leased steam-tugs, dredging machines, barges, and lighters. He was ready now for heavy salvage work and would have more than enough opportunities.

In 1884, the *City of Columbus* had sailed south from Boston around Cape Cod and through Nantucket Sound. The 2,200-ton ship was a typical early iron steamer with auxiliary sails. Although the previous evening sky had been so clear that all of the myriad stars seemed to shimmer brilliantly, a westerly gale had suddenly moved in with heavy waves as the ship angled toward the open seas. On the early morning of January 19, the 275-foot ship was off the western shore of Martha's Vineyard. The lookout suddenly yelled out that the vessel was close to the Devil's Ridge buoy. They were too close.

The ship struck the double ledge of submerged rocks at Devil's Ridge. When the captain's attempts to move the ship off the rocks by steam and sail didn't work, he gathered the eighty-seven passengers and forty-five crew members together. While he tried to explain their precarious situation to already-frightened people, a giant wave rose over the gunnels, struck down the boat with a thunderous roar, and swept overboard nearly all of the men, women, and children on deck. The seas were so rough that they smashed the two lowered lifeboats against the ship's sides, and its masts angled toward the raging seas. Screaming people tried to stay afloat in the rough waters by holding onto the vessel's rigging.

A local lighthouse keeper and others from the Gay Head Indian tribe courageously approached the wreck in rowboats to save those who were clinging to the swaying, wave-engulfed vessel. Although the waters were rough, cold, and deadly, the Indians were able to save those who could make it to their boats. A revenue cutter also appeared and tried to maneuver around the wreck to pick people off the swinging masts and rigging. One man, Lieutenant Rhodes, saved two men who were unconscious. He tied a rope and swam through the debris and frothing ocean to the wreck. Even after a piece of wreckage slammed into him, he continued to climb the rigging and bring the two men back to safety.

Although twenty-nine persons were saved, approximately a hundred people drowned or froze to death in less than half an hour. Those who managed to hold onto the rigging long enough for the rescuers to come were saved. It was reported as one of the worst ocean disasters of its time, not to mention that of the New England states that ringed the disaster area.

When Scott arrived on the scene, the *City of Columbus* was on the shallow, rocky bottom three-quarters of a mile from the cliffs, and the seas were breaking violently over its superstructure. Already hovering around the wreck were five steamers, of which Captain Townsend, the New Bedford diver, was representing the Boston Underwriters' interests. Although the men somberly noted the high death toll and sent surfboats to pick up the dead, there was a job to be done in saving what property they could.

While they waited for more favorable conditions before diving below, Captain Baker and his Baker Wrecking Company crew had also arrived from Boston. Scott saw that Baker was in charge of the wreck; then, despite the stormy conditions and bad currents, Scott dropped over the ship's starboard side in the early afternoon to examine the stricken vessel. He located one hole that was "three feet square," as well as several smaller ones forward and aft; a perpendicular crack appeared near the foremast, while fragments of jagged rock—evidently broken from the large boulders on which the ship struck—were scattered on the bottom.

After completing his initial survey of the sandy floor, Captain Scott swam up and slid onto the deck, now awash with foamy water. Making his way carefully through the sloshing ocean, he dove under at the forward hatch and found that it and its deck were still in good condition. The angry seas broke against the ship with powerful "smacks," and he had to be careful when the ocean crashed down on the deck. Looking up, he saw the crest of an immense breaker surging over the ship. Scott had no time to react, as the pounding ocean quickly crashed down, hurled him "feet foremost into the air," and carried Scott with hissing surf over the ship's bow. Realizing that the heavy seas prevented further work, he motioned for his waiting surfboat to pull him from the ocean.

On the next day (Friday), Captain Scott sailed out to the sunken ship in his steam-wrecker, but discovered a stiff breeze blowing and the water again too rough. He managed to pick up three cases of boots and shoes near Wood's Hole as salvage, however, which had floated away from the *City of Columbus*.

The winds blew fresh from the northwest on Saturday, but the sea was moderate with clearing weather. Scott was able to remain underneath the water for two hours and complete his survey. He "went down well aft on the port side" and examined the seabed, finding parts of the smokestack and machinery, lines, sails, and other wreckage strewn along the port quarter by the main rigging.

Aft of the boilers near the bottom, the hull showed more cracking and several holes forward. The extent of the damage increased toward the bow, where the hull was cracked and pierced with "innumerable" holes. Scott worked his way past the wreck "another forty or fifty feet" and found himself in a submarine channel or sluiceway. This discovery indicated the vessel had struck a distance ahead of her present position, and the strong tides on that slope had pulled the wounded ship back, leaving her keel's imprint on the sandy bottom. Knowing this ship could not be saved, Scott headed home, but the wreckers that stayed did reclaim some cargo and parts from the vessel.

Six years later and nearly to the day, on January 12, 1890, the *City of Worcester* grounded ashore on the rocks outside New London, Connecticut. Within an hour of his receiving the news, Captain Scott was speeding to her assistance in his tug *T.A. Scott, Jr.* He was soon alongside the big, helpless steamer. The officers reported that the *Worcester* was fast on the rocks with the ocean pouring into her second, third, and fourth compartments with her boiler fires out. After life preservers had been handed out, the surfboats were readied and the passengers lowered in the lifeboats. This time all of the passengers were taken to shore without incident, and most of the cargo, including 1,250 bales of cotton, was transferred to shuttling lighters. As the weather conditions were moderate and the ship in good condition, but now quite lighter, Scott waited for the tides to sweep in and raise the water level. Twenty-four hours after the grounding, his tug hauled the endangered steamer from the rocks during the high tides. Captain Scott's ship towed the *City of Worcester* into New London Harbor and anchored her "within a stone's throw" of his residence.

Merritt was equally busy. Among his company's salvage opportunities was a race between two very large steamers that resulted in more business. The *Campania* and *St. Paul* were steaming toward New York Harbor on January 25, 1896. The *St. Paul* was 554 feet long, could carry 1,370 people, and had quadruple expansion engines that powered two propellers. It reached a service speed of nineteen knots. The *Campania* was a larger and more powerful ship at 601 feet long; it could carry up to 2,000 passengers and had triple-expansion engines that delivered a speed of twenty-one knots. Competing companies owned these two ships, and newspaper accounts called them the "second and third largest liners in the world."

The largest ship ever built then was the *Great Eastern;* at her launch in 1858, she was 692 feet long with a carrying capacity of 4,000 passengers, but was slower, at thirteen knots, with sail, screw, and side-wheel propulsion. Although broken up for scrap in 1888, it would be years before a larger ship would be built.

Captain Walker of the *Campania* gave his version as to what had happened between the *St. Paul* and his ship:

> It was about 8:30 o'clock Friday morning when we sighted the *St. Paul* fifteen miles ahead of us on our port bow. We watched her smoke for some time without being able to determine who she was, and about the time we recognized her, she must have recognized us, for we both went at it as hard as we could. We kept following her, but did not have her abeam until about one o'clock P.M.
>
> We steamed on until about 8:30 o'clock in the evening, when we ran into fog, and then ran at a fair rate of speed until one o'clock. From one A.M. until 5:30 A.M. in the morning, our movement was slow, and we then anchored. The lead at 5:30 indicated only ten fathoms of water, so I bucked the ship until I found fifteen fathoms, and then we dropped anchor.
>
> After the anchor was down, I knew we were fast to America, and was determined to stick to her. I was satisfied with this position. The fog lifted at 9:30 A.M., and we then again got underway. I had no idea where the *St. Paul* was until the lifting of the fog, and then I saw her on the beach.

Although Walker's description is factual, his statement downplays the fact that both huge ships were racing recklessly in the fog. The *St. Paul* was approximately 400 miles from New York City on its voyage toward Sandy Hook when the *Campania,* westbound from Liverpool, England, to New York, began to overtake her. Captain John Jameson of the *St. Paul* sighted his competitor in pursuit of his ship and ordered that all possible steam power be generated from the engine room. The race for New York was now at full speed as the giant ships produced "all the revolutions they could" throughout that Friday. By pushing to its maximum power, the *St. Paul* was able to keep abreast of the *Campania* for the bulk of the day, even though it had less engine power.

When a fogbank rolled in and obscured visibility, the conditions changed very quickly. Without regard for this development, the second and third largest liners in the world continued to speed through the fog, ignoring everything except their competition. Foghorns shrilled out warnings to one another at regular intervals, but this appeared to be the only safety concession made under this blind race.

As the vessels hurtled through the night, passengers reported that they constantly heard the other liner's foghorns. The officers on the vessels were so caught up in the race that they lost all reckoning of where they were or where their ships should be. As a result, both liners were fifteen miles off course. Even though they had slowed down appreciably in the blackness of the early morning hours, the two ships were still steaming away at several knots, feeling their way for the entrance to New York City. The *St. Paul* was "somewhat in the lead" when she suddenly slid over the sands at East Beach, New Jersey. The impact was gentle enough that some passengers didn't even know this until they awoke that morning.

Lifesaving crews were close by and had seen the lights of the *St. Paul* approaching the shoreline. They "frantically lit beacons" to warn the ship away from the close beach. However, the officers didn't see the signals until "she had struck or was about to strike" the sands. Worried about the *Campania*, the lifesaving teams burned a red light, which was finally answered by the large ship as it safely passed south of the beach.

Although the weather was moderate and calm, the seas came in high and dashed against the *St. Paul's* sides. The rollers sent spray high over the decks and the crashing sounds carried down to the passenger quarters, waking those who were not already up. When people ventured outside, they incredulously saw that the ship had grounded close to the sandy beach, and the continuous pounding waves had swung her around broadside. Long breakers rolled from the ocean toward them and boomed onto the ship and beach with unsettling regularity. The huge ship stayed firm on the sands, however, only moving a little when a particularly hard wave smashed in. Despite the conditions, Captain Jameson on the *St. Paul* made the decision to wait it out until a tender arrived from New York City to take the passengers off.

The race for the salvage was on. The International Navigation Company was close and quickly sent steam-wreckers to the scene; the tugs of the Merritt Wrecking Company quickly steamed into place; and the New York Tugboat Company sent three of its ships—all looking to earn a potentially very large salvage fee. Although the Chapman Derrick & Wrecking Company's ship arrived first, the insurers felt the wrecking companies should work together to refloat the vessel. Furthermore, this wreck was too entrenched in the sand with the ship's salvage value too great for one company. A coalition of wreckers joined together with their steam-tugs and men to work the salvage—and share the fee.

The salvagers quickly set heavy anchors offshore and moored them with large hawsers to the *St. Paul* to stop the dangerous push toward land. The ship was about one-quarter mile north of Iron Pier, almost "beam onto the beach," with her bow pointed to the southwest. As the news spread, thousands of spectators sped to the scene to watch while the huge vessel off-loaded its passengers and the salvage operations began.

The bow of the *St. Paul* was embedded below the sand in sticky clay, which would make it very difficult for the huge ship to be pulled off. The tugs were able to move the ship a little at times, but a "good storm" was needed to help move her along. For one week, the wreck-tugs and steamers pulled the *St. Paul* out "a bit" more each day. But this was an agonizingly long and slow process. The heavy ship had grounded in very shallow water, and each day's progress ranged from six to twenty-eight feet.

A strong nor'easter on February 3 rocked the vessel "a little" and made it possible for the tugs to shift her twenty-eight feet seaward in the morning and then 196 feet during the night. The tugs of the different wrecking companies pulled in tandem: Two ships shared one cable while two others were pulling on a second. The salvagers might have accomplished more had the waves not been so high that their ship's propellers were out of the water when they rode the wave crests. Throngs of bystanders watched the ship move the longest distance yet on that Monday, February 3, in spite of the driving rain and blustery conditions. Finally, on Tuesday morning, after having been grounded for ten days, the hull loosened from the clay and sands.

When the wrecker tugs resumed work that Tuesday, 200 feet still remained between the stranded liner and deep water, but the high tides, storm waves, and ship's heavy rocking made the salvagers confident. The coordinated effort by everyone was set for 9:00 A.M., and the *St. Paul* powered up with a full head of steam. By now, the tugs had moved the vessel to where it was more head-on to the shoreline. Her giant propellers began thrusting full astern as the tugs powered up with all available steam. There was "a long pull, a strong pull, and a pull all together," and the big ship moved from her bed, grating her keel though the sand and bumping and jolting over the bar. When she finally slipped into deep water, the shrill blasts of jubilant tug whistles cut through the air. People streamed to the beach to wave farewell to the famous ship as she made her way to New York City.

Captain Jameson, of course, was greatly relieved, since the loss of this ship would have certainly cost him his command—but he still had an inquiry to survive. In the subsequent hearing before the Board of Inspectors of Steam Vessels, the captain testified that he had on "several occasions" cast lead down to determine the depths. At the time the *St. Paul* grounded, she was steaming at less than five knots, and a recent heaving of the lead (or weighted lines) had indicated the water level to be seventeen fathoms. With his officers supporting Jameson's claims, the Board of Inspectors exonerated him. The issue of whether the *St. Paul* and the *Campania* had been racing was never raised.

For its efforts on the *St. Paul*, the Merritt Wrecking Company's salvage claim landed with others in court. In April 1898, the U.S. Circuit Court of Appeals affirmed the decision of the lower district court, deciding that $131,000 was owing to the firm for its effort on the ship, along with an additional $29,000 assessed for cargo work that included removing bags of gold. The American Line argued in court that the ship's value at $2 million was too high, but the Merritt Wrecking Company produced records showing that the vessel had been built for over $2.5 million just two years earlier.

The wreckers received nearly everything they demanded for their services, since the cargo itself was valued at a high $2 million, although more than half of it was gold packed in bags and easily handled. Deciding that those who were safeguarding the gold should also receive a fair payment, the judge ruled in favor of Merritt (who would share its fee). When the *St. Paul* was nudged into a dry dock at Newport News, Virginia, the inspection showed the hull was virtually undamaged and its machinery in perfect order. One month after hitting the shore, the *St. Paul* was in New York to prepare for its next scheduled sailing.

Collisions, fires, wrecks, and capsizing were always a risk of ship travel. Although vessels continually ran into threatening situations, fortune or misfortune seemed to depend on the fates. Whether people lived or died, or a ship survived, depended on the weather conditions, what object was hit, where the ship was, and other factors beyond the control of mere mortals. Being moored securely to a dock would appear the safest place to be—but not always—and this became a legend of ghost ships and their crews.

● ● ●

RIDING LOW due to the heavy cargo of coal she carried, the large, square-rigger British ship *Blairmore* arrived in San Francisco Bay in February 1896. After discharging her cargo, the sail ship lay idle at anchor, empty except for 260 tons of standing ballast used to offset the lost weight of the unloaded coal. Because the charter market for maritime hauling had softened, the *Blairmore* tugged in the ocean swells at her chains well into the spring.

The early clipper ships, such as the *Flying Cloud* and *Champion of the Seas,* were sleek, tall-masted greyhounds. However, by this time the fierce competition from the ever-growing number of steamships had forced the builders of sailing ships to design for even more speed. This led to sail ships with no dead rise (the angle between a ship's bottom and its widest beam), no depth of keel, and a heavy top hamper (the weight of rigging and spars on top) that combined to bring about a dangerous instability. The *Blairmore* was such a ship.

To overcome this problem, ship captains lashed spars, masts, and logs about midship to minimize the risk of their vessels capsizing when docked. When unloading the *Blairmore,* the stevedores off-loaded the cargo but didn't haul in enough compensating ballast. A charter to haul cargo was later secured, and the crew began loading goods back onto the vessel, but then they removed the ballast. They decided to rely on the strong hawsers that tied the tall-masted vessel to the wharf, instead of strapping spars to its middle and adding more counterweight.

On April 9, a squall from a southeast storm blew into the bay. The sail ship was lying in an east-west direction at the dock, pointing toward land, and the high flood tides were catching her broadside as they surged against her iron hull. The ship was drawing little water, and with her towering masts seemingly touching the clouds, the conditions were combining with a deadly effect. "The stevedores miscalculated," Whitelaw observed later, "as they threw off so much ballast that the ship was now top-heavy."

Men were working busily on the deck moving cargo, but most of them were inside the ship's hold, and as the wind occasionally gusted hard, a few looked up at the whipping sails. Lonely seabirds squawked loudly while they searched for shelter. The overhead, dark gray skies and "whomp" of the waves against the ship were forebidding, but the vessel was docked in the usually quiet bay and this fact comforted those working on the *Blairmore.*

But as a strong tidal current, large wave, and strong winds hit her simultaneously, the sail ship trembled along its length and then slowly heeled dangerously over with a deep aching, groaning sound. The hawsers attaching the ship to the dock held as they stretched taut with a twang. Time seemed to stop. With the vessel suspended at an angle, the seamen inside the ship yelled in surprise or shouted oaths.

With another sailing vessel in tow, the captain of the steam-tug *Active* saw the *Blairmore* start to heel over. He ordered his men to drop the connecting ropes to its charge and steam over to the ship's side. As the tug chugged closer, the *Active's* captain yelled through a megaphone and asked what help was needed.

The master of the sail ship, Captain John Caw, flatly refused the offer of assistance, more than likely because he was afraid of the ensuing salvage claims. Although most of his crewmen were working below in the hold when the ship pitched over, a few had managed by now to scramble on deck, but the shifting ballast and cargo had trapped others inside. The sharp cries of pain echoed up from one man caught by the pitching crates. While the tug stood by, the ship's fore, main, and crossjack yardarms were dipping into the ocean.

As another wave surge hit with a large smack, the vessel surged away from that side and the large hawsers parted from the dock with sharp snaps that cracked through the air. The *Blairmore* careened over with its masts becoming parallel with seas that inundated its sails. The overturning vessel threw shocked men into the ocean, while others found themselves sliding fast over the rough surface of hard, wooden decks. A few cried out terror-stricken yells, but most of the men simply slid or were thrown silently off the ship into the shifting seas.

When the *Blairmore* began pitching over, mate Thomas Ludgate and several seamen were cleaning inside one of the holds. They suddenly found themselves thrown wildly to the floor with loose cargo and equipment. With the hold's deck at a crazy, seaward angle but still upward, workmen frantically tried to crawl up the sides to the open hatch. However, they couldn't get there, as the ocean began pouring through the opening. When the final horrifying death roll of the ship happened, the sea surged inside and the sailing ship flipped completely upside down. The men tumbled down wildly from the open hatch, but with the rushing waters pouring inside, they were forced upward with the ocean's roar to the hull.

The tsunami-force of sea also hurled what was on the deck back inside the hold with the avalanche of water. A large capstan bar flew back and struck Ludgate on the head, knocking him unconscious. A flying plank smashed another apprentice and instantly killed him. The sailing ship stopped its roll when her masts snapped into the rocky bottom. Only her bilge-bottom was above water, and the air captured inside the *Blairmore* kept her partly afloat. Inside the ship's hull, the sea pushed bobbing men to the top of the overturned keel. There they gasped for precious air in the darkness through nostrils and mouths that were filled with saltwater. Gusts of wind and smacks of the sea surrounded the men who were imprisoned inside a small, lifesaving bubble of air.

Due to the accident's suddenness, no one on the dock knew how many men were trapped inside the hull or had escaped. Ships in the harbor lowered small lifeboats that were quickly rowed or motored over to assist, and the different crafts circled around the stricken ship like pilot fish around a dead shark. With the water and winds being cold, the men in the ocean treaded water slower and slower, while hypothermia began to set in and eventually shut down life.

British, Italian, and American crews, however, were able to pluck from the sea those men who had fortunately managed to survive their fall or jump. As rescuers pulled shivering seamen into the safety of small boats, the saved men knew that others were still trapped inside.

When the first rescuers jumped onto the *Blairmore's* slippery hull, ocean still dripping down its sides, they heard metallic, staccato sounds. The noise came from inside the hull. The trapped crewmen were frantically hammering against the ship's sides, and this eerie clamor resounded throughout the vessel. Men from the nearby Union Iron Works raced over to cut a hole in her bottom plates, unfortunately assuming that the ship rested on the bottom. The workers marked an eighteen-inch square on the *Blairmore's* hull and began swinging hard sledgehammer blows against chisels tightly held to the iron plate. After repeated smashes, the men finally succeeded in knocking in the plate.

Immediately, the massive hulk gave a strong lurch and a geyser of water shot high into the air. The motion knocked workers from their feet as water poured out of the opening with the last of the escaping air. The ship settled deeper into the water and the hammering stopped. The would-be rescuers had succeeded in opening a hole that allowed the last of the breathable air to gush out. Seawater had flooded through the hatch at the bottom and filled the entire ship.

The smell of death hung over the wreck. The first mate, sailmaker, two seamen, an apprentice, and a steward drowned terribly within that iron prison. The steward found himself trapped in the galley, but drowned before he could unlatch the door on the upper side. Captain Caw, the second and third mates, and five crewmen had escaped.

The *Blairmore* was tipped neatly upside down, as if she had been dropped into the bay on her rigging instead of her keel. The ship's deck was entirely underwater, and only a portion of the vessel's curved bottom was above the surface, "nearer the keel than the rail [at the bow]." After the storms passed, the ship owners had to decide what to do about the *Blairmore*. Even if the wreck wasn't valuable enough to be raised, it still had to be brought up. The vessel was a hazard to navigation and had shut down all operations on the long dock.

With the sail ship's rounded hull pointing to the skies, the owners consulted Captain Whitelaw. Just how do you salvage a large sailing ship that has its masts stuck into the bottom? To make matters worse, the ship's ten-story masts were at least twice that depth, and no one knew precisely what had happened there. Even if a way could be found to roll the boat back up, another tough problem was that it had heeled over toward the ocean. From its position close to the dock, salvage vessels couldn't find a decent angle from which to pull the ship back. Whitelaw knew "the ship had to save herself, as is done in all ship-rescue operations." Exactly how became the highly debated question.

Captain Whitelaw remembered his experiences a few years back with the *Newbern* and *Earl of Dalhousie*. The *Newbern* was a steam-powered coal cargo/passenger vessel that was 198 feet long. Winds and instability had caused her to partially sink and roll over at her San Francisco Bay dock. Whitelaw was able to right her in four days with tugs and hawsers through a series of pulling and holding maneuvers.

The 1,677-ton steel *Earl of Dalhousie* was 264 feet long and wrecked also in San Francisco Bay, when her ballast spars weren't securely lashed. The winds and waves had "turned her like a turtle," just like the *Blairmore*. Whitelaw's crews had managed to right the vessel by combining enough winch, hawser, and steam-wrecker pull to wrench the ship back. These techniques were usable here; however, those ships didn't have their masts buried in the bottom, nor were they positioned so close to a dock that it limited a tug's pull angles. Righting the *Blairmore* would take more than salvage vessels could provide alone—and new approaches were needed.

As the vessel's hull lay close to dockside, seamen walked by silently. They stared at her, some in disbelief that friends could die so suddenly while simply loading a ship. The vessel looked like a beached whale, decomposing in the sun, the only remains being the ribs of its bleached bones. A few stevedores already reported hearing metallic noises echoing from its insides, like those of trapped men still frantically trying to escape their watery tomb. Over drinks in waterfront bars, seamen began telling the stories about the ghosts on the *Blairmore*.

Whitelaw came up with what seemed to be a workable solution to this ship's particular problems. On the exposed part of the hull, his men would build a long platform for the ship's entire length. The wood structure would extend "from the portion nearest the submerged rail" out over the keel at an angle of forty-five degrees; at the platform's end, his plan called for the workmen to construct four open water tanks. Whitelaw believed the raised stand would operate as "a kind of huge lever, with which, if weight enough could be placed on the outer end, we could finally right the ship."

When filled with water, the tanks would put a strong, downward push on the vessel's dock side. Salvage tugs would moor on the opposite ocean side and pull in that direction with hawsers attached to the sunken masts and ship. Whitelaw further designed pontoons that created more lift from below, while the tanks, platform, and pulling salvage vessels would bring an angled or combined vertical/horizontal thrust. When divers confirmed the *Blairmore's* masts had cracked away from their impact with the rocks, the job of cutting them away could be crossed off the list.

As workers scurried over the overturned, bleached hull with their assignments, most of them didn't have time to think about the men who had died so tragically—at least during the day. When evening fell and work was done, some of them again said that they had heard strange sounds echoing from inside. It was as if the dead were still trying to get out. The construction superintendent assured the anxious men that any noises heard were simply the underwater currents swirling around the confined, loose goods. The workers still felt uncomfortable: Bodies were trapped inside and couldn't be recovered until the *Blairmore* was.

Divers reported seeing strange lights inside the vessel when working around it. Others dismissed those reports as being caused by the refraction of sunlight or the men's eyes firing with flashing spots when they worked too hard. One diver said he felt someone touch him on the shoulders. When he whirled around, he didn't see anyone in the dark gloom. The diver quickly surfaced.

Descending several stories down into the murky waters, divers attached heavy lines to the *Blairmore's* masts and "other parts" now underwater. Seamen rowed these thick ropes over in surfboats to different wreck vessels nearby, and their crewmen lashed the hawsers to bollards.

When all was readied, a steam-tug and barges with cranes pulled the slack from the tied ropes. As they tugged on the attached hawsers, steam-engine-driven pumps clanged into operation and filled the tanks on the platform with tons of water. With the additional weight on the lifting lever and strong pull underwater, the ship slowly turned on her long axis, and this rotation moved the water tanks toward the ocean's surface. While the barges held the *Blairmore* in that upward position by the stretched hawsers, steam pumps emptied the water from the tanks in powerful thrusts. Workmen scrambled on board the dripping hull and moved the platform with the now-empty tanks farther up the hull toward the keel. This time-consuming step took several days as workers removed planking, rebuilt the supporting platform, and moved the tanks with their waterlines. Once this work was completed, the tugs' stacks again belched thick smoke into the sky and water once more surged into the holding tanks. The process started again.

The heavy weight of water on one side, coupled with strong pulls from underneath the vessel and the force of the tied pontoons, ripped the masts away from the bottom. The *Blairmore* grudgingly righted herself by another five to ten feet, and the process was repeated once more. With the water tanks positioned further up the hull with more leverage, the sailing ship finally rotated to where her masts sliced from the ocean and came to rest parallel to its surface. With the tight ropes from the barges holding the ship in position, workers then boarded up the holds and pumped out more water.

Since the wreck barges with their equipment couldn't gain a sharp enough angle to bring the *Blairmore* completely upright, a donkey-engine-driven steam winch on dockside chugged and slowly inched the ship upward. As the ship was being uprighted, seawater began draining noisily from its masts, spars, and hull into the bay and long strands of seaweed hung in eerie patterns. Green-and-brown algae covered the derelict, but over time, the hot sun would bleach this away. When her sails were nearly upright, the vessel bobbed to a standing position, but as the water ballast sloshed, it angled over toward the dock. The ship floated, although her bow pointed up with the stern low in the water.

Lines and rigging lay jumbled on the ship's decks, and the steel railing around the bow was twisted and bent with broken spars thrust through, showing where frightened men and loose equipment had pummeled the handrails. Windows in the pilothouse were broken and fish strewn inside. The smells of rotten decay pervaded. Algae and seaweed were attached to the masts and woodwork, their long strings hanging down as if the ship had been sailing in another ethereal world.

With the ship upright, the wreckers pumped water from her hull, leaving just enough to counterbalance the shortened masts and top hamper. Concerned about the danger of "her pulling away and getting upside down again," Whitelaw decided to have a waiting tug drag the *Blairmore* to shallow water and ground her by the repair facilities. During a calm day without wind, a tug and wrecker gently pushed the ship on its side, while another ship pulled a distance away on the attached hawsers.

Once the ship was beached, pumps labored continuously and forced the ship to give up the rest of the ocean she had swallowed. Workmen then repaired the damage from her long immersion underneath the sea. The ship was worth several times the cost of the salvage and refurbishment, and workmen repaired the damage caused by the nailing of the planking and construction activities. They stripped away the rusted metal, replaced rigging, rebuilt railings, repaired broken windows, and changed wood stripping. Whitelaw's salvage yard provided the masts, spars, rigging, and whatever else was needed as the *Blairmore* received a paint job and new lease on life.

Although the bodies had been recovered and given decent burial services, this fact didn't stop the ghost sightings. Workmen bumped their heads on cabinet doors that they thought were closed—but were in fact open. Passersby saw lights moving about the decks at night, with more clanking noises echoing from its hull. The lights seemed to flicker on the deck like swarms of fireflies buzzing around a lamp, but there were no lights on that ship. The noises could have been brought about by the vessel's swaying in the ocean swells, but then again, what caused the metallic sounds? And the sparks of light? The stories abounded.

Once the *Blairmore* was seaworthy, the wreckers attached hawsers and eased her back into the water, ready to sail again. One night, a dock watchman made his rounds checking the ships tied at that wharf. As the bearded old man swung his oil lantern around, the shadows and silhouette of the vessels—some tall and slender with masts that disappeared into the night, others with squat smokestacks and small sails—appeared and then were lost. When he walked by one ship, the startled man heard a tapping sound. Turning around to investigate, he recognized the vessel as being the *Blairmore*. The sharp staccato noise became louder and cut through the foggy night air.

The watchman walked slowly up the gangplank to investigate, curious, yet still afraid. The deck was refurbished and his steps sounded dully while he crept toward the noise. It was coming from the hold that Thomas Ludgate and his men were working inside that fateful day.

The man hesitated and looked back toward the dock. No one was around. He shuddered as he looked around the cold, dark vessel with its unfamiliar shapes so close at hand. He peered inside the hold, but couldn't see anything in the darkness. More metallic hammering joined the other sounds. Lowering his lantern into the open hatch, the man once more stared hesitantly down.

A dark shadow jumped toward him and strong, whirling winds gusted up. The rush of air extinguished the flame and everything around him suddenly became dark. The watchman scrambled back over the gunwales like a man "twenty-five years his junior" and threw the lantern into the ocean in his mad flight back to the safety of land. Shouting for help from the heavens, he ran away from the waterfront like a crazed marionette. Although the ex-watchman was never again seen working the docks, he spent the rest of his time in pubs telling about his experience.

As to the *Blairmore's* recovery, Whitelaw later observed:

> After we completed the pumping, stored her with ballast, and towed the ship back to her berth, she was repaired, filled with cargo, and sent on her way. Probably more than half of the ships

rescued during my years of this work are still in service, some of them being sailing ships, out on remote trade routes, and others being iron and steel steamers, which, apparently, are just as good as they ever were.

Completely renovated, the *Blairmore* returned to the sea-lanes when a charter could be found. Seamen refused to sail on this ship, however, because of its stigma of death and reputation of a ghost ship. The tall-masted vessel was renamed the *Abby Palmer* and later was known as Alaska Packer's *Star of England*. Her ghostly name was still inscribed on the bell and capstan, and crews still felt the specters' presence on their journeys.

The owners eventually gave up. In a time when sails gave way to steam engines, the once-proud sailing ship was reduced to the ignominious role of a sawdust barge in British Columbia. No one there had any reason to know that it was the *Blairmore*; it was just one of many other once-magnificent full-sail vessels that were now passing into history.

CHAPTER TEN

NO REWARDS
WITHOUT RISK

S hip salvaging was just one of the various businesses that the
Whitelaw Wrecking Company and T. P. H. conducted. As seen
before, he was into maritime activities such as commercial shipping, towing, chartering, building vessels, reselling ship parts, and buying and selling scrap, not to mention whaling, sealing, and commercial
fishing. He also repaired buoys and moorings, inspected ships, ran a
pumping service and quarry, owned gold mines, and invested in mining
claims, land lots, and real estate.

He and his crews worked on nearly anything, ranging from laying a
pipeline across the bay to installing cannons that protected the Golden
Gate. Whitelaw laid moorings down the coastline for the government
with three-inch chains and six-ton anchors. When T. P. H. raised the
barge *Martinez,* he saved the oil tanks and shipped them to Richmond for
storage. His grandson said that he was "quite the operator and would
tackle anything. He'd put in a well for you if you needed one."

As to the cannons, he floated the heavy artillery over the bay by barge,
and then "parbuckled" them up the steep slopes. He had his crews construct heavy timbers up the inclines and build large skids. Tying thick

hawsers to the wood platforms, the men roped the cannons to the frames. Horses with block-and-tackle dragged the "guns on skids" up the slopes. Horse-drawn wagons hauled the cannons along the coast to where they were finally installed.

T. P. H. conducted underwater work for the movie industry and rigged vessels for Hollywood productions. For example, he constructed what was needed to film the storm sequence in the 1920 movie *Shore Acres,* with silent-screen notables Alice Lake and Robert Walker. Whitelaw constructed a large wood tank on a wharf, filled it with water, and pulled a smack through it as pumps shot water over the boat. The scene was for the movie's climax, when a fierce storm blew over a boat during a dark night.

According to his grandson, Whitelaw's prime yard was his one-acre junkyard between Folsom and Harrison on Main Street, two blocks from what's now the waterline at the Embarcadero and close to the present Bay Bridge. This location had "everything that was maritime," from ten-foot propellers and large centrifugal pumps, down to the smallest shackles. It was a "real wonderland" of marine parts, diving suits, pumps, buoys, anchors, chains, wire, metal drums, rope, parts, and machinery salvaged from vessels. According to Ken Whitelaw, "Old Jake Evans, who had his own marine chandlery business in London, England, was in charge of the yard."

Captain Whitelaw owned another yard on Bay Street, with Main Street "then following Bay." Back then, Main Street was a maritime center, as Ken recalled, with the "Main Street Iron Works, a blacksmith business, McCarthy's (secondhand anchors), Matson's (ship line) people, iron works, ship-work repair facilities, Wolcott sailmakers, Greenberg Copper Works, and everything associated with ships."

The Captain also owned a five-and-a-half-acre open estuary where he anchored his salvage ships, such as the *Catalina* and *Greenwood.* The barge *Catalina* was a "bald-headed, four-masted schooner." Whitelaw owned 500 lots in Visitation Valley, according to his grandson, not to mention a gold mine and mansions (including the "Whitelaw Mansion" on Lincoln Hill). He loaned $10,000 another time to one Mr. Laurel who started a machinery company that bore his name and developed gasoline engines for cars.

Whitelaw loved to be active and was very energetic, by his grandson's recollections. Although T. P. H. always enjoyed the challenge of something new, he embraced the sea above all. He operated from "British Columbia, the Puget Sound, and Columbia River—where he made a million dollars," and was well known for "operating seal ships in Alaska and raising ships down the West Coast to Acapulco." He kept his divers and a skeleton crew on salary for any emergency, and then subcontracted out for the dozens of workers that might be needed for a particular project. When he heard about a ship in distress under difficult situations, such as the *Umatilla*, his "eyes would light up."

He retained the best divers, from George Kristoferson to Jack Whitelaw (his nephew), including one Ricardo Bernardi, who happened also to be a lion tamer. He hired well-known captains and officers who would later develop their reputations. They had names such as Captain Hoffman, Tanglefoot Pete Bertelsen, Captain Pillsbury, Captain MacLean, and the "old salt" Captain McGuinn. Whitelaw's typical approach was to stay on a wreck site for the tough work, but then steam back to San Francisco when the job was under control, leaving a trusted seaman for the remaining operations. Once he figured out a challenge, he looked for another one.

One of the stories told about Whitelaw on the waterfront was called the "battle over a rusty old anchor." This story included a furious captain, Whitelaw, a smirking crew, a stern policeman, and one aged anchor. Jake Rauer was the captain of the *Point Arena*, a steam schooner that was due to sail one day at three o'clock in the afternoon. By the time the crew had loaded the "huge old anchor" onto the ship's deck, the clock struck three. Seamen pulled in the hawsers while others prepared to take the schooner out.

A shrill whinny suddenly pierced the air, as a horse-drawn buggy carrying Whitelaw and a policeman screeched to a stop on the dock, coal dust flying from the horse's hooves. "Stop that craft!" shouted the patrolman, as he jumped to the planking and waved a search warrant with one hand up in the air. The boat stopped. The officer ordered that the anchor be taken off and put back on the dock. Once that was done, Rauer and Whitelaw argued for a long time in front of everyone.

Rauer shouted loudly that he bought the anchor two years ago from Whitelaw, while the Captain yelled back that Rauer had only rented it a year ago—and never paid the money. Rauer claimed it had been lying in a lot for seven months, and that he had finally decided to use it to moor the *Point Arena*. While the heated exchanges were taking place, the crew members smiled at one another, as they didn't care, one way or the other: They had already signed on and didn't have to work.

After three hours of angry words, Whitelaw decided to change his approach. The law provided that anyone who delayed a steamer's departure without good reason could later be held liable for the ship's damages. He silently walked away and found a telephone in a nearby shed. A horse-drawn dray soon arrived with a much smaller anchor, and the two men started up again with their strenuous arguments. After crewmen had loaded the small anchor on the schooner, Rauer and his vessel left.

The patrolman guarded the old casting all night until the following day, when the two pressed their claims in court. Rauer claimed Whitelaw had given the second anchor to him because he knew he was wrong. Whitelaw argued that he had loaned it so that the vessel could sail. Although there was no record on how the judge ruled, others claimed Whitelaw held onto that rusty old anchor as long as he lived.

❦ ❦ ❦

HE ALSO took the odd jobs that came along, including one of diving for a $50,000 brick made of solid gold. Workers at a smelting company in Selby, California, had just removed the hot, golden ingot from its form and carefully placed it on a steamer's gangplank. Guarded on both sides by men, the brick was sliding down the metal runway toward the waiting ship.

A longshoreman happened to be standing by the runway and spotted the "glittering fortune" that was going by. The man leaned over to give it a gentle touch of affection. To his pained surprise, the golden brick was still intensely hot from the furnace's heat. The man's reflexes took over, as he shoved the brick savagely away. It slid off the gangplank and disappeared with a sharp sizzle into the water.

When Whitelaw happened to be working nearby, the smelter owner called on him to retrieve the gold bar. He dove down himself, expecting to find it where the heavy piece had disappeared into the shallow waters just a short time before—but the brick was nowhere in sight. The near-priceless bar, worth at least $5 million in today's dollars, couldn't have been stolen, as the area was too carefully guarded. The gold was too heavy for the tide to have moved it very far.

This annoyed Whitelaw, because he could see the "big dent in the mud" where the brick had hit the bottom. He ordered his divers to dig down at the spot. "They dug and dug," said the Captain. "They kept at it for five days, moving barrels and barrels of mud." He changed divers to keep them fresh, since digging underwater was hard labor. Although the waters were relatively shallow, even the divers showed their frustration at not being able to find something this valuable—especially when it was so close.

On the fifth day, a diver signaled victory. The man had found the thick gold bar thirty feet below the surface of the oozy bottom. The heavy brick had hit the mud with such speed that it sank three stories through the mud layers. As Whitelaw later observed:

> It had apparently escaped the divers by a few inches each time they got near it. The gold sank a little farther every time they opened the hole a few inches more, until it finally rested on hardpan and couldn't go deeper.

He and his crews had a similar experience in Washington. A workman was boarding a steamer with two sacks of silver, each containing a thousand dollars worth of precious coins. The gangplank was frosty that morning, and the man slipped, his feet shooting out from underneath him. As he fell back on his elbows, the heavy sacks slammed his wrists down hard on the gangplank's edges. The worker let go of the bags.

After the owner tracked him down, Whitelaw dove into the water and quickly found one sack. "I'm in luck today," he thought to himself. He had agreed to another one of his contingent deals: The owner received the first sack, and he was to have the second. There was no compensation if he didn't find both. "I went down again for my sack," he said. "Well, sir,

I dived there for two entire days looking for the other one. I even crawled on my hands and knees and felt every inch of ground—but no sack."

Whitelaw continued:

After every other possibility had been exhausted, I noticed a few feet from the spot, a lot of old waterlogged slab wood [what's sawed from a squared-off log]. I began to shift it around. Nobody ever stacked wood with more interest than I did in this operation. I had dropped into a routine in doing this, when up came a board that had been covering the sack of silver. The silver couldn't have been hidden any better than if someone had put it there.

In 1913, the underwriters for the steamer *Corcoran* hired T. P. H. Whitelaw to find a safe with $51,000 in gold pieces—worth millions of dollars today. Another steamer had rammed the ship, and it had sunk in San Francisco Bay. He found the ship and the sought-after object. Attaching a buoy to the safe, it slowly rose to the surface, where he claimed it and received his fee.

Another time, Whitelaw discovered what he called a "coal mine" at the bottom of San Francisco Bay, "provided the vein didn't pinch out" and he could raise it economically to the surface. The old American ship *May Flint* had been lying in twelve fathoms of water for seventeen years. The wreck was supposed to have 2,500 tons of coal inside its holds, and with the fuel's high price, this recovery made sense to him.

On the evening of September 9, 1900, on Admission Day, the full-rigged *May Flint* had sailed into the harbor and up the bay. A pageant had taken place that evening to celebrate the day when California officially became a state in 1850, and thousands of sightseers admired the *May Flint* as she passed up "majestically under full canvas." A strong flood tide current, however, swept her by the Ferry Building and against the sharp prow of the battleship *Iowa*. The collision pierced a large hole in her hull, and the ship sank in ten minutes; as the sail ship swung free from the *Iowa*, however, the *May Flint* struck the bark *Vidette* and almost sank her. Surfboats from the battleship rescued the crew.

The *May Flint* carried at first 5,000 tons of coal. Another salvor later raised about one-half of the precious cargo. After complying with the federal government's requirement to clear the wreck to a depth of thirty-five feet, so the hulk wouldn't obstruct navigation, the wrecker abandoned his efforts. After checking to ensure that its holds were intact (only the masts and above-deck structures had been removed), Whitelaw received the government's permission to work on the wreck.

After consulting with other experts, he concluded that coal improved in its quality due to the chemical reactions when immersed in saltwater. He was told that a cargo of coal submerged for fifty years on the Atlantic Coast was in apparently better condition than when it first sank. For several days, Whitelaw and his wrecker *Greenwood* hovered over the scene. Although his men brought up scrap iron, as well as more coal, it isn't known how much money he made. However, his salvage attempt was newsworthy.

Another time, he decided to find a valuable Hart automobile from the bottom of San Francisco Bay. On a whim, Oakland millionaire H. H. Hart had directed his chauffeur to "drown it." (Although the names are identical, H. H. Hart was not associated with the car's manufacturer.) The eccentric man was on board the San Francisco/Oakland Ferry at the time, and his chauffeur dutifully backed the car off the ferry's end. Hart told reporters that whoever found the car could keep it. Hearing the offer, T. P. H. raced to the scene. He thought he might make a tidy profit by finding the $4,500 car in the fifteen fathoms of water and putting it up for bid.

After sailing to where the ferry was said to have been, Whitelaw brought his boat to where he thought the car had entered the water. Making allowances for the underwater currents and where the car would have hit bottom, he anchored at another location. Using grappling hooks, his men found an object that was a car, and Whitelaw's divers attached a red barrel buoy to mark the spot. When they came back later, the crew discovered to its chagrin that the buoy had disappeared.

Bright and early that next morning, commuters were crossing on the ferry steamers again to San Francisco and watched the operation in progress. Whitelaw's divers and grapplers were successful again, and he fastened the automobile to another red buoy. Whitelaw quickly returned to shore with his men to find a stronger hawser that wouldn't break away.

As unexplainable as before, upon their return the men were disappointed to find that the second red barrel had vanished. Whitelaw and his diver searched again for any sign of the buoy—but in vain. Cappie told a reporter he was going to find the car, since the vehicle was worth "a lot of silver" in those days. The reporter took Whitelaw's statement: "A dinna ken hoo the buoy got awa', but A'm gaun' tae hae anither try fur it. Ye see, Maister Hart has tell't me thet A can hae the machine fur massel' if A can fin' it. Automobiles are worth a lot o'siller thae days an' A canna afford tae lose a chance like this yin." (It's doubtful that T. P. H. usually talked like this, but the newspaper printed his response this way.)

The third time would be the charm, he thought. Whitelaw was now ready for the tricky currents with the strongest cable possible. As before, they found success—or so they thought. Just after noon, the grappling hook caught "in some object" amid the cheers of the wrecker and his men. A fully equipped diver was also "close at hand," and before the tides could possibly turn, the helmeted diver disappeared beneath the choppy bay waves.

When he returned to the surface and took his helmet off, T. P. H. wanted to know if the saltwater had damaged the car's metal. "Automobile!" exclaimed the diver. "There's no automobile down there," the man said. "It's an anchor with about fifteen fathoms of chain attached to it." Whitelaw was perplexed at the disappointing find, but he was not discouraged. He raised the anchor for salvage and renewed his search for the now-famous Hart motorcar.

Reports, meanwhile, about the movements of the red buoys began to surface. Captains of steam schooners reported they had seen a red buoy floating out to sea. Several skippers told Whitelaw that they had glimpses of a red buoy barrel. One captain said he had steamed into the bay in the early morning darkness. He was "feeling his way" into the harbor when he heard a horn honking. When the lights switched on from the Alcatraz lighthouse, the skipper saw a red buoy floating in the bay, but he couldn't get to it in time.

After learning that the gasoline in Hart's car was still "active," Whitelaw told the press he had solved the mystery of the disappearing buoy and car. He said:

> When Hart had his chauffeur back the automobile off the ferry-
> boat, by a queer combination of chemical energy, this gasoline

became active, and the car, by some queer process righted itself and began to race along the bed of the bay. The car would continue out to sea and defeat all attempts to rescue it.

The reporter observed in the article:

It must be distinctly understood that this is Captain Whitelaw's own impression of what had happened. When he said it, there was a twinkle in Cappie's eye and a bounce to his step, because he had brought up an anchor from one of the ancient windjammers when this port was the rendezvous for sailing craft.

The appropriate headline for that December 1912 *San Francisco Examiner* article was, "Motor Car's Buoy Starts for China: Mermaids Out Joy Riding." No one ever found the automobile.

T. A. Scott also had his share of odd wrecks to raise. Finally incorporating his business in 1903 as the Thomas A. Scott Company, his stationery stated that the company performed "Towing, lightering, dredging and pile driving, wharf, bridge and foundation building, submarine work, and wrecking." One time, the general manager of a railroad line asked him to recover a locomotive. The engine had tried to cross a bridge trestle, but it had toppled over instead into thirty feet of water and a muddy bottom. The good news was that underlying rock was only a few feet farther down and still supported the heavy locomotive.

"Get her up?" answered Captain Scott. "Certainly, but where do I put her?"

"Back on the rails," said the general manager, with a laugh, as he thought about the impossibility of the task.

"All right—she'll be there in the mornin.'"

Scott had his workmen rig a pair of sheer poles and put on his diving gear. He then dropped down in the murky water beside the locomotive. He passed heavy chains under the boiler and between her axles, hooked a block onto a ring, and had his men pull the rig and chain up. They attached the rig to a nearby tug's hoisting engine.

With the boiler fired up, Scott turned on the hoisting engine and opened a steam cylinder. The derrick slowly winched up the locomotive.

Heavy rivulets of water drained noisily down onto the surface as the engine was hauled upward onto land. The powerful crane lifted the locomotive ever so carefully and slowly onto the railroad tracks. Using a hose attached to his steam pump, Scott cleaned off the engine as the last part of his service.

"There!" he told the overseeing manager. "Now git a fire under her and pull her out—she's in my way." As he told the story, Scott's work took "but half a day."

● ● ●

DURING THE 1900S, several important developments affecting transportation took place. The Wright Brothers made the first airplane flight at Kitty Hawk in December 1903. The first production run of the Model T occurred in late 1908 in Detroit, Michigan—and the car quickly became the most popular line of the time. This vehicle was the first that was truly affordable due primarily to Henry Ford's innovations and the introduction of modern assembly-line production methods. The United States finished building the Panama Canal in 1914, allowing ships to dramatically cut the distance from the Atlantic to the Pacific Ocean.

In the maritime salvage world, however, no advances had enabled wreckers to raise the 331-foot *San Pedro*, which still lay on Brotchie Ledge near Victoria Harbor. The spectacular wreck had occurred in November 1891, but Whitelaw was not successful and left after months of work at his own expense, having accepted again a fee contingent only on success (see Chapter Eight, "Failures Follow Accomplishment"). Two years later, Captain Lachlan took on the job of raising the *San Pedro*. Armed with the ship's plans, Lachlan told the press he had built this ship and other vessels for his company and the owner, Southern Pacific Railroad.

In the first week of August 1893, Lachlan made his initial attempt to raise the ship; however, as the ship lifted "a little," the pumps broke down. Another attempt was made the following week with twenty-three pumps operating for fourteen straight hours, along with numerous ships and two tugs to pull the wreck. However, when the largest tug used its maximum power, the nineteen-inch thick towing rope snapped "like a piece of twine," and still the *San Pedro* hadn't moved. When divers discovered holes that were sixty-five feet long, Lachlan gave up, deciding this ship would never be pumped dry.

Soon to be known nationally as premier shipbuilders, the Moran Brothers Company from Seattle next tried to raise the *San Pedro*. After repairing the cofferdams that encircled the ship, they used more powerful pumps—and endured two more unsuccessful tries that November. When storms destroyed their equipment, the ship's stern disappeared, and another attempt failed in 1894, it became clear that this wreck would never be raised. The Moran Brothers left.

Until then, the Southern Pacific Railroad had been convinced that the *San Pedro* could be refloated. After three years passed with large amounts of money and time expended, they rethought their decision. Despite Whitelaw's efforts, Lachlan's cofferdams, and the Moran Brothers' pumps, the heavy ship had failed to move one inch. In his own way, T. P. H. had been vindicated. He said later, "I might have bitten off more than I could have chewed," but then again, very few tried to tackle these jobs.

The owners finally gave up. Erecting a temporary warning light on her bow, the railroad announced that the ship would be removed and a lighthouse built on the reef. The San Pedro disaster had proved more costly to wreckers than any other in the Pacific Northwest, and Whitelaw later said he had lost nearly $100,000 on his attempts. The eyesore of the vessel's bow, foremast, and underwater outline continued to be visible.

With the ship being a hazard to navigation, the man called upon to remove the *San Pedro*—piece by piece—was none other than Whitelaw. Signing a new wreck contract in September 1896, he couldn't start until the following May. A severe storm in March then blasted her bow away, and only the forward mast stood, "as if the only resting place for a lantern man's light."

The Canadian government in Ottawa granted him permission to take his new wrecker *Whitelaw III* and equipment across the border for the salvage. (When the *Whitelaw* was placed on charter—and later to be lost off Alaska—T. P. H. had by then commissioned two others with his family surname.) With more design improvements based upon his experiences, the construction of *Whitelaw III* was almost complete, and this job would be its first large undertaking.

Due to the continuing cold conditions and risk of dynamite freezing in water "around forty-two degrees," Whitelaw would wait until at least mid-spring. It wouldn't be until April that the icy waters of the Juan de Fuca Strait would begin to warm. And as the channels were exposed to the Pacific Ocean's westerly winds and storms, the seas were rougher there than in the more protected inlets.

In May 1897, Whitelaw and his steamer arrived in Victoria to begin demolition. He would use explosives to cut the derelict in sections as large as his derricks could lift, believing the recovered iron could more than repay his costs. Large explosions began to disrupt the ocean's surface, and one blast threw a wide expanse of water fifty feet into the air.

Dynamiting the *San Pedro's* most "visible section" was planned for the Queen's Diamond Jubilee—the sixtieth anniversary of Queen Victoria's reign—and as per Whitelaw's contract. This occasion was subject to elaborate celebrations by British subjects around the world, and so the demolition would take place in front of crowds of spectators. On June 21, 1897, the *Victoria Daily Colonist* reported:

> The explosion was a very pretty one, a column of water being sent a hundred feet in the air, but those who looked for the obliteration of all traces of the *San Pedro* were again disappointed. The landmark still remains and will still give the wreckers a profitable occupation.

Whitelaw brought in the *Alexander* to haul away the cut-up iron. The four-masted British schooner had formerly been a huge side-wheel tug. Lying idle at Port Townsend for some time, the vessel was purchased and converted into a barge that carried logs from island camps to Victoria mills. The old craft was then sold to another Victoria-based company for $1,000, or one-half of one percent of its original construction cost of $200,000. Whitelaw then took it over, removed the engines and wheels for scrap, and built the schooner rig.

His team eventually completed the contracted demolition, and T. P. H. finally ended his connection with the *San Pedro*. During the six years that the large ship was skewered on the reef, the vessel itself was a navigational marker, as a warning light was hung every night from its masts. A sturdy concrete beacon was built in 1898, replaced ninety-one years by another, and what was left of the *San Pedro* remained on Brotchie Ledge. Scuba divers still explore the wreck today, searching for souvenirs and spear-fishing for the large cod lurking under the pieces of iron Whitelaw left behind.

❧ ❧ ❧

ONE OF THE most unique salvage operations involved the Columbia River Lightship Station No. 50, the first lightship (a vessel that served as a "floating lighthouse") to serve on the West Coast. Constructed at the Union Iron Works in San Francisco for $61,150, the 250-ton ship was 121 feet long and built with a composite steel frame. Planked with Puget Sound pine and sheathed with white oak, the vessel had two masts with two coal-fired boilers that produced the steam for her twelve-inch fog whistle. Three lanterns topped the ship's masts to warn vessels away at night. The ship didn't have an engine or propeller, but was equipped with sails to use if the anchor gave way.

A steam-tug towed the LV-50 into position in the Pacific Ocean on April 11, 1892, roughly five miles west of the Columbia River's entrance. When the ship's lights beamed out and its foghorn boomed, vessels heading into the river knew their precise position. Otherwise, the ships could run aground on the beach or a reef. This fate happened so often that the Columbia River was justifiably called the "Graveyard of the Pacific." From 1870 to 1930, more than a hundred major shipwrecks occurred in the vicinity of the Columbia River's mouth, where ships stranded, sank, or completely disappeared.

Anchored off the treacherous, continually seething bar, the lightship had a crew of eight who kept watch, maintained the kerosene lights, and shoveled coal into the boilers to power the massive fog signal. Their wave-tossed perch with its booming horn drew hardy men who—like those at the remote lighthouses—"endured modest pay and isolation."

Held securely in place by a 5,000-pound mushroom anchor, the lightship endured a strong gale on November 28, 1899, with winds of seventy-five-miles per hour. The storm slammed cresting rollers against the ship, which strained against her chains. In the afternoon, the two-inch mooring lines finally snapped, leaving the vessel and crew at the mercy of the gale's full fury.

The men quickly set her sails to keep the lightship from grounding. Using their skills to match the forces of nature, the seamen at first were able to stand offshore under sail. But the conditions soon became so treacherous that the captain decided the next morning to make for the relative safety of the river. The shrieking winds shredded the sails, however, and the ship drifted aimlessly but angled with the currents toward land.

Receiving the news about the ship's distress, the district inspector of lighthouses quickly ordered two steam-tugs and a tender to rush to the scene and aid in the rescue. The crew of the tug *Wallula* was able to attach a hawser to No. 50, but the extreme conditions soon strained the thick line until it gave way.

With the winds screaming and cresting waves smashing against the ships in the Columbia River's wide expanse, the tender *Manzanita* carefully approached the wallowing lightship. Under pallid skies and gray, grim surroundings, the men shot another cable through the salt spray and heavy rain to land across the lightship's bow. Once attached to a bollard, this line held momentarily, only to also snap. While the gale drove the ships from one another, debris curled underneath the ship and fouled its propellers. The rescuing vessel was now another victim.

While the crew desperately tried to retain control, LV-50 drifted away toward the shoreline. The captain of the third ship, the tug *Escort*, had a difficult decision to make: try to save the lightship or save his tug. Her sails shredded and near capsizing, the lightship was in great danger. The tug steamed cautiously toward it; once close enough to the vessel, the men managed to get a cable onto her.

With the lightship in tow, the *Escort* had nearly succeeded in pulling it over the treacherous undertows and waves crashing from different directions that mark the Columbia River Bar. Then that rope snapped. With the huge, rough rollers breaking over and inundating No. 50, its captain didn't have a good alternative: The winds and waves would either drive the vessel to its destruction on the rocks of nearby McKenzie Head or onto the southern part of Cape Disappointment. He chose to save his crew by trying to maneuver his vessel onto a sandy shore between the two points.

The vessel drifted into a line of high breakers on the seaward side of Cape Disappointment, north of the Columbia River Bar. Death and destruction seemed imminent. As the currents and winds drove the light-ship to land, the captain frantically tried to maneuver his craft around. At the last moment, his attempts proved successful. The ship grounded fortunately on a short, sandy stretch of beach between McKenzie Head and the cliffs at the end of the cape, where the lighthouse at Cape Disappointment flashed its light.

Before running onto the beach, the captain managed to swing the ship around so that its bow pointed toward the sea—its high forecastle giving some protection against the crashing surf. Once the ship grounded, its crew safely left by a high-wire breeches buoy set up for shore. The crew of the Cape Disappointment Lifesaving Station had raced there with a line gun. They shot a rope across the lightship's bow on their second attempt and worked the breeches buoy. Although the tender and tugs managed to survive the storm's onslaught, LV-50 remained beached and at the storm's mercy.

Spectators flocked to watch the efforts to pull the ship from the beach, which each time proved fruitless. After six months of attempts, salvage bids were finally requested, and most bidders proposed to pull the craft back into the ocean. Three contractors suggested, however, hauling No. 50 overland to Baker's Bay—located some two-fifths of a mile away—by lifting the vessel onto blocks and pulling her across the narrow point of the peninsula from the Pacific Ocean. This cove was situated on the north shore of the Columbia River, just inside the river's entrance, 700 yards from where the lightship grounded.

When U.S. Light-House Board officials in Washington, D.C., decided that the land approach wouldn't work, they awarded the bid to a Portland shipbuilding firm that planned to tow the ship into the ocean. Although armed with heavy cables, anchors, a large crew, salvage barge, and a tug, this firm's efforts also proved to be unsuccessful. Realizing that going by sea wasn't possible, the lighthouse service called for more bids, but this time only for the land route.

The winning bid of $17,500 came from Allen & Roberts, who were Portland house movers. The two men naturally agreed to move the ship as if it was a residence and complete the task in thirty-five working days. The plan called for erecting heavy timbers as braces under the ship. Jackscrews would lift the vessel up, and a large cradle built underneath it. This cradle would hold the ship while men and horses pulled the lightship over land on rollers. Whether this plan would work was another consideration.

On February 21, 1901, workers began clearing the sand away from the ship's hull and swung her bow around so it pointed to land. Another crew lifted the ship with jackscrews and built the cradle. Multitudes of workmen with horses tugged, pulled, and strained to move the ship—inch by inch—through the woods from Cape Disappointment to Baker's Bay. Weeks passed. The strange apparition startled unaware travelers who happened upon this lightship on tracks, weaving its way over a path cut through the forest and being pulled by horses with sweating, straining men.

Work proceeded much slower than anticipated, and the thirty-five-day period expired. Although the contract called for a $100-per-day late-delivery penalty, the board decided to give more time, especially since the contractors were doing their best and working around the clock.

While the ship and its cradle creaked over sets of large rollers, men with horse-drawn wagons carried more of them ahead to set in front of the slow-moving expedition. Horses labored to pull the attached hawsers and block-and-tackle around rotating capstans that inched the ship over the newly constructed heavy-planked roadway. Work camps were established ahead at predetermined locations, so the workmen could rest there with food and bedding, ready for the next day's efforts.

Although people flocked to see the sight every day, large crowds usually congregated on Sundays to watch. This spectacle became the major event in the region. After all, it wasn't usual, to say the least, to see a large "high and dry" ship moving overland. The curious "came by the hundreds," with widely advertised excursions leaving from nearby Astoria, Oregon. The cost was one dollar, with "bicycles checked for free."

There was no record that the firm used steam donkey engines, as would be employed in logging camps or on docks. Two horses on a capstan seemed to be able to move the 250-ton ship. Uphill routes were quite difficult, however, and three sets of block-and-tackle with more horses were then used. With tie ropes stretching ahead, like something out of *Gulliver's Travels*, the caravan of laborers, thick planked tracks, and one lightship on rollers made its slow tortuous path over the contours of the land. More weeks passed.

Finally, the men saw the river's edge at Baker's Bay. When the ship was within 250 feet of the bay—and the salvagers knew they would be successful—repairs were hastily made where, over one and a half years before, the pounding waves had knocked in holes and fractured parts of the ship's rudder and hull. At 11:45 P.M. on June 2, 1901, the movers launched LV-50 from its bed of rollers and planking into the bay's calm waters. After being marooned for eighteen months and enduring an overland trip of over three months, she had finally been set free. A waiting tug then towed the lightship to Astoria for the needed repairs.

The Light-House Board spent nearly $14,000 to repair the craft. Once completed, she was resupplied and towed back to her station in mid-August. Three years later, however, harsh winds again drove the ship aground, this time onto the beach north of Cape Disappointment. Workmen again repaired the ship, and one year elapsed before the lightship was back in operation.

After seventeen years of duty, the lighthouse service "mothballed" her in Astoria and then finally sold her six years later, in 1915, at public auction for less than $2,000. Subsequent owners used her as a freighter in Alaskan waters under different names for another twenty years. She was then scrapped, but the stories of her overland transportation were still being told.

❦   ❦   ❦

ANOTHER WIDELY followed salvage was that of the *Minnie A. Caine.* The Moran Brothers built this four-masted schooner, but she ran into problems when first being put into service. A tug was towing the ship south from Victoria, British Columbia, when, on December 25, 1901, the infamous "Christmas Storm" swept over the Puget Sound region with great fury.

The savage winds and waves forced the tug to cut the schooner loose and run for shelter at Port Townsend, Washington. The gale soon shredded and ripped away every canvas sail, and the bad conditions drove the *Minnie Caine* during the night onto the rocky beach at Smith Island, which lies at the eastern extremity of the Juan de Fuca Strait.

The schooner struck at extreme high tide, and being light, she ran far up the beach. When morning came, the craft was high and dry. The men easily climbed down the ship's ladder to the beach, where a nearby lighthouse keeper hospitably received them.

Being a new vessel of 780 tons, the insurance companies and owners were loath to write her off as a total loss. Although the vessel was not badly damaged, the long distance she would have to be moved over the rock-strewn beach—and full exposure to fierce westerly winds—made this salvage a very difficult one. All of the bids offered for her release were considered too high, and Robert Moran consequently decided to handle the salvage operations himself.

The undertaking started in February 1902, and the plan was to raise the vessel above the beach, and then force her seaward along a short track of heavy timber "skids," with hydraulic jackscrews being used. The gang of forty laborers first worked at clearing away the sand from the schooner's hull while ships brought in provisions, fresh water, heavy timbers, jacks, blocks, tackle, and other equipment. Most of this was carried on scows from Port Townsend, located some fourteen miles away, and with the wreck being in an isolated location, laborers built a cookhouse, lodging, and supply sheds.

After removing the sand, workers constructed blocked supports for the jacks. They nailed cleats to the vessel's hull that would control the upward lift of the screws. After their first towing efforts moved the schooner a short distance from her sandy bed, the men discovered that the sharp rocks had cut through the hull in several places and the keel was broken.

The crew nailed planks over the holes and placed rows of heavy timbers beneath the keel. The salvagers next dynamited the boulders lying seaward, removed the rubble, and built the skidding farther down the beach. By carefully operating the jacks, the vessel was shoved seaward some forty-five feet along the improvised way. Since high tides hampered the beach operations, all work had to be done at night during the prevailing low tides.

The salvagers were optimistic. The weather had been favorable so far, and only a few more days would be needed before the schooner was afloat. A strong gale unexpectedly sprang up from the west, however, and in a few hours, the heavy seas destroyed the work that the weary workers had completed over the last weeks. The combers washed out the wood skidding and threw the vessel back onto the beach. The tides then changed and were too high to permit any repair work for the next six weeks.

When the ebb tide began occurring during the day, operations again resumed in April and work progressed well. The men replaced the skidding, put the jacks back into position, and moved the ship a second time down its path to the open sea. But another violent wind soon ripped into the area. This gale and high seas again tore out the timber work, but the vessel held to her position, as Moran had set heavy anchors in place.

Laborers continued shoveling the sand away from her hull, and they constructed new skidding. When everything was in order, the crew waited for the "flood" or high tide to come. At that precise time, winches on board the schooner strained in pulling at the wire cables connected to the sea anchors; a steam-tug simultaneously made several strong pulls on the thick hawsers tied to the stranded vessel. The *Minnie A. Caine* disappointedly stayed right where she was, however, when another windstorm swept in and disrupted operations.

The next tides were too low, which meant waiting until May for the next launching. Two powerful tugs steamed there to take advantage of the highest tides of the year and make a "supreme effort" to float the craft. Fighting for every inch of cable that would yield, the winches tightened at their maximum power while the tugs strongly pulled on their hawsers.

On the evening of May 9, the steady pressure finally took hold. *The Caine* slid back quietly into the sea after being held prisoner on land for nearly five months. The steam-tug *Tyee* hurried up and took her in tow to Moran's dry dock in Seattle, where the ship received a complete overhaul.

The salvage operations cost in round numbers $20,000 with a repair bill equaling $10,000 more. Since the vessel cost $65,000 to build, her owners and insurers congratulated themselves on making the right decision for a bad situation.

●　●　●

TWENTY-FIVE years passed before another ship became a maritime legend similar to the *Minnie Caine* and the LV-50. Launched in 1920, the *North Bend II* was a 204-foot-long, four-masted schooner and the last tall ship built in Oregon. In January 1928, the *North Bend II* had sailed over the treacherous Columbia River Bar toward Astoria. While making this crossing, the winds suddenly died and left the ship becalmed. She drifted aimlessly in the strong currents until eventually grounding on Peacock Spit. After several failed attempts to pull the ship off the sandbar, the crew finally abandoned the vessel. High winds and waves pounded away at the ship over time, and most believed the *North Bend II* would soon break apart.

Thirteen months later, however, the wind-swept currents finally forced the sail ship from the reef to where she literally "walked" away from it. The strong winds and waves had carved a deep channel in front of the ship, and the combination of powerful high and low tides then pushed the vessel over one-half mile into nearby Baker's Bay, the same cove where lightship No. 50 had been relaunched.

Sustaining only slight damage, the *North Bend II* became the only ship in recorded history—according to *Ripley's Believe It or Not!*—to refloat and salvage herself in such a way when every man-made attempt to free her had failed. It was as if the vessel had followed her own calling and spirit to be free. The ship was in service for eleven more years before finally being lost at Coos Bay, Oregon.

CHAPTER ELEVEN

USED PARTS, SCRAP, AND A NEW BOW

I n 1900, the Captain, now fifty-three years old, and Elizabeth were still living in San Francisco with their married son, T. Andrew, daughter-in-law Emma R., and grandsons Milton (four years old) and Ken (two years old). The Captain still listed himself as a ship chandler—although being considerably more than that—while his son Andrew was now twenty-nine and shown as the bookkeeper. Andrew worked for his father his entire life, and regardless of how the census listed him, he ran the San Francisco operations and yards when Cappie was away on a salvage job. Their company was listed in the telephone directory as "Whitelaw, T. P. H. & Son, Salvors."

Whitelaw was still assuming risks the same as he did nearly thirty-five years ago when he started diving, but the year 1904 was troublesome. For example, the *Respigerdo* was a four-masted iron ship used as a coal freighter that had grounded on Point Montara off the California coast. She was stuck fast, but apparently could be saved, provided the salvage crew could work faster than the destructive tides and winds.

With the sea being calm, the salvagers felt no great hurry or excitement. In fact, when the noon hour came, all of the workers except one left to eat lunch on the nearby anchored steam-wrecker. The man who remained wanted to study the wreck more and be sure the plans to refloat her were workable.

Captain Whitelaw sat down on a hatch midway on the wreck and began to work over the plans in his mind. The vessel creaked a little and then groaned, but there seemed to be nothing unusual about that. He suddenly heard a "terrific ripping sound and great splintering," and this seemed like a volcano was heaving underneath the wreck. The *Respigerdo*—a 220-foot-long ship—then broke in half.

Whitelaw was by himself, and it was as if a jagged, invisible knife had sliced across the *Respigerdo*. The seaward half cracked down so fast under T. P. H.'s feet that he almost fell down. As Whitelaw started to step across the crack, the rupture suddenly widened from a few inches to five feet. He backed up, ran several feet, and jumped as hard as he could—to land successfully on the grounded half.

The moment he landed, however, Whitelaw heard a clatter "more terrifying" than the ship's splitting. He looked up to see a confusion of masts and yards falling down toward him, as if an earthquake had shattered "tumbling telephone poles" to the ground. The shocking sight instantly became larger, followed by the sounds and shocks of crashing wood against decks. Seeing and hearing the destruction, the crew hurried over in a small boat to the floating debris. They expected the worse.

His men found Whitelaw lying underneath the mess of canvas, thick poles, and splintered wood. Miraculously, he was unhurt and without a scratch. A sudden list by the wreck had swung its railings into a position where they stopped the heavy timbers from crushing him. Cappie's reaction to making his long jump and surviving the crashing rigs was to happily exclaim later, "That was the greatest thrill of my fifty-six years of salvaging wrecked ships!"

In the same year, the Captain worked on another ship, the *Drumburton*. As he reflected back, he said:

Remember that any ship on the rocks is hauled and tugged at ceaselessly by the tides. This racking goes on every fraction of a second, day and night, as long as a single stick of the vessel remains upright.

A ship on a rock will sometimes age twenty years in one week. Every beam, every bolt, every joint is disarranged, because there is no mercy from the power of the sea. A vessel may look practically safe, and yet be only five minutes from disintegration. However, this adds a sporting element to the business of salvaging a wreck.

The *Drumburton* had wrecked off Point Pedro in a dense fog. Four men were working with Whitelaw at the time. The first hint of danger they had was when the sea began carrying away pieces of the ship: A high wave pushed a cabin off, and it drifted away; part of the railing disappeared from one side, as another roller took away the pilothouse. Every wave seemed to be taking away a part of the ship.

The salvagers watched the process silently for about a minute. When they heard a loud "pop," the sound drove them into action, and the five men quickly jumped over the gunnels into their boat. They pulled away just in time to keep from being splattered by "a lot of flying wood." Thirty minutes later, Whitelaw said, "You wouldn't have known there ever had been a vessel on that spot." The waves were so strong that they didn't leave a piece of wood or a steel plate on the rocks. An hour before, the *Drumburton* seemed perfectly solid with the hole in her side seeming to be a comparatively easy fix.

By this time, seamen and residents alike applauded his efforts. Whitelaw was seen by reporters as "the man who has braved the dangers in handling the big wrecks of this long period and is nothing short of a hero." They wrote that "the tales of his prowess are passed on from lip to lip." Other accounts maintained that "among the most superstitious of seafaring men, Captain Whitelaw is often accredited with having super powers."

He didn't let the adulation or successes go to his head, because he remembered the times when he hadn't been successful. A record of "win some, lose some" was the wrecking business. Although he had a much better score, Whitelaw was motivated by the game, risks, and challenges. It was about life and he lived it.

According to his grandson Ken, Cappie was kind to his family and a cheerful, dedicated family man. He practiced a strong rule of no drinking or smoking. Holidays were the only times when the "old man" made an exception, and the only spirits served then was a glass of port wine. On days such as Christmas, Thanksgiving, and New Year's Day, the whole family came over with grown children, spouses, and grandchildren, and Captain Whitelaw cooked the turkey every time.

The family always lived well, and Ken remembered growing up in the mansion on Rincon Hill, between Second and Third streets. Rincon Hill was where the "upper crust" lived, and his grandson recalled that they had horses, stablemen, maids, servants, a gardener, and "magnificent apartments." Thanks to the servants, his grandson said, "For eight years, my mother didn't even know how to wash a dish." No trace of the once exclusive neighborhood remains as it is now buried under concrete, a few buildings, and the James Lick Skyway that leads to the Bay Bridge.

This change was due more to a natural calamity than "urban progress." On the morning of April 18, 1906, a powerful earthquake shook the proud city of San Francisco for two full minutes. The quake and ensuing fires over three days left an estimated 3,000 people dead, destroyed over 80 percent of the city, and decimated over 500 city blocks of the downtown. Although the destruction was greatest in San Francisco, its effects were felt in every city from San Juan Bautista and inland Santa Rosa to the coast at Mendocino. The Whitelaw Mansion was completely "burned out" by the inferno, and the family later moved to Oakland.

San Francisco was the largest city then on the West Coast with a population of 410,000. As a financial, trade, and cultural center, it operated the busiest port on the West Coast. The city was the gateway to the Pacific for U.S. trade and influence from the Pacific Rim to Asia. When firemen finally put out the last fire, over two-thirds of San Francisco's population was homeless. It was estimated that half of the homeless fled across the bay to Oakland and Berkeley, while makeshift tents and refugee camps sprouted up all over San Francisco. More residents left for the north and south and started new lives in other cities.

During the conflagration, ships evacuated 30,000 panicked residents. The waterfront was relatively free of damage except for a few freight sheds that had burned and piers that had collapsed. During the rebuilding that followed, the ports were lively with the increased shipping of building materials, food, and other essentials. Although San Francisco would rebuild relatively quickly, the catastrophe shifted trade, business, and population growth south to Los Angeles. Although San Francisco retained its maritime significance, during the twentieth century Los Angeles would grow to become the largest and most important urban area on the West Coast.

As to Whitelaw's counterparts back east, Merritt and Chapman continued their competition. They finally solved their competitive problems in the spirit of the era by merging their businesses together in 1897 to form the Merritt & Chapman Derrick & Wrecking Company with headquarters in New York City. The T. A. Scott Company was still based in New London, Connecticut, but at the time of its incorporation in 1903, Captain Scott appointed his second son, Thomas A. Scott, to take over the operations as president. Under the vigorous leadership of the younger Scott, the firm didn't neglect its salvage operations but turned increasingly to construction. In 1904, T. A. Scott Company designed and built a chemical plant to manufacture bichromate of potash and soda (used in printing photographs to producing dyes) for a business in Jersey City, New Jersey.

❦ ❦ ❦

AROUND THIS time, a steel-hulled ship came into trouble and gave Whitelaw another "interesting" job. The SS *Pomona* was built in 1888 at the Union Iron Works in San Francisco for the Pacific Coast Steamship Company and then assigned to the weekly northern run from San Francisco to Eureka, some seventy-five miles from the Oregon border. As one of the first steel-hulled vessels constructed on the West Coast, the *Pomona* offered significant competition against the wooden-hulled side-wheelers and barks that were prominent during the 1880s. This "magnificent" steamer was 220 feet long with a 33-foot beam and a 16-foot depth.

Owing to her 1,500-horsepower, triple-expansion engine, she cruised between twelve and thirteen miles per hour. An early photograph of the *Pomona* shows she carried auxiliary sails after her construction, like other ships of the time, indicating the owners' distrust of the reliability of the newly introduced triple-expansion engines. Later photos of the vessel indicated no evidence of the sails.

The vessel carried nearly 1,200 tons of freight, and an Edison "patented dynamo" could "burn" 175 incandescent lights that were placed around the decks, one in every stateroom and "all over the ship." Although the new electric lights were run by a steam generator, each room also had an oil lamp in case it didn't work—which at times happened. The *Pomona* had a large social hall with overhead chandelier, large French plateglass mirrors, and upholstered, plush red seats. With these amenities, the *Pomona* was virtually a luxury liner compared to what people had before on these coastal runs.

Two rows of cabins lined the deck in long corridors with the ship's large smokestack in the middle. The *Pomona's* upper deck housing extended from the stern to the rear of the forward mast. The housing was made of wood and painted a glossy white, while her two masts were built of iron, as was the single black smokestack. The hull was painted jet black, while the awning above the main deck was white.

Her design called for five water-resistant bulkheads, which meant that they didn't run all the way to the main deck. Realizing this problem later, the Union Iron Works began building special vessels with watertight bulkheads that ran from the keel all the way to the main deck.

On both coasts, steamship lines employed shipping agents in their ports of call. These agents represented and marketed the line, organized the cargo, and worked with the passengers. They dealt with the weight, costs, and taxes on all goods being transported. The agents answered the everyday questions of the paying public, tracked lost receipts, collected what was due from the shippers, and negotiated rates. Owing to the marketing of this line and railroad competition, the *Pomona* usually carried fewer passengers and more cargo, including mail and an occasional automobile strapped to the deck. The fare for a paying passenger ranged from $50 to $500, depending on the length of the trip and the desired stateroom class.

Along with each ship's operations came the inevitable accidents, which were a common occurrence given the extensive maritime traffic, and wreck reports indicated the *Pomona* had been involved in several. On route to Eureka in a thick fog on one voyage, the $250,000 ship ran into the side of a wooden schooner, the *Fearless*. The steamer sustained

$500 worth of damage, but nearly cut the bow off the smaller ship and forced it to be towed away for repairs.

In 1903, the ship collided with another vessel in San Francisco Harbor during a thick fog. At this time the vessel was insured at $125,000, although still valued at $250,000. One year later, the *Pomona*, under its newest master, Captain Swanson, rammed into a ship in a dense fog, causing another $500 in repairs. It then rammed into a wash rock in Fort Ross Cove. In all these cases, the *Pomona* sustained relatively minor damage. Operating a steel ship made a great difference, especially when it collided with a wooden vessel.

On St. Patrick's Day, March 17, 1908, a rising wind off Northern California swept the sea from the northwest. A large swell was running. The wind, waves, and whitecaps caused an uncomfortable chop, and it was into this sea that Captain Swanson and the *Pomona* sailed after leaving San Francisco to steam north for Eureka. The captain and his ship had sailed up and down the redwood coast for years, but none of the 147 passengers and crew knew that this well-known ship—known as the "Pride of the Coaster [Coastal] Fleet"—would never again cross the Humboldt Bar into Eureka.

The weather became cruel, cold, and windy. To avoid the rough water, Swanson steamed farther inland toward shore. After setting the course past the Russian River, Swanson retired to dinner and left instructions for the second mate to "haul her out a little more if necessary." Choppy white water clouded the entire ocean as the ship came so close to shore that a passenger later reported, "You could see the color of a cow on the hills."

Shortly after six o'clock in the evening, the ship lurched violently when she struck an uncharted pinnacle two miles offshore and south of Fort Ross Reef. The whitecaps that dotted the ocean made it near impossible for the lookout to spot this particular rock. Reports later indicated an earthquake had thrust the rock up to create the hazard, but no concrete evidence supported this theory.

Although the ship was free of the reef, the collision had punched a gaping hole into the steel hull. As water gushed between the decks, the engineers activated the steam pumps to keep the vessel afloat. However, the pumps couldn't keep up with the amount of ocean rushing in. The water-resistant bulkheads couldn't stem the flow of the sea as it flooded inside. Captain Swanson quickly decided the only way to save his ship was to make a run for the shore in Fort Ross Cove and beach his vessel.

He ordered full steam ahead and maximum effort on the pumps. Despite her wounds, the steamer reached a speed of 13.2 knots (nearly 15 miles per hour), and the *Pomona* pulled toward the cove while frightened passengers gathered up their belongings. Although the skipper and crew appeared not overly alarmed, some of the passengers ran nervously "about the ship in near panic."

By the time the *Pomona* approached Fort Ross—a two-mile trip—her hold had drawn in more than four feet of water. As she was down by the bow, waves poured over her front, and the ship's helm was nearly unresponsive. As Swanson tried in desperation to maneuver the sinking vessel into the cove, the outline of a wash rock suddenly appeared in front. Whitecaps covered the uncharted reef with a "snowy white blanket," and the ship headed to it like an out-of-control freight train. People gasped and braced for the impact. Within seconds the rock dealt the fatal blow to the ship. With a full head of steam, the *Pomona* rode over the reef by her keel with a metallic squealing and smashed down with a sickening "thud." Some people were thrown to the deck by the impact, while others grabbed railings and walls. Part of the rock cracked through the hull and tightly impaled the ship in the swirling sea—another victim of this "stern and rock-bound coast."

When the steel steamer hit the rock in the cove, the captain ordered the engine shut down, but the electric lights were kept burning. While the crew handed out life jackets to the anxious passengers, the winds howled and large waves crashed into the ship. She slowly twisted by her bow to eventually face the sea. The cold ocean continued to pour into her holds as the *Pomona* settled lower into the water.

Swanson had a sickening feeling inside with the knowledge that his ship was doomed, but he had to save his passengers and crew. Knowing that a sheltered area was on North Point on the shore, he ordered the ship to be abandoned. The chief stewardess, a Mrs. Matthes, commented about the women and children, "It was amazing how quickly they forgot about their seasickness."

Swanson ordered one surfboat to leave first and survey the beach area in the dark. The people on board watched intently as the lantern in the boat became smaller while it bobbed up and down with the swells. Then the lamp didn't move. The seamen had safely made shore and set it on the beach to guide the others to safety. As people milled on board the vessel, the six lifeboats on the *Pomona* made three trips each before finally getting everyone to the shore. Captain Swanson, three officers, and nine crewmembers returned later to remove the navigation instruments and valuables.

People built bonfires to stay warm during the night and attract passing ships. Most of the passengers spent an uncomfortable night on the windy shore even with the fires, until another ship took them back to San Francisco, many with just the clothes on their backs. A few impatient people marched thirteen miles inland during the night and stumbled across railroad tracks. They flagged down an oncoming train and headed back to San Francisco, again with no luggage or warm outerwear. Others decided to scale the cliffs behind the beach. They formed a human chain to climb up the steep precipice and actually lifted others to the top. There they waited out the night in the house of a local rancher, who fed them and gave the people "fresh produce from the dairy located conveniently on the premises." No lives were lost.

The wreck held only 300 tons of general cargo, some mail, and an automobile that had been lashed to its deck. The crew was able to off-load much of the loose gear and cargo, but the company considered the vessel a complete loss. Numerous claims about negligence and faulty lifesaving equipment were later made.

A few passengers believed the boilers should have been able to provide more steam against the strong headwind and currents. Two months before, the boilers had developed a leak, and the repair work was completed only twelve days before the ship sank. Divers later reported that some boiler plates had been altered and crimped, as if the leaks hadn't been properly repaired. Although they might have been right, these claims were never proved and not upheld.

The insurance company wanted to have the ship raised. Despite an expert's report that the fractures in the hull were too large and the ship was a total loss, the insurer gave the Pacific Coast Wrecking Company twenty days and a $10,000 budget. Its plan was to remove the remainder of the cargo and refloat the vessel by inflating canvas bags inside the hull. A wreck-tug would then tow the ship back to San Francisco for dry-dock repairs. To accomplish this, divers in clumsy, heavy diving gear descended into the waters to start patching the hull. Using canvas bags and compressed air, the men tried to float the ship off the rock.

The problem with this wreck and any other salvage was not just the underwater work. Predators abounded in the sea, whether they were sharks, lingcod that mistook a diver for a meal, and octopuses. Martin Lund had worked for Whitelaw and other diving companies; later he tried to salvage the long-lost *Brother Jonathan* farther north. Lund was now diving for the Pacific Coast Wrecking Company in late September of 1908.

While working in seven fathoms of water (about forty feet) at Fort Ross Cove inside the *Pomona's* hold, a "monster devilfish" swept after him. It seized Lund's leg tightly by one tentacle and snaked the startled diver toward its parrot beak. Lund lashed at the octopus with his knife and jerked on his line the signal to be hoisted up. His assistants began to haul him toward the surface with strong pulls. The devilfish had too strong a hold on him, however, and he had to signal the helpers to stop hauling. The tug-of-war between the octopus and his assistants above was making his helmet "give way."

Another tentacle quickly twisted out to grab Lund about the waist, as another ripped around his neck. When the third one tied the diver around his legs, Lund knew he was in for the fight of his life. With strong motions, he slashed through the water and severed two of the "tough tentacles that grasped him in a deathlike embrace." When the diver saw the creature preparing to strike at him with its beak, he lunged his knife at its head just in time to deal it a "death blow."

Lund was also the diver involved in the *Umatilla* incident with a devilfish (see Chapter Five, "Dynamite Johnny and the *Umatilla*"). Whitelaw's divers by now had made thousands of dives and the Captain noted his bias:

> In that entire list of dives made, I never heard of a diver being molested by a shark. But while sharks are leery of divers, octopuses are not. When we were raising the *Umatilla*, one of my divers had a thrilling encounter with one of these dreadful creatures.

Although no further reports were made of similar encounters, efforts to save the *Pomona* continued. More time passed. Even though the company had filed a $300 bond long ago to extend the time limit, these attempts were not successful. It was now clear the *Pomona* would never leave Fort Ross Cove.

Using his steam schooner *Greenwood*, "salvage master" Captain Whitelaw (according to newspaper accounts) bought the salvage rights and did the recovery. As the price of scrap steel and iron had increased, he believed that this would be a particularly "useful" salvage. The *Greenwood* had been built in San Francisco in 1886; she was 192 tons, 114 feet long, had a wide 30-foot beam, but drew a shallow 9-foot draft. Whitelaw had bought her for a low price and then converted the ship for his wreck purposes.

One of his steam-tugs moored over the wreck with two eight-inch stern lines and two eight-inch bow lines. His workmen yanked off anything of value above or below water, including the many salvageable steam valves, ventilators, compasses, blocks, boats, davits, winches, pipes, fittings, tools, and instruments—which were estimated to be worth $5,000. With the parts and equipment safely on board, T. P. H. and his Whitelaw Wrecking Company began working for the scrap.

Blasting the wreck with hoses filled with black powder, he cut the ship into whatever scrap sizes were wanted. The *Greenwood* then brought the equipment and scrap to San Francisco. His men only missed the anchor, which divers recovered decades later. Believing in the value of the scrap and saved equipment, Whitelaw again invested his free cash into hard assets. The divers finally dynamited the half-sunken wreck as a menace to navigation, and the *Pomona* broke in two on November 21, to slip forever beneath the waves.

● ● ●

MEANWHILE, the salvaging continued unabated on the Great Lakes. The *William C. Moreland* was a large, 580-foot-long bulk carrier built in 1910. Powered by triple-expansion engines and with a 58-foot beam, the steel ship cost $450,000 to build. On October 18, 1910, on what was only her fifth trip, the two-month-old ship was carrying 11,000 tons of iron ore over Lake Superior. The weather was good, but large forest fires had blanketed the area with smoke.

Incorrectly concluding the *Moreland* was farther away from the Michigan shoreline than it actually was, the captain continued the heavy vessel on its course. At 9:00 P.M., the ship struck the Keweenaw Peninsula's unlighted Sawtooth Reef at full speed. She slid over the first rocks that formed the reef about one mile offshore of Eagle River and ended up on the second line of rocks. Twenty-three crewmembers, including the captain, were on board.

The crew promptly tried to free the vessel, but she remained hard on the reef and began filling rapidly with water. After the captain left in a small boat for land, a strong northwesterly gale swept the next day into the area. As heavy seas began to rise with high winds, the Portage Ship Canal lifesaving crew motored out and rescued the crew. When the captain returned on October 20, he found the vessel crewless and sagging badly on the reef.

The master brought his men back onboard. When the ship raised sufficient steam to move off, the seas and motion caused the ship to crack between two hatches. The crew left for the last time, and three days later, the *Moreland* broke a second time, this time farther toward the stern. The wreck was now split into three weakly connected sections.

This was the sixteenth wreck that had happened at the same spot in sixteen years. The reef was dangerous, hidden by rough water, and at a place that ships constantly steamed by. In addition to many accidents of a "minor" nature, several steamers—including one that was towing a barge—hit the rocks and were lost.

Once wreckers were on the scene, the men patched and pumped water from the stricken ship. Before the weather worsened, the workers were able to remove some 7,000 tons of ore. However, the white-capped waters soon drove the workmen off the *Moreland* and forced the salvage ships to find safe harbor. On November 2, the owners abandoned the ship to the insurers, and the *Moreland* had the distinction of being the largest vessel "lost" on the Great Lakes up to that time.

The insurers gave the contract for salvaging the ship to Captain Jim Reid and his Reid Wrecking Company. Arriving at the scene three weeks later with their wreck-tugs, the crew continued to remove cargo from the derelict freighter. This work went slowly, as the salvagers were frequently forced to retreat to the shelter of the Portage Canal due to very bad weather on the open lake. The captain's son, Tom Reid, then took over the operations.

Because the *Moreland* was new and one of the largest vessels on the lakes, the extensive salvage efforts continued. Although winter curtailed their activities, workmen that spring completed patching and repairing bulkheads on the breaks, and they then lashed the sections together. The ship finally floated clear in June 1911.

Although the engineer could generate enough steam to move her off the reef, the ship didn't steer well due to the damage. She soon collided with the tug *James Reid,* which had steamed close by to guide her. Filling up with water, the *Moreland* sank slightly to the west of Sawtooth Reef, but in much deeper water. Only a part of her superstructure could be seen now above the lake's surface.

When another severe storm howled through in July, the severe conditions completely severed the 278-foot stern section from the rest of the ship. Reid was forced to concentrate his efforts on raising the valuable stern. His men floated that section in early August and towed it to Portage Harbor. The rest of the wreck wasn't salvageable.

The ship's stern remained in Portage for more than a year. Although the salvage contract specified delivery at Superior, Wisconsin, it was decided to take the remains to Detroit for dry-docking. In September 1912, two of the Reid Wrecking Company's tugs set out again on the voyage that had started almost two years earlier. When the ship began leaking again, the wreckers beached her at Port Huron for pumping and, two days later, brought her to another safe harbor when they removed the last of the iron ore.

Repairs were made on the stern section at Ecorse, Michigan. The wrecking company had entered into a "no cure, no pay" agreement with the underwriters, and although Reid delivered to them a stern, it wasn't considered to be a full ship. The insurance agents gave his company the stern in full payment for its services.

The wreck company's tugs finally towed the stern to Port Huron, where it stayed for three years, and Reid pumped the vessel out again and cleaned the section up. Despite Reid's attempts to sell the stern, there wasn't a market for one-half of a ship—that is, until World War I came. The Canadian Steamship Lines purchased the half for $55,650—a high price—and decided to build a bow onto the salvaged stern section at Superior, Wisconsin.

Two of Reid's tugs towed the long portion through the Poe Locks at Sault Ste. Marie, Michigan. Large crowds lined the piers at the canal to catch a glimpse of the *Moreland* being pulled, stern first, through the locks. When another windstorm swirled into the canal, the winds pushed the ships around so hard that the towing lines snapped.

Once the hawsers were reconnected, the stern was left at Superior, where the new bow was being built. Workers then attached the *Moreland's* stern to its new bow. In November 1916, the "new" 580-foot-long ship was christened the *Sir Trevor Dawson*. Soon afterward, she left for South Chicago with a cargo of iron ore, a little over six years after her eventful last voyage. After a succession of owners, names, and voyages, the stern of the *W. C. Moreland* spent another fifty years in service with its new bow. She was finally scrapped as the Canadian steamer *Parkdale*.

The Reid Wrecking Company had its successes and its failures. In the late 1890s, the salvage company made a number of costly attempts to raise the 290-foot-long steel steamer *Cayuga*, which had sunk near Skillagalee Shoals on Lake Michigan. The continued windy weather in the straits greatly delayed operations, while the incessant winds kicked up the sea. This rocked the steamer on which the air pumps were located, and the sweeping pulls on the hoisting ropes and air hoses were dangerous and delayed the divers when they were working.

The salvage company continued working on the wreck off and on, "at great expense," for several years and without success, although the *Cayuga* was towed closer to shore while submerged. During this time the wreckers suffered serious diving accidents. Although these risks are part of the business, the Reids suffered more than their share on this one wreck. The ship dragged down the wreck barge during the recovery efforts, and this incident gave rise to a ghost story about a lost diver whose torn air hose could be seen for many years trailing underneath the sunken barge.

In 1900, the financial losses on this wreck came to light in court. A judge ruled that Edmund Hall owed money to the Port Huron company that rented the wrecking "apparatus" to James Reid. Hall was the money-man for these efforts and he kept "wrecker James Reid at work, on the thus far vain attempt to raise the *Cayuga*." These were risky ventures, not just physically, but financially as well.

●　●　●

ON THE EVENING of March 20, 1909, the wooden steam schooner *R. D. Inman* ran aground on the rocks near Duxbury Reef about fourteen miles from San Francisco. The ship grounded when the captain mistook a bonfire on the beach for the signal of a distressed ship that was adrift and on fire. A subsequent inquiry found that "negligent and unskillful navigation" caused the disaster.

The *R. D. Inman* settled and washed over the reef, resting parallel to shore 500 feet from the beach in a shallow basin and listing heavily to starboard. The crew from a nearby lifesaving station could do nothing except land the insurance company's underwriter on the beached hulk, carefully navigating their surfboat through the breakers.

The vessel was wedged so tightly in the rocks that no attempts to free it were successful. After the owner collected on his $100,000 marine insurance policy, the underwriters took possession and contracted with the Whitelaw Wrecking Company for the salvage work. Whitelaw promptly set up a camp on the beach and started work.

The *Inman* appeared to be in perfect condition except for a slight list to port, but on closer inspection, the divers could see she was stuck fast on a rock. The lower portion of the hull was actually cut in two, and the stern had sunk so that at high tide, waves broke over the ship's railing. A swinging rope-ladder or a boatswain's chair (a wooden seat with rope attached like a swing) was the only way to get on and off the vessel.

The salvage work progressed slowly. Workmen loaded the smaller pieces of machinery, fittings, and furnishings of value into a rowboat that then took them to shore. Wagons hauled the finds three miles to the wharf at Bolinas, and from there they were stowed on board Whitelaw's scow-schooner *Catalina*. Steam-tugs towed the *Catalina* back to San Francisco, where she was off-loaded and then towed back to the wharf.

Divers worked to remove the machinery that was fourteen-feet underwater. When they finished cutting the larger pieces of machinery out, the *Greenwood* steamed from San Francisco and anchored as close as possible to the wreck. A strong hawser was attached between the steamer and the wreck, and a smaller lighter moved back and forth carrying the heavy pieces to the *Greenwood*.

This work progressed slowly with long delays when the booms broke under the weight of hauling up a particularly heavy piece. When a strong crane finally hoisted the huge, thirty-ton steel boiler over the wreck's side and onto the lighter, after which another crane transferred the huge object to the *Greenwood,* the wreck-tug then steamed back through the Golden Gate.

Three months after the disaster, a charge was placed onto the lower part of the stern and the blast loosened the "tail shaft" so that it could be salvaged. Once this work was completed, the wrecking crew broke camp and returned to San Francisco, "leaving the hull of the ill-fated schooner *R. D. Inman* a prey to the ravages of time and tide."

Whitelaw continued unabated to purchase and salvage wrecked ships. He continued to bet on his favorite "no float, no fee" contracts. If he needed money to pay for one of these ventures, he would sell off a ship, land, or some asset: He loved the action. Whether or not he was involved in trying to save a ship, Captain Whitelaw would more than likely buy it for the scrap value if the efforts weren't successful. He was a passionate collector of sunken ships and their stories.

In 1903, the coastal collier, *Progresso,* became another disaster while moored at the Fulton Iron Works in San Francisco. The vessel was being converted into an oil-tank carrier when for some unknown cause the tanks exploded. Causing deaths and devastation, the explosions tore the vessel up badly, and the resulting flames practically completed the ship's destruction. The Whitelaw Wrecking Company purchased the remains. After he spent money and time trying to reconstruct the ship, Whitelaw abandoned those efforts and broke the wreck up for its salvage value.

With the *Pomona* and *R. D. Inman* as examples of the wrecking he took on, Whitelaw continued this work into the next decade. For example, the *James Rolph* was constructed specifically for the Pacific Coast trade. The schooner had made a number of coastal voyages before she was lost in 1910. She was sailing from San Francisco with a cargo of general freight, lime, hay, and 14,000 board feet of lumber bound for the sugar plantations at Hana and Maui, Hawaii. Plagued by a weak breeze, the currents swept the powerless *James Rolph* toward shore. In the thick pea-soup fog, her captain didn't see how close the schooner was coming to land. The twilight evening then turned into the blackness of night.

When the ship's master at 10:00 P.M. heard the nearby crashing of surf, he ordered the ship tacked to sail offshore—but it was too late. The *James Rolph* crashed into the rocks at Point San Pedro. The vessel actually grounded fifty feet from the same spot where the four-masted bark *Drumburton* was lost. Although the *Rolph's* crew managed to reach shore safely, the vessel couldn't be pulled from the rocks. When tugs were unable to haul the ship free, the owners contacted Whitelaw. His salvage firm stripped the wreck of its usable fittings before abandoning the ship to the waves.

There were different ways of being compensated for salvage work: refloat for a fixed fee; be paid a good amount, but only if you were successful (which Whitelaw favored); or buy the ship for its scrap value, if it couldn't be refloated (another T. P. H. preference). The price between what the owner demanded and wrecker wanted was at times substantial. For example, when bidding for the "reviving" of the steamer *Excelsior,* Whitelaw wanted $70,000 for the work. The owner, Thomas Crowley, offered $20,000. They didn't work out their differences.

When the price of scrap iron and steel on the market at this time took a sudden jump and was quoted at $26 a ton, it was estimated that Whitelaw owned 20,000 tons of steel, iron, equipment, and ship parts that were stored in his yards or under the sea in wrecks that he owned. If he sold the scrap and items off then, Whitelaw stood to make more than $10 million alone in today's dollars. He was quoted as saying, "It's a wise hunter who doesn't shoot at every bird he sees, but waits for a fat one within easy range." Believing the value of his holding would only continue to rise, he held onto nearly his entire inventory. When he did sell, he used the money to purchase more wrecks, iron, scrap, and sunken ships—plus invest in the contingent contracts on raising vessels.

◉ ◉ ◉

MEANWHILE, Cappie would take grandson Ken down to the San Francisco wharf to see the ships. He told Ken that someday he would be running the business. Six years old at the time, Ken commented that instead of seeing the bears at the circus, he was talking to "these old guys in whiskers." His grandfather took him down the line of maritime shops and operations that sold sails, wires, and anchors, Cappie obviously checking on his competitors' prices while taking his grandson on a walk.

Life was very good. The Whitelaws enjoyed family picnics, traveled together to the Scottish festivals, and, if time permitted, they would go to the circus or see some event. A photo in the picture insert shows the family as they await the arrival in 1908 of Admiral Dewey and his fleet of battleships into San Francisco Bay. Captain Whitelaw enjoyed these times with his family.

One year later, Ken's father, T. Andrew, was injured while working at sea. A cable snapped and struck him savagely on the shoulder and neck. Needing heat treatments, he was recuperating at home with this therapy when, unfortunately, both he and Ken came down with deadly typhoid. Andrew should have been taken to the hospital, but because he also had a "bad" lung from the accident, he remained at home. He died about a year after his injuries on board the ship—but from typhoid fever. "They had a German doctor and two nurses, but my dad died at age thirty-nine on August 17, 1910," Ken said years later.

The family, of course, was heartbroken over the loss of their oldest son. They had only two grandsons, Ken and his older brother Milton, and one grown sibling, Margaret Elizabeth, (Daisy). Grandson Ken was now twelve years old, and T. P. H. took him under his wings to seriously groom him for the business.

T. Andrew had worked for his father his entire life and was quite helpful in running the San Francisco operations during Cappie's absences. T. P. H. had to first work in people to watch over this part of the business. Although it isn't known why he picked Ken, his youngest grandson started working for the Whitelaw Wrecking Company in earnest after school and during summers. The lad ran errands, was a mess boy, washed the dishes, operated the pumps for the divers, picked up parts for galvanizing, and did other work when he was young.

As Ken grew older, he spent more time in the business, including diving on different operations to patch vessels when he was twenty-one. In a later interview with the San Francisco Maritime Museum, Ken gave his insider's view as to how he and the other divers patched ships "in the old days."

The divers measured the dimensions of the underwater patch by a stick and a knife. They cut the stick underwater into the lengths that were needed to cover the hole. Using the cut sticks as guides, workers on the docks or boat next nailed "four by fours" into the required wooden frame. Covering the frame by nailing "two by twelve" wood planks over it, the men covered that structure with felt and canvas. The divers next attached one-foot-long "hook balls" into the frames. Lowering the patch down to the bottom on chains, the divers placed the covering over the hole and attached it to the hull. The underwater workers then inserted the hooks through the hull. Using a wrench, the men secured the ends of the hook with a nut and bolt. They weighted down the patch from the inside or later used quick-drying cement. Chains were attached to tighten everything up.

The salvagers temporarily stopped leaks by using plugs, stuffing the cracks with pillows, building the patches, closing bulkheads, building cofferdams, and "doing whatever worked." Although pumps, air bags, and other equipment were used to build buoyancy, pumps were the weapons of choice. The divers first closed the openings (portholes and doorways) and activated the pumps. After attaching the patches, the men pumped out more water while the cranes or tugs tried to pull the ship away.

In the 1910 census, Captain Whitelaw was listed as still working in San Francisco as a ship chandler. He was sixty-three. Married for forty years, he and Elizabeth were now living alone. Whitelaw would have to

rely on his grandsons, Ken and Milton, to help run the Whitelaw
Wrecking Company when they were older, since Daisy wasn't interested.
The question was whether they had the interest, and he wouldn't find that
out until later.

CHAPTER TWELVE

THE DECADE OF THE GREAT WAR

T he U.S. economy during the 1910s was excellent, due to the demands of war and thrusts of innovation. Edison's development of electric power was revolutionizing entire industries around the world, and the maritime world equally benefited. In the first decade of the twentieth century, generators powered lights on ships, electric pumps sucked out huge volumes of water, and wreck cranes operated without the cumbersome donkey steam engines. Diving bells had already been invented, and this discovery expanded the depths at which ships were salvaged. Divers could work by the electric lamps on their helmets, as well as at night under the illumination of high-intensity lights. The development of acetylene underwater welding and cutting torches was underway.

With the expanding electrification of the country, technology was changing transportation: Electric trolley cars were fast replacing horse-drawn streetcars and buggies. In San Francisco, the last horse-drawn streetcar disappeared in 1913, thanks to Henry Ford's work. Although the first automobiles were manufactured in 1901, buggies, cable cars, and horse-drawn wagons predominated. It wouldn't be until 1913, when Ford used assembly lines, that cars truly became mass-produced. Just one year later, his Model T dominated the automobile market, selling more than all other makes and models combined. The constraint on automobiles and trucks being major factors in moving goods and people now was the lack of highway networks and service stations.

Seeing cars now appearing on city streets, Captain Whitelaw soon bought one. "Come on over, Ken," he said to his grandson, "I'll give you a ride." The trip was like Mr. Toad's wild ride in the *Wind in the Willows*. Ken tightly gripped the car door while Cappie sped down a road, careened around a street corner, and ran right into the back of a streetcar. As there was little damage, he apologized to the conductor and took off again. Chuckling in between pointing out the scenery, Whitelaw continued his touring San Francisco in his vehicle, before nearly running over one of the few traffic police. The cop whistled him to a stop, and it took him time to stop the car. While the policeman strolled to the vehicle, Captain Whitelaw remained behind the wheel in the middle of a major intersection at Third and Mission. Traffic backed up. The policeman recognized Cappie and put his hands on his hips. After thinking for a moment, the traffic cop exclaimed, "Hey, Cap, please don't come around here again in an automobile." Whitelaw was lucky—he was better sailing over the ocean.

Vessels were becoming safer. Steam-powered iron and steel ships were replacing the graceful wooden sailing ships of old that had been mainstays. Greatly improving maritime safety, large vessels came equipped with wireless radio. In 1910, the naval wireless station at Newport, Rhode Island, made the first broadcasts of weather information. However, two years later, the *Titanic* disaster showed that tragedy could strike in an instant. The outcry over what was one of the worst disasters in maritime history led to the establishment of the International Ice Patrol in the North Atlantic and improved ship design.

In 1915, President Woodrow Wilson signed the Coast Guard Act, which brought about the merger of the U.S. Revenue Cutter Service and the U.S. Life-Saving Service into a single maritime agency, the Coast Guard Service. The construction of more lighthouses contributed to the safety of seamen and lessening of accidents, as captains could more easily avoid deadly reefs during fogs or storms by following their navigational points and warnings.

During this time period, however, the seeds of World War I were sown and war between numbers of countries would erupt. Military alliances would change dramatically and set the stage for more developments affecting the maritime world.

● ● ●

THE STEEL-HULLED oil tanker *Rosecrans* impaled itself on a reef off the Oregon coast during a gale on the night of January 7, 1913. Twenty-three men died in the maelstrom, and as the white-lipped waves rolled spray so thick and high that the tanker—whose distance from keel to mast top was 143 feet—became entirely hidden at times from view. The towering wave explosions and storm conditions were best described as "ferocious."

Since this was a memorable salvage, Whitelaw discussed the difficulties of the *Rosecrans* in depth—as well as his experiences with the *Respigerdo, Umatilla, Dumbarton,* and *Blairmore*—in different widely distributed national magazines. This culminated in a 1925 *Literary Digest* article and, three years later, with another lengthy one in *Popular Mechanics,* in which he observed:

> Occasionally a ship is in collision in comparatively shallow water, with either her bow or her stern stoved in as a result. In these days of ship construction, watertight bulkheads confine the damage to one compartment, but in the older ships, it is necessary to send divers into the dark and dangerous hold to put in a wall of planks, two to four inches thick and a foot wide, set on end, to keep out the water. Then again, by applying pumps to the interior, behind this wall of planking, the water which the ship has swallowed is sucked out, her buoyancy restored, and she floats.

> But without the divers, the ship salvor would be almost powerless. And the diver in this work is a highly specialized man. He must be not only a competent diver, thoroughly familiar with all underwater work, but he must be a carpenter, a steelworker, a riveter, and, to some extent, a shipwright. He also must have at least an elementary knowledge of how water pressure operates, and be able to

estimate the strength he must build into bulkheads, patches, and cofferdams, while working in total darkness.

With a rocky spire "higher than your head" skewering the empty-tanked *Rosecrans,* the problem was to find the best way to save the ship, especially when the only passageway inside was too narrow to allow a diver through in his full gear. Showing the differences between patching wooden and now steel ships, T. P. H. thought about the problem and came up with the solution. He had his divers place an explosive underneath the steel plates of the deck that covered the part they wanted to reach. The explosion lifted the designated area and loosened bolts so that his men could take off one plate, "like lifting the roof from a house."

When the divers could enter from the deck, they placed an explosive "shot" on the rock's pinnacle. The controlled tiny blast blew up the rock inside the ship, but was surgically placed so that the *Rosecrans* wasn't damaged inside. The men next used "magnetized bolt-holders" that allowed them to hold the bolts in place as they guided them into predrilled holes in the steel plates. The plates were then bolted over the holes.

The next problem was how to repair the long leaking cracks in the hull where steel plates wouldn't fit. The divers pressed half-filled sacks of cement against the fractures with their feet. The tides continually heaved in and out, however, and the sweeping currents kept the cement from drying. Whitelaw then installed pumps to stabilize the water level and reduce this movement to a minimum. The equipment forced the ocean into the hull when the tide went out, and then sucked it out when the seawater came in. By equalizing the water level and pressures this way, the cement was able to set.

After the cement hardened and the patches were sufficiently watertight, his divers attached chains and hawsers and brought them to his wreck-steamer *Greenwood.* Its steam engine groaned at full power as the lines stretched tight. The $250,000 oil tanker hesitated for "a second" in the bed she had been for seventeen days. As Whitelaw told the story, "Then she came. As full of life as a tornado, and without a thing to control her, she literally sprang out!" The hawsers' spring, the salvage tug's power, and the force of the heavy waves caused the *Rosecrans* to leap from her bed like "some living monster of the sea"—straight at the smaller *Greenwood*.

Seeing the tanker rush toward him, Captain Whitelaw ordered the lines to be immediately cut. He didn't want them reducing his ship's maneuverability or getting tangled in its propeller. The helmsman then "twirled" the *Greenwood's* wheel until it couldn't be turned anymore. The wrecker slowly turned away in response while the large tanker loomed closer. With the derelict fast approaching its stern, the *Greenwood* smashed into the waves. The men held their breath. With spray breaking "beautifully" over her bow, the *Rosecrans* sailed past the wrecker by a mere twenty-five feet.

The next task was to control the runaway ship. With its engine pouring out all available power, Whitelaw's steamer turned in a slow curve to where the *Rosecrans* was heading. With smoke pouring from its stack, the *Greenwood* finally overtook the out-of-control wreck as it swung out to sea. When the time was right, his men boarded the bucking tanker and attached hawsers to the bollards. The thick ropes tightened with tension and the ship slowly came under control. He said later, "We roped her, just like a cowboy ropes a runaway steer."

A painting of the *Rosecrans*—his 200th salvage job at sea—was one of Whitelaw's prized possessions and hung in his living room. Immediately following this rescue, however, Whitelaw told newspaper reporters what he considered to be his worst failure. He said:

> When you fail, you fail hard. The worst failure I ever had was with the schooner *J. H. Lunsmann*, rammed one summer several years ago by a steamer. It cost me $8,000 over and above the fixtures I salvaged to find out that I couldn't save the vessel.

The *Francis H. Leggett* slammed into the *Lunsmann* in 1913, and she quickly sank in San Francisco Bay. When Whitelaw's company "took her over," the wooden ship's masts were underwater. When he had the contract to raise the schooner *J. H. Lunsmann*, T. P. H. declared, "The secret of success is the ability to be on hand at the opportune moment." The Captain was to receive 70 percent of everything "connected" with the ship and cargo that he saved, which was thought to include 3,500 tons of expensive coal. He would assume all of the costs of the salvage, as he normally did in these types of preferred contracts.

By patching and pumping her out, the Whitelaw Wrecking Company soon refloated the *Lunsmann* with her rails barely above the water. His wreck-steamer towed the vessel 700 feet toward the shore and beached her. Intending the next morning to pump her out even more, the crew left her for the night and felt that they had a successful salvage. The next morning Whitelaw looked out at the wreck as he was thinking about his salvage plan. He was shocked when he couldn't find it. The derelict was nowhere in sight.

Once the men were at the location, they looked closer: The *Lunsmann* was underwater again. Although the salvagers had grounded her at a "fairly high tide" with her rails showing, she had sunk again, even though the tide was lower. He sent a diver down to investigate, and the man quickly surfaced with the answer to their puzzle. "We had grounded her on the only patch of quicksand ever found on this piece of the coast!" remarked T. P. H. later.

That's when the real troubles started. The ship's temporary patches had burst open from the sand's weight, and huge quantities of quicksand flowed into the vessel. Whitelaw's crews "would patch and pump, patch and pump," but they never could get ahead of the ever-present quicksand. The *Lunsmann* sank deeper and deeper into the bottom of the sea.

The loose sand then nearly brought about the death of one of his divers. To keep the quicksand out of the ship, it was necessary to keep the pumps working when the worker was patching. The men on topside for some reason stopped the pumps for a few minutes, and the diver quickly signaled by sharp tugs on his cord that he wanted to be brought up. The vessel now seemed to list slightly to one side. When the assistants pulled on the diver's tie-rope, they couldn't pull the man up. It was as if his rope was tied to the ship.

The crew worried that the vessel had pinned the hapless man underneath it. Another diver immediately jumped in the ocean and went down to aid his comrade. They were right. The first diver had been caught—but by the quicksand. When the pumps stopped, the "treacherous stuff" had flooded in and buried the surprised diver against the ship's side. The operator immediately started the pumps up again, but they needed to be kept going "some minutes" before the sands subsided enough for the others to be able to haul up the exhausted diver.

Once this round of patching and pumping was completed, Whitelaw brought his wreck-steamer to haul the ship from the rocks. One morning when the crew tried to drag the *Lunsmann* off, the workmen had an unexpected (but, to Whitelaw, another "thrilling") experience. When the steamer *Harvard* passed into the bay, the large ship threw off a series of huge waves due to its direction into the currents. After several bumpy waves rolled into the wreck, a "big fellow" came along that struck the "poor old wrecked schooner" with a terrific whack.

Whitelaw saw the large, rolling wave approaching and yelled a warning to his two nephews, who happened to be working with him. The Captain then quickly climbed up the rigging. Once there, he felt the wave slam into the *Lunsmann* and crash over its decks. When he looked down, he saw a horrifying scene. The roller had hurled Jack Whitelaw—one of his nephews—twenty feet to one side. The dazed man had somehow landed safely on his back on a raft that was sailing in the currents toward the shoreline. The roller had swept another nephew, Tom, overboard as well into the ocean.

Tom had managed to swim to the stump of the vessel's mainmast, although it was now over the ocean and "slapping up and down." As T. P. H. checked the ocean, Jack seemed to be out of immediate danger. He turned his attention to Tom. Captain Whitelaw climbed down from the rigging, grabbed a rope, and tried to get the line to him. Cappie's footing was unsteady and the waves were sweeping into him. Despite his tries, he couldn't get the rope over to Tom.

A crewman grabbed the line without hesitation and walked over the slippery rail toward Tom. While the vessel swayed with the swells, the man tiptoed over the metal, nearly losing his balance and pitching into the sloshing waters that were inches away. As others watched silently and prayed for the best, the crewman managed to toss the line to Whitelaw's nephew. The seaman then turned around, walked back over the railing as the vessel dipped and rose, and helped to pull Tom back in.

Whitelaw said later:

In this business, rescues of drowning persons are common, but that was one of the bravest things I have ever seen. Only supreme courage kept that man's feet steady as he tiptoed across the plunging rail.

A pilot in an open cockpit, multistrutted biplane flew spectators over the *Lunsmann* to watch the operations, charging $5 per flight with a two-flight limit. This was twelve years after the Wright brothers had made history with their first flight at Kitty Hawk. Countless thousands of curious spectators also took to charter boats or watched from their own boats. Motion-picture companies took pictures of the salvage attempt and played them as spots in theaters. It was said that film clips of the fleet of wreckers surrounding the top of the *Lunsmann*'s masts became a classic and were inserted as scenes in movies. Whitelaw's effort had taken on a life of its own.

Divers meanwhile started the construction of a cofferdam by setting up frames, securing them with bolts, and building the wall of planks around her. Although this wooden schooner wasn't as valuable as the expense Whitelaw was incurring—even with his high percentage of the take—the ship was a navigation hazard and the Captain wanted to save the vessel. When everything was ready to float the ship once more, unfortunately, another winter storm crashed in. The gale destroyed what had been completed and left the *Lunsmann* with "every seam of the vessel now yawning." It would be impossible to pump the wreck free of enough water to save it.

In December, Whitelaw abandoned his attempts to bring the *Lunsmann* safely from the bay. He had fought for nearly six months to salvage the schooner. Skilled divers dove hundreds of times into the seas to patch over the leaks. The "grizzled old wrecker" gave the word "scores of times" to start the powerful pumps in the hopes of seeing the hulk of the schooner rise up from the sea. But none of the attempts was successful.

When the U.S. Army Corps of Engineers agreed to blow up the wreck and remove its hazard to the shipping lanes, Captain Whitelaw gave the reluctant order for his wreck barges to leave. His hopes of realizing a tidy amount had vanished like "another dream of treasure island." He concluded:

> This is one of the times that the weather and tide fooled me. This is the only time I have really failed to make good. Perhaps I am a bit older than I was, but despite the loss of a few thousands, this old man will be ready to make another gamble when it's needed.

Whitelaw was motivated by the challenge, as were presumably other salvagers. This was his "worst one," since he had been unsuccessful on a well-publicized salvage effort in his home port. He didn't put much emphasis on the financial aspects of his salvage failures or successes, however. Whitelaw had spent $8,000 before he realized he couldn't save the *Lunsmann;* later estimates put this figure higher, at upwards of $20,000. But Whitelaw had lost much more money on other ventures, such as the $100,000 spent on his attempts to save the *San Pedro* (see Chapter Ten, "No Rewards without Risk"). In retrospect, given the extent of his undertaking to refloat the *Umatilla* (see Chapter Five, "Dynamite Johnny and the Umatilla"), it is entirely possible Whitelaw broke even or lost money on that venture. For Whitelaw, it seems, it was all about the "gamble" in overcoming obstacles or doing what was said to be impossible.

One good thing came from the attempts, though, as the ever-optimistic Whitelaw told the story. He was at Crowley's Vallejo Street dock, waiting for the return of the *Lunsmann's* wrecking crew, and spotted Captain Weikunat, the master of the submerged schooner, that same day. Asked what he was doing there, Weikunat answered, "Waiting for the diver."

T. P. H. questioned suspiciously, "What do you want with the diver?" The skipper told Whitelaw that it was of no concern to him and only a "personal matter." Captain Whitelaw didn't accept the answer. He said pointedly the diver was on his payroll on this job, and any discussions would require his permission. He pressed Weikunat further.

Weikunat finally answered, "I asked him to look for a little thing of mine in the schooner's cabin."

"You have no right to do anything of the kind," T. P. H. responded. "Seventy percent of everything on that ship is mine." The skipper then divulged there was $550 in coinage in the schooner's cabin and the diver had agreed to retrieve it for $100.

"So you see," said Whitelaw later with a smile, "how being on hand at the right moment saved me $385." He received his 70 percent cut of the $550 when the diver brought the gold coins to the surface.

●　　●　　●

ONE OF THE worst disasters in maritime history was then destined to take place in the Midwest. The *Eastland* was a 269-foot-long passenger ship with four decks and a thirty-six-foot beam. Built in 1903 in Port Huron, Michigan, the vessel had twin smokestacks, a white exterior, and was powered by twin screws. In 1915, the ship was owned by the St. Joseph-Chicago Steamship Company. By that time, it had acquired a reputation of being unstable.

After the *Titanic* disaster, a new federal Seaman's Act was passed, and among other provisions, this required ships like the *Eastland* to be retrofitted with sets of heavy lifeboats—which she hadn't been designed for. Already so top-heavy that the ship could only sail with restrictions, the new gear made the ship even more unstable. The vessel's decks had also been loaded with several tons of concrete in a recent repair of rotten wood.

On July 24, 1915, Chicago's Western Electric Company leased the *Eastland* and two other cruise ships to take its employees to a picnic across Lake Michigan in Indiana. Passengers began boarding around six-thirty that morning at the ship's dock on the Chicago River. The vessel had reached its capacity of 2,500 passengers by 7:10 A.M.

When the gangplank closed, most of the passengers settled on the port side of the upper deck so they could view the river. Few passengers paid attention to the ship's lean as they boarded on the starboard side, or the ship's subsequent list to port when many people moved to that side. The crew attempted to stabilize the leaning by increasing the amount of water in the ballast tanks. When loading passengers from the wharf on the starboard side, for example, the engineer partially filled the port ballast tanks to compensate for the weight when people boarded.

The ship had just pushed away from the Clark Street dock when it listed badly enough for water to start pouring inside through the open portholes and hatches on the port deck. The unsteady vessel began to "bob and weave" because of its top-heavy state, the ballast, and the lopsided distribution of so many passengers. The ship's list to port became so severe that a refrigerator behind the bar toppled over with a loud crash, and passengers had a difficult time standing upright with the deck's steep angle.

By 7:28 A.M., the *Eastland* was slowly rolling over, and onlookers couldn't believe their eyes. A large steamer was slowly turning over on its side in calm water with no wind, explosion, fire, or any other indication of a problem. The people on board fell, slid, and were swept down the continually tilting deck, and then the *Eastland* completely turned over into the mud.

The ship came to rest on its port side in twenty feet of water. It was a mere twenty feet from the wharf on the river's south bank between Clark and LaSalle streets. The rollover happened so fast that no lifeboats could be deployed or lifejackets handed out. When the ship upended, a heavy grand piano pitched over, crushing several people to death, and many others were trapped inside the massive ship.

Panicked passengers on the upper two decks were instantly immersed in cold water. Some could swim; others couldn't. Pulled down by soggy clothing, coats, and shoes, terror-struck people flailed their arms and seized stronger swimmers as they sank beneath the murky waters. Those trapped inside cabins, lounges, and gambling rooms were horribly imprisoned in filling tombs of water.

Rescue attempts immediately began. Another cruise ship stopped alongside the *Eastland's* hull to allow some passengers to reach safety. Onlookers dove into the river to try and rescue more. Quick-thinking workmen grabbed produce crates and threw them down as floats. A deliveryman rescued several people by pulling them out of the river with ropes from his wagon.

A tug from the Dunham Towing and Wrecking Company rushed in and saved "fifty to a hundred" people. A wholesaler of produce tossed down chicken coops with ropes attached for the struggling people to grab onto. Workers cut holes into the ship to let some people out alive. Hoping to find air pockets with more passengers, divers jumped into the river and worked their way into the dark, water-filled ship.

But the Chicago River and *Eastland* were quickly clogged with the dead. Nearby warehouses and even a nearby steamer were converted into morgues that day. Bodies were piled up in rows as they were pulled from the water and cut out from compartments. Stripped to the waist, divers treaded water inside the hull. When they kicked a body, they called to workmen above, who then retrieved it with pike poles and grappling irons. Rescuers pulled bodies from watery compartments and passageways.

A total of 841 passengers and four crewmembers died in mere minutes in the disaster. One of every three passengers who boarded that day died. Husbands lost wives, and wives lost children and spouses. Kids lost parents. Decisions that people made in an instant—to stay on the deck or walk down the stairs to a warm inner lounge—made the difference between life and death. Where you decided to sit, or whether you leaned against a loose object, now made the difference for survival. Whether you left your child at home or not had lifelong implications. The fates continued to rush in with their ironies. One sailor dove into the river to save a woman and died, while another man saved a woman and later married her. Two people met while trying to help the survivors and also married later.

The *Eastland* sustained one of the worst death totals ever from a United States ship disaster, behind the *General Slocum,* the *Sultana,* and the *Titanic* (1,517 perished). The *Sultana* was a Mississippi river paddle-wheeler whose boiler exploded in 1865, and an estimated 1,500 to 1,700 persons died. Most of those who perished were Union soldiers just released from Confederate prison camps.

The worst East Coast marine disaster was the burning of the paddle-wheeler *General Slocum* near Hell Gate in New York City. In 1904, hundreds of churchgoing families boarded the steamer on an excursion cruise for the Sunday school classes of St. Mark's Church. The ship was just underway when a fire started from an explosion in a cookstove. Whipped through the vessel by a strong breeze, the flames leaped through the dry wooden beams and quickly consumed the wooden steamer. Panicked passengers jumped off the *Slocum* for safety, only to drown or be crushed by the churning paddle wheels. The death toll was shocking: 1,021 people died, primarily women and children. This disaster resulted in the firing of lax marine inspectors, a prison sentence for the ship's captain, and the upgrading of standards for steamboats. Merritt-Chapman raised the burned-out hull of the *Slocum,* and it was converted to a coal barge.

As for the *Eastland,* many of the bodies were taken to a nearby cold storage warehouse, which has since been transformed into Harpo Studios, the soundstage used today for *The Oprah Winfrey Show.* According to reports, some studio employees over time have had strange encounters they can't explain, such as the sighting of an apparition they have dubbed the "Gray Lady" and hearing the sounds of crying babies. Additionally, others maintain they hear whispering voices, old-time music, the clinking of phantom glasses, and the marching of invisible footsteps.

The exact cause of the *Eastland* disaster is still a mystery. After months of hearings, authorities officially blamed an obscure engineer who they said neglected to properly fill the ship's ballast tanks. Other theories ranged from the sudden rush of the passengers to the port side to an overloaded, top-heavy ship that was resting on a sloping river bottom. Still others blamed the tug, which they said was pulling on the *Eastland* before her lines were released from the dock.

Starting the very next day, Commonwealth Edison provided 125 tungsten-nitrogen lights to assist in the rescue and recovery efforts. These lights were set up along the starboard side of the *Eastland,* which now faced the sky. Ten floodlights were installed around and on a nearby building to illuminate the wharf area. The St. Joseph-Chicago Steamship Company gave the bid to right the *Eastland* to Captain Robert Young of the Dunham Towing and Wrecking Company (the local "affiliate" of the Great Lakes Towing Company) for $34,500.

A 181-foot-long steel salvage vessel, the *Favorite,* steamed to the site on July 28. It was equipped with salvage equipment, including large ballast tanks that could be filled to lower the vessel in the water and then pumped out to right a ship moored to her. Owned by Great Lakes, the *Favorite* also carried underwater "sealed' lights to aid the divers, along with deck searchlights.

The divers first had to cut off and remove the obstructions to righting the ship, such as funnels, spars, smokestacks, masts, lifeboats, and other deck obstructions. They then sealed these areas to keep the water out. The men next patched the holes in the hull's side that had been made by rescuers using acetylene welding torches; the rescuers had cut these openings when trying to free people.

Closing the openings on the vessel's underwater side came next, with more difficulties. Owing to the great piles of luggage, ship furniture, and debris in the way, the divers had to clear away these muddy obstructions before further work could be started. While the workmen were closing hatches, port holes, and gangways, they discovered more bodies in grotesque positions. These finds were disturbing at best, especially when they next had to move the dead out.

Although the salvage work was proceeding on schedule, complications always seemed to arise, no matter what the job. When workers dove into the murky waters to seal the aft bulkhead, they found more work to do. The rescuers had broken down the metal partition in their haste to rescue trapped passengers. When these repairs were completed, the pumping began and the water surged out of the *Eastland;* however, the aft bulkhead weakened due to the loss of heavy water pressure. The workmen were sent back into the water to further brace it.

The ship's coal moved en masse to the port side during the capsizing, and salvagers needed to remove tons of it and the mud that had surged into the hull. Once this work was accomplished, the wreckers completely filled the *Favorite's* ballast tanks with water to provide rolling weight in righting the *Eastland.* The filled ballasts would also help balance the ship when the derelict was finally raised.

In early August, a 100-foot pontoon boat carrying hoisting equipment left Cleveland and arrived in Chicago. Three tugs also came on the scene to move more salvage gear and provide the needed steam power in running the pumps. On August 11, the pumping—which several days earlier had been suspended—resumed and pumped the water out of the *Eastland.*

The *Favorite* moored to the sunken ship's bow. Its crew looped strong cables under the *Eastland's* hull; the cables were then attached to the salvage ship's starboard side. The large pontoon boat tied up to the stern. Workers next ran cables from this boat to the *Eastland's* upright side and fastened them close to the stern.

On August 13, the harbormaster suspended all shipping activity on the Chicago River, and a barge with coffins stood by in case more bodies were recovered. The sterns of the *Favorite* and the pontoon boat were flooded with water until each lowered eight to nine feet into the water. The winches drew up the cables until both wreckers were pulled as deep into the river as possible. Pumps then removed the water from both salvage ships while they were "mated" with the wreck.

With the salvage ships' buoyancy and tightening cables, the *Eastland* rolled from the water. With the ship coming to a forty-five-degree angle, the taut cables kept the vessel upright, especially since it was so unstable for starters. The righting continued the next day until the vessel was nearly upright, but with a slight list due to the coal, mud, and debris still weighting down the port side. Once the *Eastland* was completely trimmed of this weight, it was turned over to its owners for repairs. A crew of thirty-two men had worked twelve to fourteen hours per day, for sixteen days, in righting the ship.

An Illinois grand jury brought indictments charging negligence and manslaughter against the ship's captain, chief engineer, two steamboat inspectors, and others. A federal judge later rejected the petitions for lack of sufficient evidence. Hundreds of lawsuits were filed, but nobody ever collected. Twenty years after the disaster, the U.S. Circuit Court of Appeals in Chicago upheld in 1935 a lower-court ruling that the St. Joseph-Chicago Steamship Company was not liable for the deaths.

Under existing maritime law, *The Eastland* decision (78 F.2d 984) by the appellate court held the company could be liable only to the extent of its interest in the ship's salvaged value—a very limiting amount. The judges affirmed there was no negligence as the *Eastland* was seaworthy, the operators had taken proper precautions, and the responsibility for the disaster rested with the engineer who hadn't filled the ballast tanks properly. In upholding the findings of the appointed special commissioner and lower court, the appeals court wrote that the *Eastland* was in every respect seaworthy, "if properly handled."

Legal observers commented the courts erred by ignoring the true cause of the disaster: the ship's top-heaviness. There is no question that a different result would happen in today's legal world, and there would be multimillion-dollar settlements and plaintiff-favorable decisions. The shipowner would have been forced into bankruptcy, if not completely put out of business —but the passengers and their families would have been much more fairly compensated for their losses.

●　　●　　●

BY NOW, THE threat of war in Europe was in the air, and this soon became a reality. In June 1914, a member of a Serbian secret society, which demanded total independence from Austria-Hungary's influence, shot and killed Archduke Franz Ferdinand, the heir to the Austrian throne, and his wife in Sarajevo. The assassination set in motion the events that in one month escalated into full-scale war. Austria-Hungary declared war on Serbia; Germany joined Austria and other countries took sides.

When Germany declared war on France and invaded Belgium, this action brought France and England into the conflict. Japan, which was committed by treaty to support Great Britain, declared war on Germany in late August. Although the war was primarily fought in Europe, it was a global military conflict that lasted for over four years and finally forced the United States to enter.

The worldwide conflagration was fought on land, in the air, and on the ocean. When Japan entered the war, its navy put to sea to trap the Imperial German fleet in the Pacific. Although Japan's alliances would totally change in two decades, this move was designed to bolster the near-nonexistent Allied forces that were deployed along the West Coast of the Americas. The United States had a relatively large naval force, but the country was then committed to neutrality. The British, French, and German navies were amply represented in this region with their cruisers and other warships, and all of them made use of remote Mexican and Central American harbors to coal and supply their ships of war.

Receiving intelligence that indicated the Imperial German Navy would move further north toward the U.S. Pacific coastline, Japanese ships steamed closer to the United States to patrol the West Coast and its neutral American ports. Japan planned to establish its base of operations in an isolated bay halfway up the Baja California peninsula, known as Puerto San Bartolome, or Turtle Bay.

On January 31, 1915, the Japanese cruiser *Asama* struck an uncharted, submerged rock in "moderately heavy" seas while steaming into the harbor at Turtle Bay. The vessel ran aground and sustained a hole in its bottom nearly fifty feet long. The captain couldn't move the ship from the reef, and the ship's boiler room became completely flooded. With the resulting lack of power, the pumps stopped and the ship sank. Only the underwater rocky formation kept the warship from plummeting to the bottom.

When the seas turned worse, the captain ordered his crew to sink kedge anchors to stabilize the *Asama* and keep the ship from rocking off the reef. In answering the Japanese ship's calls for assistance, the British collier *Lena* anchored close by. The injured men, food and supplies, fresh water, and other provisions were then moved to the British ship. Worried about a possible German attack, the Japanese readied their stern guns and moved the ammunition to the upper decks before the lower magazines became flooded. The captain posted sentries and positioned picket boats for more protection.

While the *Asama's* crew struggled to keep their ship afloat, the *Idzumo*, another Japanese cruiser, was patrolling off San Francisco, unaware of what had happened. Two British colliers and a Japanese schooner began assisting the *Asama*. The captain, while thankful, declined the offers of assistance by the crew of the USS *Raleigh,* which had steamed to the bay after learning about the disaster.

The *San Diego Union* reported on February 18, 1915 that Japan, being an ally, had retained the "veteran Pacific Coast wrecker, Captain T. P. H. Whitelaw" to assist in the salvage of the wrecked *Asama*. At that time, however, Whitelaw was directing the salvage of the Danish motor ship *Malakka* off Natividad Island and Baja California, as the same storm that had swept over the *Asama* had driven the *Malakka* onto another reef. Five days later, the *San Diego Union* carried Captain Whitelaw's denial of the reported news that Japan had hired him.

The contract was awarded to the British Columbia Salvage Company, which then outfitted two barges in San Francisco and arranged for a U.S. tug to tow them south. The German ambassador to the United States issued a sharp protest over this breach of neutrality and demanded the U.S. government halt the sailing of the rescue ships. Although the government declined to intercede, it did place conditions that denied the Asama's access to U.S. ports. When one of the barges became disabled, however, the tug was forced to put into Monterey, just south of San Francisco—and the British efforts came to an end.

The captains at Turtle Bay were concerned, however, that German raiders could attack their ships, destroy them, and then steam to neutral U.S. West Coast ports. This risk lessened when British cruisers finally cornered one German cruiser, the Dresden, in the Pacific and brought about its surrender. The threat ended when England's warships forced two other German cruisers to put into U.S. ports on the Atlantic Coast, where they stayed for the war's duration. With the arrival of the Japanese repair ship Kanto on March 24, the task of refloating the Asama began. Its force went to work on the disabled warship two days later, and in three weeks the workforce had removed 1,200 tons of equipment.

The New York Times next ran an errant Los Angeles Times article that "exposed" the presence of five Japanese cruisers and six colliers at Puerto San Bartolome. The newspapers declared that Turtle Bay was to become a base of operations where one-half of the Japanese navy could anchor and easily "serve" against the United States. The reporter described the Asama as simply "having her nose stuck in a soft mud bank near the mouth of the harbor since December 31."

The same article also stated that Captain Whitelaw with his steamer Greenwood was at the bay, and quoted the veteran salvager as saying the Asama could not have been badly damaged and "with a good try the boat could be pulled clear in a few hours." The narrative continued that the harbor was heavily mined, a radio station was operating from shore, and 4,000 Japanese sailors and marines had already landed. The danger was so serious, the reporter wrote, that the Japanese now had a naval base within easy striking distance of the United States and its Panama Canal. The articles concluded that running the Asama ashore on a soft mud bank near the entrance of the harbor was just an excuse for the Japanese to send its warships and soldiers to the remote bay.

In actuality, despite thirteen pumps operating around the clock, the cruiser was still taking on seawater faster than its pumps could remove it. The cruiser in fact had settled so heavily onto the reef's pinnacle that her forward berth deck was now underwater. The *San Diego Weekly Union* labeled the *Los Angeles Times* article a complete fabrication, and it ran contrary statements by a recently returned American captain. Although the captain reported there was no armed camp and the *Asama* was seriously damaged, the speculation from the earlier erroneous accounts continued.

The *San Diego Weekly Union* finally carried an exclusive interview with Captain Whitelaw. Aware of the controversy and his potential involvement, Whitelaw had personally visited and inspected the area. He said the bay wasn't mined and the Japanese had not created an armed camp there. Whitelaw stated flatly that they were doing "everything possible" at the harbor entrance to salvage the cruiser *Asama* from the pinnacle rock "upon which she is impaled."

With his reputation and repudiation, the story was no longer front-page news and virtually disappeared from the public eye. The Japanese salvagers made temporary repairs inside the hull and attached collision mats over the major holes, which allowed the pumps to finally lower the amount of water inside the ship. Using a high tide and strong surges of ocean to advantage, the cruiser finally came off the rock after being grounded for ninety-eight days.

The *Asama* was promptly moored next to the repair ship *Kanto*, and workers began to patch the holes in its bottom. The largest rupture required a twenty-four-square-foot steel sheet, and twelve temporary patches were placed on the hull. Workers poured 250 tons of cement into the ship to ensure it stayed watertight. With only one-half of the *Asama's* boilers operable, the ship's speed was reduced to six knots.

In late August, the cruiser attempted its first test run outside the bay. With this success, the ship departed Turtle Bay two days later. Escorted by the *Kanto* and another cruiser, the *Asama* slowly steamed to the British naval station at Esquimalt, British Columbia, located 1,200 nautical miles to the north. (This is the same port used in several of Whitelaw's projects, including the *Umatilla*.) During the voyage, water continually poured into the vessel from its fractures, and the ship's pumps had to run constantly to pump out 800 tons of water each hour. After ten days on the seas, the *Asama* and her escorts finally reached the naval dockyard at Esquimalt.

With the assistance of both Canadian and Japanese dockyard crews, the men attached forty-three metal plates to the ship's bottom that allowed the ship to continue on. In late October, the *Asama* and *Kanto* started the long transpacific voyage for Japan. Her men still had to operate the pumps—now pumping out a reduced 100 tons of water per hour—and the ship arrived at the Yokosuka Naval Station on December 18, 1915.

Two days later, Emperor Taisho received Captain Yoshioka and his officers with honors. The noncommissioned officers and men were received five days later at the Imperial Palace. Captain Yoshioka closed his report by noting one diver had died in an accident and two stokers had died of illness while the ship was stranded. Another diver was killed when working on the cruiser at Esquimalt. The captain's final reflection was, "It is my great regret that these men were unable to share our victorious return."

In the meantime, the *San Diego Weekly Union* had reported three months earlier that Turtle Bay was now empty. The Imperial Japanese Navy had departed for good.

● ● ●

AMERICA'S POLICY under President Woodrow Wilson of staying neutral while trying to broker a peace treaty also resulted in tensions with both Berlin and London. In 1915, when a German U-boat sank the *Lusitania*, a large British passenger liner with a huge death toll of 1,198 people, including 128 Americans aboard, U.S. sympathies changed. Former president Teddy Roosevelt highly criticized what he called Wilson's cowardice. In January 1917, the Germans announced they would resume unrestricted submarine warfare. Berlin's proposal to

Mexico to join in the war as Germany's ally against the United States next came to light and angered Americans even more. After German submarines attacked several American merchant ships, sinking three, President Wilson was forced to request that Congress declare war on Germany. It did.

On April 6, 1917, the United States joined its allies—Britain, France, and Russia—to fight in World War I with the other Allied Powers of Italy, Belgium, Serbia, Montenegro, and Japan to battle the Central Powers of Austria-Hungary, Bulgaria, Germany, and the Ottoman Empire (now Turkey and parts of the Middle East). Before then, U.S. companies were shipping and smuggling contraband to the Allies in merchant vessels in operations well known to their government. T. P. H. Whitelaw was seventy years old when his country entered the war.

Since so many ships were used for military purposes, a boon in ship construction and maritime activities began. The reduction in tonnage for coastwise and cargo service meant less competition and increased shipping rates. Ship values rose sharply. Given the requirements for war, the market for scrap iron and steel greatly increased. Whitelaw's scrap was now worth a fortune. He could buy entire cities if he wanted.

During the war, different governments contacted Whitelaw for help with the salvage of the vessels that German submarines had sunk in European waters. Feeling there was enough business to do in the Pacific Ocean—and unwilling to be away from his family—he chose not to sail to Europe. He did make it clear that he would "give freely of his many years of experience."

After millions of soldiers and civilians on different warfronts died, Germany, as the last of the Central Powers, signed a ceasefire on November 11, 1918—one and a half years after the United States entered the war. The opposing armies on the Western Front began to withdraw from their positions. The war caused the disintegration of four realms: the Austro-Hungarian, German, Ottoman, and Russian empires. Germany lost its overseas territories, and new states such as Czechoslovakia, Estonia, Finland, Latvia, and Yugoslavia were created, or in the cases of Lithuania and Poland recreated. These events also sowed the seeds for another horrible world war to start two decades later.

On the naval front, German Empire battleships, cruisers, and sub-marines had hunted down merchant ships from the Atlantic Ocean to the Mediterranean Sea. It was estimated German U-boats had sunk nearly 5,000 Allied ships. The Allied forces had been equally successful in killing men and destroying vessels.

Before the war was even at an end, Whitelaw believed that a large part of the tonnage lost would be recovered, because this salvaging would be at depths not exceeding twenty-five fathoms (or 150 feet). He said a majority of the ships torpedoed were in comparatively shallow water, such as the "greater part" of the North Sea and the British Channel. Owing to the great tonnage that sank and the large number of ships needed to be raised, he concluded that marine engineers would need to create "new and original methods" to simplify the salvaging. It was a "simple matter of calculation," he said, as if there was nothing mysterious about this proposition.

T. P. H. also forecast that at war's end, the numerous ships refloated and repaired would add a surplus to worldwide maritime shipping, given the numerous ones built during the war. He was right on all accounts. In fact, there were too many ships by then, and the United States—like all other countries—would be selling its fleets at greatly discounted prices.

During and after the war, steamers plied the coasts, connecting San Diego, Los Angeles, and San Francisco with Portland, Seattle, and Victoria, British Columbia. The war-boom years, moreover, doomed the wooden-ship builders; in 1921, only one wooden steam schooner was constructed. In addition to their other advantages, steel vessels were built larger than wooden ships, since timber didn't have the strength of steel and long wood boats tended to bow out. Longer ships meant greater carrying capacity—and greater profits.

Hundreds of brand-new steel ships were now lying idle in the back-bay waters of American ports. The United States Shipping Board had completed a program of building the greatest wartime maritime fleet the world had ever known. With the terrible war finally at an end, there was little need for these vessels. To sell the steel ships off, the government put them on the market at bargain rates. The coastal operators took advantage of this opportunity to replace their obsolete and aged wooden ships.

Wood and masts were eliminated, and twin-screws replaced one propeller. Ship operators converted their wooden steam schooners into garbage ships, cattle carriers, gasoline tankers, dredges, wreckers, gambling barges, and even ammunition carriers. These grand ships also passed into history.

❦ ❦ ❦

THE T. A. SCOTT and Merritt & Chapman companies were equally busy. During this time, Merritt continued to tow away grounded ships, refloat others, and salvage numerous ships for their parts and scrap. In conjunction with naval authorities and the Boston Towing Company, Merritt & Chapman undertook the salvage work on the USS *Maine,* whose unexplained sinking in Havana Harbor brought about American's entry into the Spanish-American War in 1898. When the salvagers decided that this ship couldn't be raised, the wreckers removed its equipment, armaments, and fittings, including what remained above water, such as the masts. The *Maine* rested on the harbor floor until 1911, when the U.S. Army Corps of Engineers oversaw the construction of a cofferdam and sufficient patching of the hull so that it floated. One year later, the Astor, Guggenheim, and other families jointly contracted for Merritt & Chapman to find and raise the *Titanic;* it correctly decided that the raising of this ship from those depths was impossible.

One of Scott's successes was refloating the barge *Manheim.* A gale blew three barges onto the Massachusetts shore in 1915; two of them were so damaged that they were stripped and burned. To ensure their success on the last one, the foreman and four assistants lived on the grounded barge for eleven months while they awaited high water. In the meantime, they rigged hawsers to three big anchors in deep water and hooked them to onboard winches. When a strong spring gale arrived later with high incoming swells, the five men used the winches to pull the barge safely into deeper water.

Six months later, Scott endured tragedy in his operations. German submarines were still carrying goods to and from the United States, owing to its neutrality at that time in the war, and during one early morning in

November 1916, two T. A. Scott Company tugs were escorting the German commercial sub *Deutschland* through Long Island Sound. In the darkness, the submarine captain lost his bearings and accidentally rammed the tug *T. A. Scott, Jr.,* causing her to sink with the loss of its five crew members.

Merritt took on a difficult salvage in the righting of the 13,000-ton liner *St. Paul,* which unexpectedly capsized onto its side in New York Harbor. Early in the summer of 1918, the ship lay in its slip on its port side with its main deck under fourteen feet of mud. The *St. Paul* slowly settled into the bottom with 2,000 tons of mud oozing inside through open doorways, portholes, and stacks.

When taking on this contract, Merritt knew the *St. Paul* well, since his company had worked with her before. His salvage group had pulled the large steamer off a New Jersey beach in 1896 after the ship grounded while racing the *Campania* (see Chapter Nine, "Wrecks—and a Ghost Ship"). The *St. Paul* had also previously collided with and sank a British cruiser; and while being refitted for war duties, sank in New York Harbor, only to be later refloated. Now the ship lay on her side at her pier.

After time-consuming attempts using pontoons and tackle to roll the vessel partly upright, the salvors built a wood cofferdam around the hull's low side and floated the vessel by pumping the water out. This operation sounds simple, but the setup work needed was extensive. The wreckers had to do considerable underwater diving to close a large number of portholes, doorways, and other openings, all of which were buried under mud and required substantial excavating. The salvagers had to remove a six-inch forward gun, as the ship was used as a troop transport during World War I. The crews also had to blast the masts and smokestacks away so that these structures wouldn't keep the vessel from turning over.

The workers put in place the wood cofferdams, cut steel bulkheads to drain compartments, and then built concrete bulkheads that allowed other sections to be pumped out. Men attached beams to the exposed side and attached cables that winches pulled when the pumps and derricks were activated. Workmen then removed 1,000 tons of mud from the ship's interior. After utilizing the pontoons and tackles to right the ship to almost an even keel, the men excavated the remaining 1,000 tons of mud that couldn't be first recovered. Once repairs and refurbishment were completed, the *St. Paul* returned to its North Atlantic runs.

After this recovery, the nation was nearing the great times of the Roaring Twenties, which would lead in turn to economic disaster and desperation. These would be the best and worst of times, and no one would be spared.

CHAPTER THIRTEEN

THE ROARING TWENTIES

Prohibition became the law in the United States. When the Eighteenth Amendment went into effect on January 16, 1920, the manufacture, transportation, and sale of alcoholic beverages (liquor, wine, or beer) was banned, and this attempt at enforced sobriety was in effect for thirteen years. However, distilleries and breweries flourished in Canada, this country, Mexico, and the Caribbean. Prohibition in fact caused some of the wrecks, when ships with lights off steamed at night to run liquor in or cruise with drinking partiers. The Coast Guard waged a vigorous battle against the rum runners, but neither side could claim victory in the end.

The 1920s were referred to as the Roaring Twenties because there was a great industrial boom and increase in the standard of living. Electric power and lights were expanding into many regions of the country, and a growing number of large companies were producing millions of cars, radios, and telephones. It was the Jazz Age. The first commercial radio station, KDKA in Pittsburgh, started broadcasting in 1922. Listening to radio became a favorite pastime, as television and stereos were decades away from being invented.

Charles Lindbergh, or "Lucky Lindy," became an international icon in 1927 when he became the first pilot to fly nonstop across the Atlantic Ocean. The first "talkie," *The Jazz Singer,* was released the same year as the first feature-length film that used recorded song and dialogue. It was the time of Babe Ruth, Al Capone, Will Rogers, Jack Dempsey, Charlie Chaplin, and F. Scott Fitzgerald.

On March 25, 1920, the Whitelaws celebrated their golden wedding anniversary with a small dinner for family and friends. In addition to Cappie and his wife, the attendees were Elizabeth's brother, their son-in-law and daughter Daisy, two grandchildren (Daisy's girls, Dorothy and Bernice), and their grandson Ken, along with a few close friends. The widow (Mrs. Emma Whitelaw Knowles) of their deceased son, T. Andrew, was also invited and there. She was said to be a "daughter," and this inclusion of the now-remarried woman speaks strongly about the Whitelaw concept of family.

When everyone sat down for dinner, they discovered an "Aladdin-like" surprise. Cards printed in golden letters and souvenirs of a small golden deep-sea diver were at each place setting. The cards let each invited guest know about the fine wines being served with each course, which was a marked departure from the Captain's very limited drinking rule.

A Sauterne bottled a "good sixty to seventy years ago" from the wreck of the British bark *Viscata* on Baker's Beach was served first. A white port "corked in 1864" was next; it was from the salvage of the British ship *Autocrat,* which also met with doom off Baker's Beach, just south of the Golden Gate narrows.

A claret and champagne accompanied the main dishes. The claret was bottled under a "sunny Napa sky and getting only as far from home as the resting place of the clipper ship *Flying Dragon* in the shallows of Arch Rock [thirty miles north of San Francisco] in the year the Whitelaws wedded." The champagne came from France and was "rescued" from the British windjammer, the *Jessie Osbourne,* that wrecked at Bolinas (close to Point Reyes and north of the city). "A bit" of scotch topped off the Whitelaw menu with their "favorite accompaniment of soda."

In 1921, Whitelaw announced his retirement through the newspapers:

Captain T. P. H. Whitelaw, the veteran wrecker who has followed this career for a half century on this coast, will dispose of his gear and steamer *Greenwood* and retire, [it] was announced yesterday. The old-timer said that he believes it time to dispose of his active interests and let the younger men take charge of the work of wrecking in this district. Recently, Whitelaw has devoted the majority of his efforts to placing mooring buoys and other work less hazardous than that of raising broken craft in rough waters.

He might have slowed down in raising wrecks, but he didn't with his other activities, such as buying and selling scrap iron. The previous year, the Whitelaw family moved to Oakland—across the bay—and his occupation was now listed as "Salvor at Salvage Company." His home was a "substantial residence" in the exclusive Piedmont section.

Captain Whitelaw's retirement took place after his grandson joined the company and had passed his second officer's examination in 1920. Ken's shipping experience had been for the required five years with the Pacific Mail, Matson, and Grace lines in different capacities. With his second officer's license in hand, he worked on setting moorings along the coast for his grandfather's government contract, but then left to head out on long voyages for other shipping lines. This development was important.

When Ken left the Whitelaw Wrecking Company this time, the Captain's handpicked successor was following in his brother's footsteps, defying his grandfather's wishes. Cappie was upset and dismayed at Ken's actions. More than likely, this was due to T. P. H. not being able to let go of his operational control to Ken. It also appears that his grandsons had a stronger desire to sail on the seas, not dive beneath it and salvage ships.

Whitelaw's retirement was consequently short-lived. Without successors to take over his business, he didn't want his operations to come to a standstill. Although seventy-five years old, Cappie also didn't have the temperament to live a sedentary life. The salvage of the *Lyman A. Stewart* was one example of how he spent his "retirement" days. The ship was built in 1914 at San Francisco's Union Iron Works as a steel-hulled oil tanker. Named for the president and a founder of the Union Oil Company, the vessel was delivered to its owners ten months after its sister ship, the *Frank H. Buck*. The *Stewart* had a quiet career in coastwise service on the West Coast. It plied a regular route for years so uneventful that the tanker became known as "the ole' lady" until the ship was lost.

Leaving the Union Oil Company's docks at the port of Oleum in San Francisco Bay, heavy with a cargo of oil bound for Seattle, the *Stewart* approached the Golden Gate in 1922. A heavy swell and strong tide added to the danger of a thick fog bank when the tanker steamed into the main shipping channel.

At the same time, the freighter *Walter A. Luckenback* was heading into the Gate at the end of a long voyage that had started from New York City. The fog muffled the warning horns and whistles that both vessels were sounding. When the long hull of the *Stewart* cut across the other's bow, their crews first heard the whistle blasts—but too late to avoid disaster. The freighter cut deep into the port bow of the heavily laden tanker, causing water to rush in and immediately sinking its bow. The captain on the *Lyman A. Stewart* ordered all hands to abandon ship, but he stayed to pilot the vessel toward shore. Trailing oil, the tanker finally grounded on the rocks and ripped its hull. All thirty-eight members of the crew were saved.

In spite of strenuous efforts to float the tanker, it remained hard aground. Eventually heavy seas picked up the hull and jammed it farther up the rocks, breaking it into two pieces. Three years later, Whitelaw told reporters that his refloating of the *Stewart* would be his last salvage—again—and that he would then retire. He stood at the time on the marine lookout near Point Lobos and surveyed the wreck on the rocks at the entrance to San Francisco Harbor. Deciding later against those efforts, T. P. H. bought the wreck, removed the machinery, and salvaged scrap along with "some oil" from her.

Whitelaw could still negotiate, though. The Health Committee of the Board of Supervisors for San Francisco decided that the wrecks piled on the rocks inside the Golden Gate were giving San Francisco's harbor a bad name. After a lengthy conference, the supervisors decided to declare "Clean-Up Week" when wreck owners needed to clean up the harbor's murky entrance. They requested the city attorney find out who owned the *Lyman Stewart* and another ship. Whitelaw confirmed he owned the *Stewart*, but had no intention of removing the wreck until the price of old iron and steel made it profitable to scrap. He did offer to remove both ships for $20,000 and the salvage rights. The U.S. Army Corp of Engineers announced it would be happy to blow the ships "out of existence," except that these vessels were not menaces to navigation and therefore not within the Corp's jurisdiction. The city apparently rejected T. P. H.'s offer.

In 1938, the wreck of the *Lyman A. Stewart* and its sister ship *Frank H. Buck,* which had ironically wrecked at the same spot one year before, were dynamited to clear the entrance of visible wrecks. The hulks of both vessels slipped farther beneath the waves, and only the engine block of the *Stewart* at times is still visible at low tide.

❦　❦　❦

THE WORST peacetime U.S. Navy accident occurred when seven of its "nearly new" destroyers crashed off an isolated California headland on September 8, 1923. Known locally as Honda Point (and officially called Point Pedernales), the location was a few miles from the northern entrance of the heavily traveled Santa Barbara Channel and what's now part of Vandenberg Air Force Base. Completely exposed to shrill winds and high waves, often obscured by fog, this rocky shore had claimed numerous vessels, but never as many as on this tragic dark evening at 9 P.M.

Just twelve hours before, Destroyer Squadron Eleven had left San Francisco Bay and formed to perform combat maneuvers of tactical and gunnery exercises. This routine was followed by a twenty-knot-per-hour, test-run south, including a night passage through the Santa Barbara Channel. Led by their flagship, USS *Delphy,* fourteen destroyers in the late afternoon fell into column formation as the weather worsened. These warships were 1,190-ton Clemson class destroyers, longer than a football field at 314 feet, and armed with torpedoes, depth charges, shells, and four-inch deck guns.

Due to poor visibility, the squadron commander, Captain Ed Watson, and two other experienced navigators on board the *Delphy* had to work by the time-honored, if imprecise, technique of dead reckoning, whereby they could only estimate their position by using course, speed, time, and distance from a known place. Soundings couldn't be taken at the ship's speed of twenty knots, and the men checked their charted position against bearings obtained from the radio direction finding (RDF) station at Point Arguello, located a few miles south of Honda Point. At the time they expected to turn into the channel, the Point Arguello station reported that the fleet was still to the north. Since the RDF technology was still new and not completely trusted, its accurate information was discounted. The fleet was ordered instead to turn eastward, and each ship followed the *Delphy*—one by one.

The squadron was actually moving several miles north and farther east, however, than *Delphy's* navigators believed. Undergoing an exercise that simulated wartime conditions, the destroyers steamed ahead through a dense fog in the dark night while encountering abnormally strong currents. (These currents were believed to be caused by an extremely severe earthquake in Japan on September 2, whose strong aftershocks and effects continued afterward.) About five minutes after making her turn, the USS *Delphy* slammed full speed with a rending crash into the Honda shore. A few hundred yards astern, the *S.P. Lee* saw the flagship's sudden stop and turned sharply to port side, but quickly struck and swung broadside against the bluffs to the north. Following her, the USS *Young* had no time to turn before she ripped her hull open on jagged rock spires. She slammed to a stop just south of *Delphy* and quickly capsized onto her starboard side. The next two destroyers in line, the *Woodbury* and *Nicholas*, turned right and left, respectively, but also smashed into the offshore rocks.

Steaming behind them, the officers on board the next two destroyers heard the shrieks of the alarm sirens and slowed their ships down. Although these warships scraped along the bottom, they were able to back off with relatively minor damage. However, the USS *Fuller* piled up near the *Woodbury*. When the USS *Chauncey* tried to rescue the men clinging to the capsized *Young*, this warship also grounded. The last ships steered completely clear of the coastal rocks and weren't damaged.

In the darkness and choking fog, several hundred crewmen were suddenly thrown into the cold ocean water, fighting for their lives against crashing waves and a dangerous, rocky shore. Hurled unexpectedly down passageways, from bunks, and onto metal decks, sailors picked themselves up and raced topside into the damp air and drenching breakers. Punctured fuel tanks spurted flammable oil over seamen thrown into the ocean. When boilers and engine rooms flooded, the power to the ships was cut and the last vestiges of light ended. The cries of injured sailors, crashing surf, and sheering metal cut through the air; no one knew where they were, but everyone knew they were fighting for their lives.

On board the *Young*, many men were trapped inside her engine and fire rooms or swept away when the ship heeled over within a minute and a half. Twenty men were lost from the *Young*, the highest death toll of any of the ships lost. Waves easily swept over the wreck and threatened the rest of her crew. Men were clinging to the now-horizontal port side, portholes, or deck fittings. As oily surf battered the cold men, one seaman—Boatswain's Mate Peterson—yelled he would swim the 100 yards to a rocky outcropping and haul a life rope.

The *Chauncey* had grounded between the capsized destroyer and the rocks, and its crew members were safely fighting their way through the crashing ocean to shore. This ship was also aground, but it was on a relatively even keel with the ocean. Seeing that the two vessels were seventy-five yards apart, Peterson unflinchingly dove into the seething waters and swam instead toward the ship. Hurled about by the tumbling surf, the seaman slowly fought his way toward the *Chauncey* with a thick rope looped around his body. When he finally reached the vessel, others hauled the exhausted Boatswain's Mate on board and tied the rope to it.

A seven-man life raft was tossed into the ocean and was used as a makeshift ferry between the *Chauncey* and the *Young*. The seamen completed eleven trips to bring seventy of the *Young's* crew to safety. When the operations were completed by 11:30 P.M., the two remaining officers left the overturned, battered destroyer, including one who later returned to the ship after ensuring himself that the raft ferry was workable. Crew members from the *Chauncey* during this time swam ropes over to the cliffs and rigged a network of lifelines. As the pounding ocean battered the *Chauncey*, the surviving crews from both ships used these ropes to get safely to the crags.

The *Woodbury* had firmly grounded by a tiny offshore reef, soon to be named after the impaled ship. Volunteers again risked life and limb, this time to carry hawsers from this battered destroyer across the churning, chilling ocean to those rocks. Although the ocean was cascading into the boiler and engine rooms, the officers and men stayed on board while trying to float the ship from the rocks by reversing its engines. This effort failed when the sea engulfed the engine rooms and the *Woodbury* lost all power to settle down by its stern. The order to abandon ship was given.

As thundering breakers smashed over the vessel, the ship's bow carried toward the sky and then down with the waves. Holding to a thick line with legs and arms—the rope swinging wildly with the surf—the men pulled themselves toward the safety of "Woodbury Rock." At the same time, the crew from the *Fuller* tried to send a whaleboat and later a rubber raft to rig a line between its bow and the *Woodbury.*

When the crashing, hissing cauldron of breakers prevented these attempts, seamen jumped again into the chilling sea and swam to Woodbury Rock with another thick rope. The sailors from the *Fuller*—which later broke in two and sank—shuttled over this hawser to the same reef. They joined the *Woodbury's* sailors in trying to keep warm while the seas continually crashed over the rocks. The rough log entry for the *Woodbury,* dated "9 September 1923," reads: "*Woodbury* on rocks off Point Arguello, Calif., abandoned by all hands and under supervision of a salvage party composed of men from various 11th squadron ships."

Three of the destroyers had grounded near the tip of Honda Point. The squadron's flagship *Delphy* was worst off, broadside to the cliffs and rolling violently in the surf. As her fragile "tin can" hull was in danger of breaking apart, her crew had to get off as soon as possible. The ship's stern was close enough to the lower rocks that some men jumped ashore and fastened a line down, which allowed nearly everyone else to safely follow. Three *Delphy* sailors lost their lives, however, when the ship suddenly sheered in half and the forward section rolled over into the seething ocean.

Hidden by a rocky corner to the north, the *S.P. Lee* also grounded near the cliffs, and her crew members fortunately were able to ferry themselves to shore in their life rafts. Once on land, however, the *Delphy's* and *S.P. Lee's* men had to pull themselves up the sharp rock walls. Some lost their slippery holds, fell back onto the rocks, and were injured. The USS

Nicholas had bottomed further out with her stern toward the *S.P. Lee*. This destroyer's crewmen had to stay on board—despite their precarious situation—since the crashing waves, churning surf, and long distance prevented any system of rescue from being established. When daylight came, another life-raft ferry system was established and safely brought her crew ashore in the morning.

Exhausted, cold, and coated with oil, the crewmen who had reached land began to stumble in groups into the interior. Shortly afterward they heard the sound of a train whistle. Traveling toward the noise, the men discovered Southern Pacific's coastal railway and a well-staffed maintenance house that was less than a half-mile inland. Workers from this facility sent out a call for more volunteers, who were soon on the scene to help. They built bonfires with used railroad ties to warm the shivering sailors and tended to the injured.

As the word of the tragedy went out, ships, trains, and cars sped to the scene. A Santa Barbara fishing boat motored by in the morning and rescued the men who had been marooned on Woodbury Rock. More rescuers came by rail from the towns of Surf and Lompoc, some miles up the line, and these people brought medical aid, food, and blankets. Departing quickly from San Francisco, a special train arrived in the mid-afternoon to take more than 550 shipwrecked sailors back to the naval base at San Diego—their original destination. Navy vessels arrived. A wreck patrol of eighteen Navy men set up camp to protect the wrecked ships from looters and recover bodies. Searchers over time discovered seventeen bodies, but another six were presumed to have been swept out to sea or were otherwise unaccounted for.

Twenty-three lives had been lost. When word of the disaster reached Lompoc, two doctors volunteered to treat the injured—of which more than a hundred "ambulatory" cases were counted. That day, a train transported the seriously injured to Cottage Hospital in Santa Barbara. Most of the wounded had badly cut feet or contusions and suffered from exposure. Five doctors then boarded the same train for Point Honda to join the first physicians in tending to the wounded on site.

When word of the disaster reached Washington, officials immediately telegraphed Captain Whitelaw for his advice and recommendations.

Whitelaw quickly traveled there and accompanied naval officers during their inspection of the disaster scene. Captain Curtis of the salvage firm of Pillsbury and Curtis in San Francisco, who was working on a wreck on nearby San Miguel Island (twenty miles from Honda), joined the team when he learned about the disaster. Curtis's company was also a West Coast agent for the Merritt-Chapman & Scott Corporation.

For the first time since the destruction, however, the overhead skies were clear. Whitelaw knew the area from his "connection" with the nearby salvage operations on the SS *Santa Rosa,* and on September 16 the sea was as quiet as he had ever seen. He said the next six weeks were probably the "quietest" period on this coast, but that bad storms and heavy surf would occur several times before any salvage operations could be completed. Captain Curtis, who had worked with Whitelaw on the *Santa Rosa,* joined in this assessment.

They climbed aboard the rolling, surf-hit *Chauncey,* viewed the other destroyers from another bouncing ship, and then landed to make their assessment from the top of the bluffs. Until the day of Whitelaw's inspection, it hadn't been possible to land small boats on the beach or alongside stranded vessels. Heavily loaded with supplies for the watch patrol, a large "motor sailer" was able to cruise next to the *Chauncey* and unload provisions that day onto the wrecked destroyer's decks. A trolley hauled the supplies over cables to shore. No other procedures were possible, since the seas still weren't safe enough to moor a large boat onto land. Toward sunset, another blanketing fog rolled back in, and visibility collapsed.

After his detailed inspection, Whitelaw had grave doubts as to whether any of the destroyers could be saved. These vessels were broken in half, sunk, grounded on reefs with "great punctures," inundated by heavy surf, and hulls were ripped out. Due to the great extent of the damage, even T. P. H. Whitelaw wouldn't submit a "no cure, no pay" contract. The seventy-seven-year-old Whitelaw made the recommendation that the wrecks weren't salvageable. When receiving his report, the U.S. Navy accepted his assessment as being conclusive on the matter.

The U.S. Navy had quickly undertaken efforts to remove "confidential" material, salvage equipment, and weapons. Based at their temporary camp on the overlooking cliffs, Navy personnel concentrated on getting rid of the dangerous torpedoes. Whenever possible, they fired the disarmed projectiles out to waiting Navy boats so that they could be lifted onto a waiting mine sweeper. Otherwise, teams of men and tractors pulled them out on cables, and then hauled them on sleds over the cliffs to the railroad. After that, the Navy's efforts shifted to removing the torpedo tubes and sights, radio apparatus, detonators, and depth charges.

Two-and-one-half weeks after the tragedy, the Merritt-Chapman & Scott Corporation, acting through the firm of Pillsbury and Curtis as agent, began work under a private salvage contract with the U.S. Navy. After setting up their permanent camp on the bluffs, its men began to remove the guns, other armament, and leftover equipment from the destroyed ships. While men were struggling to lift the first gun from the nearby *Chauncey*, the "span carried away" and the weapon crashed onto the rocks. After removing the second waist gun from the ship, bad weather swept in with very high seas and ended work for a few days. During this period, however, one of the destroyers broke in two, and both sections sank from sight.

When strong swells handicapped the divers' exploration of overturned vessels, the U.S. Navy took on the task of burning holes into the destroyer's hulls with underwater cutting torches. The conditions and bad weather slowed the salvager's efforts to where the U.S. Navy formally complained to Merritt-Chapman about the various delays as the ships deteriorated further. The question became whether the seas would destroy the vessels before they could be dynamited. Some turret guns and other heavy equipment had to be left behind—particularly on the wrecks farthest from the mainland—when their recovery proved to be too dangerous. Finally, the Navy sold the wrecks in late October to an Oakland scrap dealer, Robert J. Smith, who removed more equipment but couldn't salvage anything meaningful.

A special board of inquiry investigated the twenty-three deaths and destruction at one time of seven expensive destroyers: the *Delphy*, *Chauncey*, *Fuller*, *Woodbury*, *S.P. Lee*, *Nicholas*, and *Young*. The inquiry attributed the loss "in the first instance to bad errors in judgment and faulty navigation; the clear fact being that it wasn't the compass bearings sent to the *Delphy* which were wrong, but the judgment of the men who interpreted these bearings and used them wrongly." It recommended that eleven officers on board the lost destroyers be tried at a later court-martial.

The subsequent hearing decided the issues of individual blame and punishment. Although the court martial proceeding found that Squadron Commander Edward H. Watson and the commanding officer of the *Delphy* were guilty of "culpable inefficiency and negligence," it exonerated all of the remaining officers but for one. (A reviewing admiral later set aside this conviction of the *Nicholas's* commander.)

The discipline and performance of duty seen was so outstanding that of the seven warships destroyed, only twenty-three men lost their lives to the treacherous sea—and the facts speak for themselves. In its investigation, the inquiry board commended more than seventy men for their bravery and coolness under extreme danger. Among others, it cited Boatswain's Mate Peterson for his "extraordinary heroism" in bringing the hawser through such rough seas to the *Chauncey*.

From the vast surplus of destroyers built during World War I, the U.S. Navy soon replaced the lost ships with other "tin cans." Within weeks of the Honda Point disaster and during the salvage operations, the large waves crashing against the California coast nearly broke apart all of the fragile hulls. By the end of 1924, the ocean was "substantially responsible" for shredding every one of these once-valuable warships with few remains being recognizable.

The Merritt-Chapman & Scott Corporation was now the dominant ship salvager. Prior to the merger of Merritt with Chapman's operations in 1897, these entities were three small East Coast salvagers. The acquisition of Chapman's large derrick barges and cranes well expanded Merritt's salvage capabilities. When the venerable Captain Thomas A. Scott died in 1907, his son continued the firm's operations and expanded them by gaining control four years later of the Boston Tow Boat Company.

During the boom times following World War I, Merritt & Chapman and T. A. Scott began to work together on pier construction and other nonsalvage operations such as laying submarine cable. Then, they merged in 1922 to form the Merritt-Chapman & Scott Corporation, which was well on its way to being a large, diversified industrial and construction firm with extensive salvage work. Captain Scott's son, T. A. Scott, was elected president of the newly formed firm.

By virtue of the Merritt Wrecking Company's acquisition of Chapman's and Scott's operations, the firm obtained their salvage vessels and facilities on the East Coast. After it acquired other small salvagers in states such as Florida, the entity operated salvage ships from docks located from Florida to Massachusetts while using West Coast agents such as Pillsbury and Curtis and acquiring facilities there.

The diversification of Merritt through acquisitions was important for the entity's continuation, as was the decision by Chapman and Scott to combine with Merritt. With ships being designed better and built stronger, declines in salvage work could be offset by business in other areas. The combination of these salvage entities meant the larger entity also could replace or acquire tugs, cranes, and wreck ships with geographical coverage and without having to maintain inefficient older equipment that was expensive to maintain.

Whitelaw's wrecking company didn't have these advantages, nor was there any succession in place. When his son tragically died and grandsons didn't follow in his path, he lost faith in trying to get another person to learn and manage the business. Although he continued to turn down more "opportunities" than he accepted, T. P. H. couldn't generate the substantial cash salvage work that he did in the past because of his aging equipment. The well-capitalized shipping lines and "modern salvage gear" required were too expensive. He continued to speculate on salvage work and buying wrecks.

❦   ❦   ❦

IN ANNOUNCING the celebration of the wedding anniversary of the Whitelaws in 1924, the *San Francisco Examiner* reported about them:

> In this modern day of divorce, fifty-four years of contented married life seems a dream, but to Captain and Mrs. T. P. H. Whitelaw, it is a cherished pact. They were married in San Francisco by Reverend Hemhill on March 24, 1870.

While glancing over recent pictures of her husband during the celebrations, Mrs. Whitelaw turned to her seventy-seven-year-old spouse and said, "You are a better-looking man than I thought you were." He in return said, "During all of these salvage enterprises, whether in stress of wrecks ashore or afloat, Mrs. Whitelaw is my helpmate." Those pictures showed Captain Whitelaw dressed in a three-piece dark suit with a full head of white hair and a long, flowing white beard. Wearing a floor-length matronly dress that was also dark-colored, his wife was smaller, with a stern countenance, round face, and thick white hair swept back to the sides in a bun. Time had marched on.

He had learned to relate well with the press and used the media to his advantage. Whether the occasions were anniversaries, wrecks, or personal asides, the reporters flocked to Cappie's office on the waterfront. They liked him, because he always gave them good copy. A reporter asked him one time what he had in his pockets. T. P. H. pulled out a worn button from a coat and a piece of a ship's anchor, and he then told the young man the stories of the ships involved. When the cub reporter asked what his hobby was, Whitelaw answered, "Reading." The reporter replied, "That's bully, Captain, read this," and in a rather cheeky way handed him a copy of a magazine in Chinese. Whitelaw looked at it, smiled, and then threw "a bit" of armor plate at the reporter. Laughing, the young man quickly ran out of the "little Dickensian" office.

Another time, he told the press that he was taking up golf. "I've taken up the good and ancient game of me forebears, and I'm ready to meet on the links, all comers in me class," he said. Although he probably meant this at the time, it's doubtful he had the time or patience to start golfing.

Thanks to his wife's planning, Whitelaw always celebrated his birthdays with his friends and family. Elizabeth even tipped off the press so they could report on some of these occasions. Even when he was in his late seventies and early eighties, he told his friends that despite his age, the world still looked as good to him as it did all those years ago when he first arrived in San Francisco. T. P. H. Whitelaw meant it, as he had always been an optimistic person—and he had to be, in this line of work.

By March 1924, Cappie had overseen a reported 15,814 dives in his business. From Alaska to Mexico, he had salvaged 289 vessels "of many descriptions for him and his men." From his office near the San Francisco waterfront, he still held himself ready, day or night, to answer a ship's call of distress—and he did so well into his mid-eighties. T. P. H. kept his experienced diving crew on salary for the routine work, while hiring "extras" for the big wrecks that increased his workforce to fifty or more. The *San Francisco Call* wrote on February 21, 1925:

> Seated in the little Dickensian office in the big Dickensian wrecking establishment which is stuffed, crammed, and crowded with the salvage of a thousand wrecks, until the roof bulges and the ship's gear and tackle overflows into the surrounding yards and out into the street, Captain Whitelaw, with a pull now and then at his beard, named some of the ships which sank or wrecked in and near San Francisco and received his professional attention.

> It sounds like a sample sheet from Lloyd's Register—the *Yosemite, Viscata, New York, Rio de Janeiro, City of Chester, Atlantic, R. D. Inman, Western Shore, Peril, Aberdeen, Isaac Jean, Paul Jones, Confidence, Escambia, H. L. Tiernan, Alice Timble, Elizabeth, Patrician, Rescue, Sampson, Signal, Alex Duncan, Chin See, Whitelaw, Drumburton, James Rolph II, Norway, Margaret Crockard, Alameda, Damara, Costa Rica, James Cheston,* and others whose names have been forgotten during this fifty-seven years of wrecking wrecks.

> The *Sampson* was the Captain's own wrecking steamer, wrecked while working on the wreck of the *New York,* a sister ship of the *Rio de Janeiro.* In 1893, eight years before the Rio disaster, the *New York* went ashore on Point Bonita, under the light [lighthouse]. Breaking from her moorings, the *Sampson* went ashore and her lamps set fire to the vessel.

> Within a distance of one hundred feet, but separated in point of time by years, the *Alameda,* a passenger steamer plying between here and Australia, the *Norway,* a schooner, and the *Damara,* a steamer, were wrecked on the Fort Point reef.

The *Isaac Jean,* a bark, loaded with lumber and piles, inbound from Puget Sound, was wrecked on Baker's Beach at the same point where the *Viscata,* a British bark, loaded with grain, piled up years afterward. In dead low water one can see the old ribs yet. A third vessel, the *China Sea,* a bark outbound for China with a load of lumber, piled up on Baker's Beach close to the wreck of the *Isaac Jean.* Whitelaw got her off and she sailed the seven seas for many years after that.

It is a long log, the story of these ships which found graves or were grievously hurt in and near the Golden Gate. And a varying story. Sometimes it was the fog, the wind, sometimes lack of wind, and at times tremendously strong currents which spelled their fate. And the value of the ships saved, Captain Whitelaw estimates roughly at $10 million, while those which proved a total loss were worth $6 million more.

He was seen as a "full-lunged, boyish, eager, alert, spry man" and seventy-seven years "young." Whitelaw was a "ruddy, aged Captain, whose eye, blue as the sea, twinkles as it does in noonday lights, suggesting that he has done nothing less nor found a lesser satisfaction." T. P. H. understandably did say he was slowing down: "I feel the saltwater a bit now and have to look out for my toes. Once it was all the same to me whether I was in to my ankles or armpits." But he stayed active in the business.

Despite the years in salvaging and the risks of the sea, he still believed in the ancient Greek philosophy of moderation. Even into his eighties, Whitelaw continued to find a fascination in the sea's beauty, its lure and spirituality. "The sea is even religious," he said at times. "But then the desert is that, too. Every man's life work should get into his blood and beat there—then it becomes worthwhile."

Sunset Magazine joined other national magazines such as *Literary Digest* and *American Magazine* in running full coverage stories on the wrecking experiences of Captain Whitelaw. He and his wife were living in a "substantial home in the exclusive Piedmont section of the bay region"—as described in *Sunset Magazine*—with Piedmont located across the bay, straddling a ridge of hills northeast of Oakland. He had come a long way from being age sixteen without a home and broke.

Whitelaw then stated his successful wrecking philosophy that although there were no simple cases, wreckers simply needed to pump the water out faster than the leaks let it in. As soon as the water that held the ship down was displaced, the vessel would automatically float up. Seamen on the waterfront still felt he had a supernatural instinct when working on wrecks that other salvagers didn't have.

By now, the work was easier due to technological improvements. Whitelaw owned pumps that threw out 215 tons of water a minute. Wireless radio was in use, and divers were equipped with telephones, electric lights, and safer and lighter diving suits. Underwater workers now used acetylene cutters to cut metal instead of sawing with hacksaws. Electric-powered generators and air compressors had been available for some time, and the old hand-operated pumps had gone the way of wooden ships. Caulks could now be applied to ship seams and fractures instead of patches; concrete and steel plates were used in place of hooks and wood caps. Despite these advances, however, divers still faced a very hostile environment of quite limited visibility, crushing pressures, chilling temperatures, and undersea marauders.

❦ ❦ ❦

IN LATE 1925, Whitelaw watched the court battle over his schooner *La Ninfa* in his lawsuit against the U.S. government for damages. The action dated back over thirty years to when U.S. warships were confronting seamen over the right to hunt seals and whales in the Bering Sea. Former Republican Governor (1907–1911) James N. Gillett of California prosecuted the case that dated back to the days of "wooden ships and iron men."

After a U.S. cutter seized *La Ninfa* in Alaskan waters in 1891, and an appeals court had held five years later that this action was illegal, Whitelaw wanted to be compensated for his loss of the ship's use and its repairs. Through the international courts, British owners could and did collect damages for their government's illegal impounding, but there was no similar law allowing American owners to sue theirs.

Compensation was delayed until Whitelaw and others could lobby the federal government to change its stance—and they eventually succeeded. Congress finally authorized legislation that permitted Bering Sea fishermen to recover money for their vessels and cargoes seized unlawfully so many years ago. The act was passed by Congress on June 4, 1924, and President Coolidge signed it into law. The act allowed district courts to hear and determine the claims of American citizens over their damages resulting from the "seizure, detention, sale, or interference with their voyage" by U.S. vessels over this issue.

Whitelaw didn't wait long, and on July 15 his attorney sued for damages under the new law. At the time of filing the lawsuits in San Francisco federal court, attorney Gillett remarked that any recovery "might still be in time to smooth out the last days of some sturdy old salts, some of whom, through age and poverty, are now inmates of sailors' homes and other public institutions." Captain Whitelaw sued for $90,000 and other lawsuits followed. At least fifty of the old sealing ships had potential damage claims, and Congress had authorized up to $1 million to be paid for all of the demands.

In December 1925, federal judge Frank H. Kerrigan ruled that Whitelaw was entitled to $77,110 in damages for the government's confiscation of La Ninfa. Some four months after the favorable judgment was handed down, on April 2, 1926—and thirty-five years after the seizure—the government paid checks totaling $79,000 (including court costs) for the seizure of La Ninfa. As the majority owner, Whitelaw received a check for $40,000 from the U.S. government. The remainder of the payments went to the minority owners of La Ninfa, including a check for $15,000 to William E. Thornlay, a customs house broker, as his commission for prosecuting the claims over the years.

These were large sums back then, and more than the average person could save in several lifetimes. The news caused a flurry of comment among the old-timers on the waterfront, especially since Whitelaw's check was the first one paid to any former owner—as if people should have been surprised.

By now, his San Francisco salvage yard was known as the "graveyard of ships." Although T. P. H. was a veteran of scores of sea tragedies, he could still squint at "a bit" of rusted cable, a binnacle (the stand for mounting a magnetic compass), anchor, or spar and tell someone about the ship's history. People said his accounts of these wrecked ships now on dry land were tales that matched story for story those from the Sargasso Sea.

During his wrecking career, T. P. H. had been building his heaps of scrap iron, including what he took from the 3,019-ton *City of New York* steamship. He stripped wrecks and bought old ships for the same reason. The surplus of World War I steel vessels and obsolescence of the wooden steam-schooner fleet gave Whitelaw his pick of what to buy. He brought them to San Francisco to strip and burn down for the iron and steel.

If doubts existed about his national standing, a *Popular Mechanics* article from November 1928 ended them. Even his grandson Ken said, "This was a long, extensive article and it was a 'biggie.'" The magazine called him the "Dean of the West Coast Divers" and the "man who has braved the dangers in handling the big wrecks of this long period that is nothing short of a hero." The article concluded by stating, "Among the most superstitious of seafaring men, Captain Whitelaw is often accredited with having super powers."

As these were Prohibition times, Whitelaw again saw the opportunities. In 1882, the captain of the 320-foot cargo ship *Bremen*—built in Scotland for a German company in that city—was feeling his way toward San Francisco in pea-soup fog with a cargo of coal and "other essentials." The vessel ran aground on Southeast Farallon Island, twenty-seven miles southwest of the Golden Gate. The officers and crew on a calm day quickly and safely abandoned the ship in its lifeboats. When the fog lifted, however, the *Bremen* had vanished, having slipped off the rocks into deep water.

This was not a particularly outstanding wreck, except for one thing: The *Bremen* had on board a full cargo of whiskey, valued even then at a "very high" amount. Newspaper reporters wrote about the "wails on San Francisco's waterfront. A ship full of whiskey—why, that was practically a week's supply!" Fleets of small craft soon were sailing close to Southeast Farallon as the captains continually searched for the elusive treasure.

East Coast distilleries would ship large consignments of "young" whiskey to Europe where they could be stored cheaply and aged without tax until the liquor was ready to market. The companies then shipped the cargo around Cape Horn to San Francisco, which was as cheap as sending the precious liquids from New York City. The owners of the sail ships were glad to have a paying cargo of whiskey on board—after bringing over other goods to Europe—instead of returning with only sand or rocks as ballast. Some further believed that the ship's rocking on these long voyages helped to age the liquor.

With Prohibition being the reality, T. P. H. became interested in the wreck. The 5,000 barrels of fifty-year-old rare Monongahela whiskey at bootleg prices was estimated to be worth close to $10 million, "if it could be sold—legally, of course," he concluded. Whitelaw believed raising the old German sailing ship *Bremen* was possible. He proposed a way to salvage the whiskey, but the U.S. government wouldn't allow him to proceed.

When asked what his most profitable job of salvage was, he answered that it was the French bark *Franconis,* which had also hit the same Farallon chain of rocks, but in 1887. Although the ship was lost, the men were saved. Whitelaw later salvaged fifty barrels of the priceless Monongahela whiskey. "If I had that many barrels of this particular product today," Whitelaw said with a smile, "and could dispose of it legally, mind you, it would be worth a lot of money."

Off the bleak Farallon Islands, it was said, veteran skippers were still smacking their lips after passing the grave of the *Bremen.* The possibility of finding a cask of the decades-old liquor on the ocean's surface and hauling it aboard was more than they could take.

❦   ❦   ❦

THE ELECTRIFICATION of the world was well underway, including San Francisco, and all of the city's gas streetlights were replaced by 1929. Commuters and their cars still used ferries to cross the large bays, and the river steamers shuttled back and forth by the ferry slips with passengers and produce bound for the Sacramento and San Joaquin valleys.

At the same time, the prodigious oil fields of California brought about a new economy and trade. The development of processing facilities on San Francisco Bay began, even though other oil-rich refining and storage harbors in Southern California, particularly in San Pedro, surpassed San Francisco's traffic. Beginning in the 1920s, oil, gasoline, and kerosene tankers increasingly steamed to and from San Francisco, San Pedro, and other California ports to destinations around the world.

Another major transportation change was also underway: air travel. Since most of the tiny airlines operating at the time competed for rights to carry the profitable bags of mail, passenger service during the early 1920s was sparse. In 1926, only 6,000 daring passengers had taken to the skies, and usually on very short routes. By 1930, 400,000 people had traveled by air.

CHAPTER FOURTEEN

THE CHANGE
OF ERAS

Continuing a schedule that younger people would find exacting, Whitelaw carried on his wreck and parts business. One notable operation was the salvaging of the schooner *Yosemite*. Powered by a 750-horsepower, triple-expansion engine, the *Yosemite* was an 827-ton steam schooner. Built in 1906, the ship carried passengers and lumber on her coastal voyages. Ten years later, Pope and Talbot of San Francisco, the largest lumber company on the Pacific Coast, purchased the ship for its fleet. For the remainder of its career the ship ran between San Francisco and the owner's sawmills in Washington State.

Steaming from San Francisco one night, the *Yosemite* carried not lumber, but a different cargo: twenty-five tons of dynamite. Just after midnight on February 7, 1926, the ship was in a thick fog when it slammed into the rocks below Point Reyes Lighthouse, tearing a hole in her bow. When the ship flooded, a nearby steamer picked up the crew, and Pope and Talbot immediately dispatched a tug, the *Sea Ranger*, to save the ship. Men on board the tug attached a hawser to the *Yosemite*, whose starboard side was now submerged, and the *Sea Ranger* began towing it toward the Golden Gate. The task was difficult, as waves constantly washed over the schooner and the hawser snapped at least once.

After a day-long battle with the sea, the *Sea Ranger* arrived at the San Francisco Bar around 2:00 A.M. on February 8 with the water-logged *Yosemite* in tow. The strong currents and tides then overwhelmed the derelict and tug. The ship with its deadly cargo began to drift away, and even with all of its cylinders at full speed ahead, the ocean currents pulled the tug away by its stern. An anchor was dropped to slow the movement, but it soon tore away. When the powerful seas snapped the tow ropes as if they were threads, the *Yosemite* broke free and became adrift. Fifteen minutes later at 3:30 A.M., the vessel crashed ashore on Ocean Beach and began breaking apart on the beach at the foot of Fulton Street, just below the Cliff House.

While onlookers worried about an explosion, the ship splintered into floating debris, shattered timbers, twisted posts, empty powder boxes, and broken spars that dotted the beach. Thousands of spectators crowded the shoreline for the next few days, picking up souvenirs and posing for pictures amid the wreckage. The largest intact piece was the *Yosemite's* hull, and the large swells continually smashed the "bottom-up" segment into a close-by wharf. The actions of the waves and battering ram resulted in 250 feet of the pier being torn away. Workers gradually cleared the beach of the smaller debris over a week's time, but large sections of the hull remained visible. The now-water-logged cases of explosives, some emptied by the waves, were no longer a threat.

Pope and Talbot called on Captain Whitelaw to cut up the hull and remove what was left. He sent his wrecker to the spot, and his men swarmed over the sections with explosives and torches to break them down into movable pieces. The wreckage and used parts—to the extent they were salvageable—were brought to his nearby yard.

Whitelaw had occupied the same quarters and storage location for thirty-six years. Nearly an acre of land had been "piled high with the wrecks of ships, the bones of ill-fated vessels picked clean." With what he had stripped over time from past wrecks, he had finally run out of room at his Main Street lot.

He explained to the flock of reporters that his old place now was too crowded and expensive to keep up. "You could hardly turn around on the lot for what I have gathered during the years," Whitelaw said. The old ship wrecker had thousands of pieces of vessels: anchors, chains, parts of keels, and wheels worn smooth by "hundreds of steersmen's hands"; compasses into which anxious mariners peered down at night during whistling storms; ship lights that feebly flickered a belated warning before seamen heard the rending crash; and even "the house flags of ships long gone." Over the years, he had garnered them all—including another yard that was full of scrap—and the only items Whitelaw said he didn't have were $20 gold pieces and baby carriages. He did have several baby incubators, however, he had salvaged from one of the wrecks.

A year later, Whitelaw secured a new yard at 100 Folsom Street, at the intersection of Main and Folsom, one block from the then docks. Although it took time and countless trips by his workmen, he finally removed the last of the items from his old yard at Harrison and Main streets. He wasn't spending his time refloating or saving ships now, but T. P. H. was adding every month to his prodigious inventory of ship parts and scrap iron and steel. He had sold off his real estate, fleets of ships, and wreck-steamers, keeping but one, and put the money into speculative salvaging ventures that bought more wrecks. Although he had been very successful in raising vessels, as he grew older Whitelaw took on the riskiest or unprofitable ones, as if he really wanted to own the ship and its contents, no matter what the cost or inconvenient location where it had sunk.

Whitelaw continued accepting the odd jobs that came his way. T. P. H. and Jim Searles, vice president of the Haslett Warehouse Company, made a bet about one project. Searles had let a contract to pump out the sump at a Haslett warehouse. Since he wanted the job completed as soon as possible, Searles bet Whitelaw that his company couldn't complete the work within one month. Whitelaw accepted and gave the money for holding to a third party, who at the time had been listening to the conversation. Although the Captain worked hard to win the bet, he couldn't meet the deadline. When he finally admitted to Searles that more time was needed, the vice president said, "We'll look up your friend, then, and I'll collect."

Whitelaw looked at him strangely. "My friend?" he said. "I thought he was your friend."

Searles replied, "I had never seen the man before in my life."

Neither man had seen the stakeholder since then. As one reporter observed, "Each was out of five dollars, and the stranger was in for ten."

A January 29, 1929, article in the *San Francisco Bulletin* showed how Captain Whitelaw looked at the salvage that wasn't stored in his yards. Entitled "Captain of the Ghost Fleet," this piece bears repeating:

Captain T. P. H. Whitelaw owns sixty-two ships. Tall barks, stately yachts, crack ocean liners, stubby freighters, tugs, a warship, and a pair of submarines. If they were assembled, the Whitelaw fleet would be the greatest on the Pacific Coast. The name of Whitelaw would rank with the shipowners named Dollar, Inchcape, Kyisant, and Franklin. There is a catch here. Sixty-one of his ships are sunk in saltwater. The other is the wrecking tug *Greenwood,* moored at Islais Creek.

For sixty years, he has bought his ships "as is," blown ashore in storms, sunk in various Pacific Coast harbors, some as burned hulks in the mud or as scrap iron at the junkyards. He guards his clear title to every one of his sunken fleet. Let anyone touch his property and the owner will be heard from. "Scrap iron is worth money," he explains. It was scrap iron that Whitelaw turned into his golden fortune.

For example, the *Lyman Stewart* was a fine new oil tanker of the Union Oil Company, plying in coastwise and offshore service. Whitelaw owns her now. In a fog several years ago, she lost her course and piled on the rocks off Land's End. Her broken hull can be seen now between the swells that break on the shores of the Golden Gate. "I got a few cargoes of gasoline and a lot of machinery off her. And wait until the price of scrap iron goes up," said the Captain.

The *Progresso* in other days took cargoes of fuel oil across the Pacific and never had a breakdown. One day she caught fire and exploded. Lives were lost and a once-fine ship remained a charred hulk in the mud near Oakland. Captain Whitelaw then bought her.

A white-winged Danish bark came around Cape Horn twenty-odd years ago and hove to [heading into winds to lie motionless except for drifting], in order to meet a storm off the Golden Gate. A gale started blowing, the ship drifted shoreward and was caught. She drove on the beach below Half Moon Bay and broke up. Whitelaw owns her, too.

Over on the mudflats north of Goat Island is another forgotten hulk. Some sailing ship. Whitelaw keeps his title to her in a safe deposit vault somewhere. Someday, she'll be worth something, he says.

From the Columbia River to the Mexican border, and below that, too, the Whitelaw fleet is strewn. Someday, when the price of scrap iron goes up, they'll be called back into service.

After World War I, Whitelaw bought a pair of Uncle Sam's discarded submarines, the F-1 and F-3, at a government "old hoss" sale at Mare Island in Vallejo. They had served well during the war, but the U.S. Navy retired them as obsolete. Whitelaw might have sold them to the Chinese or a Latin American republic looking to start up a navy, but the U.S. government prohibited these types of transactions. He would wait until he could sell them profitably.

After removing and selling one of the engines, he moored both submarines in Islais Creek (near Mission Bay). For nine years, they rocked at anchor there, "near the old rice mill," until one day they disappeared into the water. Whitelaw thought kids had been playing around, opened the valves, let in the water, and caused the subs to sink in the creek.

He heard a second story later that a disgruntled ex-employee had opened the seacocks of both subs. Knowing his "underwater babies" were perfectly safe with free storage in twenty feet of water until he needed them, T. P. H. left them embedded in the mud. He never learned who the responsible party was—and didn't worry about it.

The status of the sixty-two ships lying in different conditions in the ocean would soon become important. Whitelaw believed that technological developments would allow these wrecks to be later refloated or completely stripped at high prices. Rather than saving vessels and receiving his contingent fee, he put his available cash into acquiring wrecks to keep in "free sea storage" or to strip for their iron and scrap. Due to his age and physical limitations, he didn't take on the cash contracts—whether they be ship refloating or mooring buoys—that he did when younger. Whitelaw sold off his real estate assets in favor of wrecks at docks or the bottom of the sea. He didn't concern himself with financial controls, only with what seemed to be an "interesting" vessel to buy. Banks would lend him money to acquire more wrecks, and these valuations always seemed—like the stock market—to increase even more. Cash wasn't as important as being fully invested.

❖   ❖   ❖

THE CRASH of 1929 and stock market disintegration occurred in late October. The downturn on Wall Street started viciously on October 24 ("Black Thursday") and continued through October 29 ("Black Tuesday"), when share prices on the New York Stock Exchange collapsed. The days leading to the crash had also seen enormous market upheavals: panic selling and vast levels of trading were interspersed with brief periods of recovery upswings. The Great Depression was now underway, and the stock market never approached pre-1929 levels again until 1955.

T. P. H. and Elizabeth were still living in their stately Piedmont home. He continued his membership in different organizations, including being a forty-year member of the Golden Gate No. 3 Lodge of Masons and the San Francisco Chamber of Commerce. In October 1929, Whitelaw listed his occupation as "salvage, wreckage." Sixty years ago, at age twenty-three, the Captain had started his operations.

These days he strongly believed that the money was in scrap iron. He could have sold it during World War I and lived as a multimillionaire—

but he held on and added substantially more. These were now his prized possessions, and the adventurous stories of the sea when he was young.

Whitelaw exuded confidence and optimism. He didn't believe in worrying, no matter what the status of his checkbook. On the day after the stock market crash on Black Thursday, a reporter asked if he was worried about the economy. Shaking his long, white whiskers at the questioner, Whitelaw responded:

> How do you think a man like me could live to be eighty-three without plenty of food and, yes, sometimes a drink, not often you know, but sometimes. And when you get to be eighty-three, son, you can't afford to worry about anything.

He told a story of how a crew awoke him one early morning at home. They told him that his "unsinkable" wrecking barge was burning at its mooring at Harrison and Spear streets (one block from where the Embarcadero is now). Whitelaw dressed as usual, ate his breakfast without "hurry or stint," strolled the ten blocks he had walked every day, and just as slowly, came over to see the ruins of his dream barge. He discovered that it wasn't his ship. The destroyed vessel was another one that he had built for "some people who needed a barge." Whitelaw's barge was still moored next to his old *Greenwood*.

Whitelaw lit a fresh pipe. His trademark white beard spread out from his chin, looking "sawed off" and in a near circle. "Well," he said. "That just shows that the things that cause folks the most worry simply never happen. And what if the other barge had burned? I could build another. I'm a younger fellow yet at eighty-three. Hell . . ."

He then came up with a well-quoted quip about his wife: "Well, you know what wives are: Sometimes they're like an anchor on a ship, and sometimes it's a blamed good thing they're that way."

On his birthday that year, Captain Whitelaw was working as usual at his wrecking yards at Main and Folsom. He left early for his Piedmont home, across the bay, to attend a party arranged by his wife. They had been married for fifty-nine years. Whitelaw observed, "I am working on my eighty-fourth year now, but I am still in the game, strong and fit."

By then, his men had made 17,000 dives and he had saved 289 ships. "I'm going to try and make it 300 before I quit," he announced. Since his last publicly announced figures, the larger increase in dives made with fewer ships raised meant he was investing his money in ship parts and scrap. Whitelaw was no longer worrying about or trying to bolster his cash or investment accounts.

And time was working against him. On June 11, 1930, Whitelaw lost one of his best friends, the old wreck-steamer *Greenwood*. After saving many ships over its forty-four years of activity, she sank at her moorings in Islais Creek. The seams of its old wooden hull finally opened up and the ship quickly sank.

The watchman, his two dogs, and a cat were in the steamer's upper structure when the *Greenwood* slowly started to settle. They left the sinking craft by the small boat that was always moored nearby. Although the ship's mast and upper works stood well out of water at low tide, the ship was on the bottom, "gear and all."

Like he did with many others, Whitelaw had bought the *Greenwood* at a good price and then converted her into a salvage tug. As a replacement for the lost *Whitelaw*, the captain steamed the *Greenwood* on salvage tours up the coast, looking for ships to save and buying salvageable equipment. Although the *Greenwood* had been idle for the last ten years, T. P. H. had instructed the caretaker to turn the engines over every day.

He left the *Greenwood* where it sank. He didn't have the cash to raise it, and the times were financially inhospitable.

● ● ●

IN LATE October 1930, the Depression finally overwhelmed Captain T. P. H. Whitelaw: At age eighty-four, he was forced into bankruptcy. Jobs were scarce, didn't pay well, and the unemployment rate was 25 percent. Businesses and banks were collapsing all over the country. Loans weren't being made—they were foreclosed on. Prices and incomes plummeted nearly by one-half, and more than 9,000 banks failed before the Depression finally came to a merciful end.

Whitelaw had spent all his cash in his quest to salvage ships and borrowed to gamble in whatever project was appealing. He had saved many ships and salvaged countless parts, relying on their value with mountains of iron—but that wasn't good enough. His faith in their worth was checkmated by not being able to pay back the loans. He was an adventurer, not a banker; in financial hindsight, he should have kept his fleet of ships, not throwing the dice as he did. But that wasn't the way he lived his life.

When creditors pressed their claims, Whitelaw couldn't sell enough items in the bad economic climate to pay them off. A U.S. District Court judge had no choice but to declare him an involuntary bankrupt. The court ousted the master wrecker—credited with saving vessels on the Pacific valued in the high millions of dollars—from his yard at Main and Folsom.

The judge ordered that the stock of ship wreckage and scrap be sold off. The process started on a Monday in the yard at 100 Folsom Street and was expected "to go on for days to come." When the bids for the entire stock were considered too low, the decision was made to sell everything off piece by piece. As the auctioneer melodically sang out the bids, his sharp yell of "Sold!" continuously rang out.

Despite the financial setback in a time of countless setbacks, the newspapers and seamen still respected him as the "Pacific Coast Wrecker Supreme" and other titles, even when heralding his financial demise. Considered to be one of San Francisco's richest men the day before, Whitelaw now saw the tons of scrap and ship parts he had accumulated over the years being sold at a fraction of their value or cost. He became one of the legions of people who had made and lost sizable fortunes.

As he watched one business go, however, Whitelaw planned to start up anew. Not dismayed, the "gallant old captain" with seeming defiance immediately tacked up a shingle on an adjoining lot that read "Captain T. P. H. Whitelaw, Wrecker." Bankruptcy would have meant a final blow to less hardy people, but it seemed to only give him renewed strength. "I'm going to start up again, right next door. There's always another lot," he said, as he planned to create another "graveyard of ships."

Even amid financial disaster, he was still contented with a love of life. The picture that accompanied the newspaper reports showed a calm but strong man, with friendly eyes, a six-inch white beard, mustache, and thinning gray hair. He was wearing his usual attire: a bowler, three-piece gray suit, and tie.

Whether he searched for and reclaimed oil, coal, liquor, or parts, Whitelaw generally put up the money for a percentage of what he could possibly save, but then wound up investing even more. Such was his financial predicament, as his grandson commented:

> T. P. H. was a magnificent-looking man who made and lost several fortunes, gambling only on whether he could raise a ship "on the come." His great, white beard gave him a look like God. The old man was very well known, an equally proud guy, and was always noticed by the papers.
>
> It took a lot of capital to get into the salvage business, but with a quarter to his name, he did this. He started in the business by raising a few sunken launches and was successful in his early ventures. The Captain believed in scrap, but he could have been a multimillionaire forever had he bought and kept a few ships to sail to Hawaii like Matson did. [William Matson bought his first ship in 1882 at age thirty-three. This three-masted schooner marked the beginning of the Matson lines, as he bought other ships, including the grand SS *Malolo,* on which Whitelaw's grandson worked.]
>
> The company folded, when the lot with all of its equipment was sold. Had he retired twenty years earlier, he would have been a multimillionaire. He'd take down ten-ton loads of scrap, as he believed in the value of scrap iron—and this became his downfall.
>
> But he truly loved the adventure of trying to accomplish the impossible; [though] this cost him money, such as the *Lyman Stewart* disaster and others that took tons of his money.

⁕　⁕　⁕

THE MOST difficult time Whitelaw had to surmount was the death of his beloved wife on January 18, 1931. Elizabeth Whitelaw died at their home on 10 Pala Avenue in Piedmont. She was seventy-nine years old, and they had been married for more than sixty years.

He continued working as his only way to get through the grief, and despite the bankruptcy, Whitelaw found ways to continue buying ships and selling parts. In April 1931, he purchased three more obsolete lumber carriers and brought them to San Francisco—Whitelaw was still in business. After removing the machinery, his plan was to use the hulls as salvage barges or break them up. He decided to burn them down for the metal.

Whitelaw had aged due to his wife's death, and his face showed the deep, sunken eyes of mourning. Time sped by quickly. On November 9, 1932, Captain T. P. H. Whitelaw died at age eighty-six. Until ill health sent him to bed for his last three months, he had been very active in consulting on salvage operations. He was rebuilding.

When announcing the death, newspapers headlined him as the "Dean of Pacific Coast Shipwreckers," "Internationally known as a Wreck Master," "The Master Wrecker," "Wrecker Supreme," and other titles. They centered on the many ships he had saved over the years. They described him as the only surviving member of the "famous Stevenson schooner *Casco,* and as the commander and owner of the famous whaler, *La Ninfa.*" The reports underscored that he had been driven by his love of the sea. The articles were laudatory, but it was also very apparent that the reporters loved the "picturesque figure of the San Francisco waterfront" who had given them so many good stories.

The internment was private and held the following day in San Francisco. His obituary called him "Cappie" Whitelaw and ended:

We must pay deference, shipmates, to the final clearance of a sailor with a clean soul and a sturdy body. If ever anybody ever belonged in this port, surely it was Thomas Patrick Henry Whitelaw.

Three years before his death, the *San Francisco Chronicle* wrote:

He is still now the same chipper, salty kind of a young fellow he was when he was one of the crew on the first trial trip of Robert Louis Stevenson's famous schooner *Casco.* Since that day, Captain Whitelaw has been a figure on San Francisco's waterfront and is still yet. Dig into the folklore of the waterfront, the tales of its romance, its perils and its bravery, its shipwrecks and ship rescues, and you will find the name and fame of Captain Whitelaw in every chapter. Wrecker extraordinary and salvager without a peer of maimed and broken ships is what he's been.

Cappie's surviving family was small, and with his death, the operations of his company came to an end. His only surviving child was his daughter Daisy, who was now the wife of a well-known San Francisco printer. He had two granddaughters by Daisy who lived their own lives, and two grandsons by the now-deceased Andrew, Milton (age thirty-six) and Ken Whitelaw (age thirty-four). But they had taken different maritime paths, leaving him without any succession.

While Milton became an officer working for the Matson Line, Ken Whitelaw sailed with the Grace Line. He later shipped as an officer on Matson's SS *Malolo,* which is Hawaiian for "flying fish." The large passenger ship *Malolo* was the pride of the Matson fleet. The 582-foot-long ship was indeed a ship of luxury with seven decks, accommodations for 650 passengers, an indoor swimming pool, ballroom lounge, and two movie theaters. It had a dining room (with a balcony for an orchestra), beauty parlor, and several lounges. The port of San Francisco had to lengthen two of its docks by an additional 250 feet just to accommodate the vessel.

After the *Titanic* disaster, new regulations were enacted to improve ship safety, and the *Malolo* was built to these new specifications with extra hull plating and thicker structural steel, among other improvements. On May 24, 1927, Ken Whitelaw was on the "super passenger ship" *Malolo,* which had been built for a reported $6 million, and then on its trial voyage in dense fog, south of Nantucket, New York. He was the second officer and on watch as the ship steamed ahead at sixteen knots. Hearing a whistle off the port side, Whitelaw knew that a nearby ship had made the sounds.

Making a mistake on where the *Malolo* actually was, the ship's captain responded that the sounds were from the Nantucket Lighthouse—not another vessel. He ordered an erroneous course change. A large freighter, the Norwegian steamer *Jacob Christensen,* suddenly appeared from the mists and slammed into the *Malolo's* bow, slashing a fifteen-foot gash into its port side.

Racing below to inspect the damage, Ken Whitelaw watched the sea noisily rush into the ship and wash down corridors. The *Malalo* began to noticeably list to port. He and others quickly closed the portholes on the ship's now-listing side and shut the watertight doors through which the ocean was flooding in. When the ship settled fourteen feet farther into the ocean, the crew assembled the passengers, launched the lifeboats, and tethered them nearby. Later concluding the ship wasn't going to sink, they brought the people back on board.

Although the passengers wanted hot coffee, the electrical generators weren't working. Whitelaw searched through the vessel for a blowtorch while another crewmember looked for the coffee and a third went for potable water. Unfortunately, fuel oil had backed into the water supply, so everyone had to do without their cups of coffee. Sandwiches and fruit juice were in the galley, and these were handed out instead.

The dignitaries, officials, and invited friends on board were understandably upset while the vessel lay dead in the water for one and a half days. She had taken on 7,000 tons of water, and the *Malolo* was so badly damaged that a tug had to tow her to New York City. Due to her better design and strong construction, however, the ship stayed afloat.

Although the bow was crushed, after five months of repairs the *Malolo* finally made her maiden voyage to Honolulu. She was the fastest ship in the Pacific and cruised in excess of twenty knots. If built like the vessels T. P. H. sailed during his career, the *Malolo* would have quickly sunk with disastrous results, but this was a ship made in today's mold. Captain Ken Whitelaw—having by then met the experience requirements—worked four years as an officer on this magnificent vessel. After sailing with more steamship lines, the Merchant Marine fleet, the U.S. Navy, and U.S. Coast Guard, he retired in 1960 after forty-two years on the sea.

Cappie's grandson Ken settled in Atherton, located thirty miles south of San Francisco, and lived to the age of ninety-one before passing away in 1989. Milton had died years before in 1965, in Solano, California, at age sixty-nine.

◉ ◉ ◉

AS RAILROADS, highways, and airports proliferated, the dominance of the maritime industry waned, but was still important due to the huge import-export commerce between countries. When Captain T. P. H. Whitelaw died, ships like the *Malolo* had taken on the look of modern oceangoing vessels with no sails, huge steel hulls, twin screws, and multiple engines. And a litany of events and change lay further ahead.

The building of the Golden Gate Bridge began in 1933 and was completed four years later. The huge span was at first considered impossible to build, due to the persistent foggy weather, sixty-mile-per-hour winds, and strong currents that whipped through the deep underwater canyon. Before then, the construction engineers had consulted with T. P. H. over what their exploratory drilling was unearthing when boring into the waters off Fort Point—above which the bridge now soars. When the bridge opened, the need for car and truck ferries was coming to an end.

Following the stock market crash and Great Depression, the Merritt-Chapman & Scott Corporation survived the lean years by cutting back its workforce and working on public works construction of bridges, ore docks, and other building projects. The hard economic conditions continued until the start of World War II. Although continuing its ship salvaging, loading, pile driving, and diving operations after the war, the company continued to acquire other firms and diversify into more construction-related areas. The Merritt companies built bridges, tunnels, and wharves, including the foundation in the early 1950s for the five-mile-long Mackinac Bridge in Michigan, then the longest suspension bridge "between anchorages." When the company was finally taken over, mismanaged, and subsequently liquidated in 1971, the last of the great wrecker names during Captain Whitelaw's era had finally come to an end.

With the sophisticated use of radar, depth sounders, GPS, and accurate charts, ship operations are much safer than they once were. Vessels are much larger on average and more resistant to damage, owing to well-designed hull bulkheads, double bottoms and double hulls, and better engine machinery. Although the need for salvage services is significantly down from its peak during World War II, oil demand and environmental sensitivity—a result of the damage from the *Torrey Canyon, Exxon Valdez,* and other supertanker oil spills—have created salvage operation opportunities never dreamed about in those earlier days. The large salvage subsidiaries and companies now have names such as Titan Salvage, Donjon Marine Co., Gigilinis, SvitzerWijsmuller, Smit Internationale, and others that work globally.

In these modern times, octopuses and undersea predators still attack divers. Salvors find themselves buried inside shifting ships, crushed by deep-sea pressure, and working in bitter cold and darkness. Even with our advanced technology, there is still danger—and adventure. A wide range of salvage opportunities is now taken for granted: from recovering a Boeing 747 jumbo jet in Hong Kong Harbor to raising the Russian nuclear submarine *Kursk*.

From grain and gasoline to lumber and cars, vessels continue to carry the world's trade and commerce. Ships still collide, beach, and founder in storms, although not as often as when shipping was king. Although the dangers at sea are still present, they are certainly reduced by advances in technology and safer ships, since the courageous, entrepreneurial times of Whitelaw and his contemporaries. Captain T. P. H. Whitelaw started in an era of wooden ships and sails and lived to see huge cruise and cargo ships. No one could have asked for more.

SELECTED BIBLIOGRAPHY

Adams, James T. *History of the Town of Southampton*. Bridgehampton, Long Island: Hampton Press, 1918.

_____. *Memorials of Old Bridgehampton*. Bridgehampton, Long Island: privately printed, 1916.

"Aged Sea Dog Runs on Rock of Bankruptcy: Skipper Has Salvaged Millions, Sees Fortune Drip to Paltry $4,000." *San Francisco Chronicle*, October 29, 1930, p. 5. col. 1.

"Along the Wharves." *Alta California*, October 9, 1877, p. 1, col. 1

"Ancient Ship Claim Is Paid." *San Francisco Examiner*, April 2, 1926.

"Arrives at Opportune Moment." *San Francisco Daily Morning Call*, July 26, 1913, p. 11, col. 1.

Baker, Captain Harry. "Copy of Report by Captain Harry Baker Submitted to the Local Inspectors at New London on November 20, 1916." Papers in the G. W. Blunt White Library, Mystic Seaport, CT.

"Bankrupt at 84, but 'Still in Game,' says Whitelaw." *San Francisco Examiner*, October 29, 1930.

Barber, Mary D. "Salvage." *The Overland Monthly*, 54 (December 1909): 606–10.

"Barge Manheim, April 4, 1915, Wreck Memo." Papers in the G. W. Blunt White Library.

Bathurst, Bella. *The Wreckers: A Story of Killing Seas and Plundered Shipwrecks from the Eighteenth Century to the Present Day*. Boston and New York: Houghton Mifflin, 2005.

"Battle Is Waged Over a Rusty Old Anchor." *San Francisco Chronicle*, July 17, 1906.

Beebe, Lucius and Charles Clegg. *San Francisco's Golden Era: A Picture Story of San Francisco Before the Fire.* Berkeley, CA: Howell-North Books, 1960.

"Boarding the Six-Master on Tuckernuck Shoal." *The Inquirer,* December 26, 1914.

"Both Bettors Lose Wager." *San Francisco Examiner,* October 21, 1928.

Boyd, Richard. "Early Commercial Diving on the Great Lakes as Lived by Diver Pearl Purdy," Wisconsin's Underwater Heritage, 14, no. 4 (December 2004), http://www.mailbag.com/users/wuaa/Dec04.pdf (accessed May 24, 2008).

Brown, Giles T. *Ships That Sail No More: Marine Transportation from San Diego to Puget Sound,* 1910–1940. Lexington: University of Kentucky Press, 1966.

"Cappie Whitelaw to Be Buried Today." *San Francisco Chronicle,* November 10, 1932, p. 18, col. 1.

"Captain of Ghost Fleet: 61 Phantom Vessels Make Captain Rich." *San Francisco Bulletin,* January 29, 1929.

"Captain Thomas P. H. Whitelaw." *The Bay of San Francisco: The Metropolis of the Pacific Coast and Its Suburban Cities: A History.* Vol. 1. Chicago: Lewis Publishing, 1892, 700–2.

"Captain Whitelaw Has Raised Hundred of Wrecks from the Sea." *The Literary Digest* 86 (July 11, 1925), 38–42.

"Captain Whitelaw Plans to Float Tank Steamer . . ." *San Francisco Examiner,* December 2, 1925.

"Capt. Thomas Patrick Henry Whitelaw: Pacific Coast Wrecker Supreme." *San Francisco Examiner,* October 28, 1930.

"Capt. Whitelaw, Bankrupt, Will Start Anew at 84." *San Francisco News,* October 28, 1930.

"Capt. Whitelaw Has Fortune in Junk." *San Francisco Call,* May 7, 1917.

"Captain Wins $77,110 Suit." *San Francisco Examiner,* September 29, 1925.

Charlton, Edward A. "Captain Whitelaw, 'Wrecker Supreme,' Laughs at Adversity; 85-Year-Old Salvager Resumes Business After Setback." *San Francisco Examiner,* March 8, 1931.

"Circassian Shipwreck," http://thehamptons.com/indians/shipwreck/circassian.html (accessed June 25, 2007).

Clunies, Sandy. "Captain T. P. H. Whitelaw," E-mail to author, November 15, 2005, regarding census and city directory information.

_____. "Thomas Patrick Henry Whitelaw." E-mail to author, November 15, 2005, regarding background.

_____. "Whitelaw." E-mail to author, November 23, 2005, regarding 10 percent payment for recovering lost moorings.

_____. "About Elizabeth Whitelaw and Ballantyne." E-mail to author, November 23, 2005.

"Collision Between the S/S Umbria and the S/S Iberia in 1888." *Harper's Weekly*, November 24, 1888; also available at http://www.norway-heritage.com/articles/templates/greatdisasters.asp?articleid=91&zoneid=1 (accessed May 26, 2008).

"Cornish History," http://www.cornish-links.co.uk/history-smugglers.htm (accessed January 5, 2006).

Crouch, Gregory. "The Point of No Return." *American History* 34, no. 2 (June 1999).

"Daring Deeds Are Told of Famous Diver." *San Francisco Examiner,* June 29, 1924.

Dayton, Thaddeus. S. "The Wreck-Master." *Harper's Weekly* 53 (December 25, 1909): 16–17.

"Death Claims Capt. Whitelaw, Noted Wrecker." *San Francisco Chronicle,* November 9, 1932, p. 11, col. 6.

Delgado, James P., and Stephen A. Haller. *Shipwrecks at the Golden Gate.* San Francisco: Lexicos, 1989.

Donahue, James. "The Haunting of Captain McLean," http://pedurabo10.tripod.com/ships/id115.html (accessed November 5, 2007).

Eastland Disaster Historical Society. "Righting the Eastland," http://www.eastlanddisaster.org/righting.htm (accessed May 22, 2008).

Eddy, Elford. "Veteran Wrecker Estimates Value of Craft Saved at $10,000,000." *San Francisco Daily News,* November 14, 1924.

Edeline, Denis P. *Along the Banks of Salt River.* California: D. P. Edeline, 1983.

"Ends Fight to Salvage Wreck: Veteran Whitelaw Abandons His Attempt to Get Lunsmann from Bay Bottom." *San Francisco Examiner,* December 4, 1913.

"Extensive Operations Planned for Salvage of $10,000,000 Liquor Cargo in Davy Jones' Locker; Farralones as Base." *San Francisco Examiner,* June 9, 1930.

Fawcett, Waldon. "Recent Notable Salvage Operations." *Engineering Magazine* 18 (January 1900): 585–98.

Field, Van. R. "Wrecks and Rescues on Long Island," Center Moriches Free Public Library, http://www.suffolk.lib.ny.us/libraries/cmor/wrecks.htm (accessed May 27, 2008).

Flayhart, William H. *The American Line: Pioneers of Ocean Travel, 1871–1902).* New York: W. W. Norton, 2001.

Gores, Joseph N. *Marine Salvage.* London: David & Charles, 1971.

"Great Ships: City of Paris," http://web.greatships.net:81/philadelphia.html (accessed November 10, 2007).

Halsey, William D. *Sketches from Local History.* Bridgehampton, NY: privately printed, 1935.

Harding, George. "Wreckers of the Florida Keys." *Harper's Monthly Magazine* 123, no. 734 (July 1991): 275–85.

"He Fights Tides for a Fortune: Bay Baffles Veteran Wrecker." *San Francisco Post,* November 25, 1913.

Hislam, Percival A. "Salving the 'Lutine.'" *Scientific American* 108 (May 17, 1931): 450–51.

"Honda (Pedernales) Point, California, Disaster, 8 September 1923." Naval Historical Center, Navy Department Library, http://www.history.navy.mil/library/online/honda.htm (accessed May 27, 2008).

Howard, Frank. *The Florida Keys,* May 31, 1995, http://www.littletownmart.com/fdh/keys.htm (accessed May 26, 2008).

Howland, Harold J. "Wrecking." *The Outlook* 82: 663–75.

Hull, David. "Before the Bridges and Freeways: A Series of Articles." *The Port Authority,* October 1977, November 1977, January 1978 (p. 1–2), February 1978 (p. 1–2), March 1978 (p. 1–2, 11), June 1978 (p. 1–2, 14), September 1978 (p. 1–2, 11), October 1978 (p. 1–2, 4), November/December 1978 (p. 1–2, 15).

Hunter, Lois M. *The Shinnecock Indians.* Westhampton Beach, NY: Hampton Chronicle, 1958.

Hyne, C. J. Cutcliffe. "How Ships are Salvaged." *Discovery* 5 (July 1924): 129–31.

Johnson, John A. "Declaration Regarding Damage to Tug T. A. Scott, Jr., June 18, 1912." Papers in the G. W. Blunt White Library.

"Kelley House Archive," http://www.men.org/ed/CUR/liv/ind/mark/arch.htm (accessed October 27, 2006).

Kemble, John Haskell. *San Francisco Bay: A Pictorial Maritime History.* New York: Cornell Maritime Press, 1957.

"Key West Shipwreck Historeum Museum," http://www.shipwreckhistoreum.com/WreckAshore.htm (accessed May 27, 2008); also http://www.shipwreckhistoreum.com/August1856.htm (accessed May 27, 2008).

Kimball, James H. Letter to Ernest S. Clowes, December 2, 1941, describing weather conditions at the time of the Circassian tragedy. Bridgehampton Historical Society, Bridgehampton, NY.

Koster, D. A. *Ocean Salvage.* New York: St. Martin's Press, 1971.

La Ninfa; Whitelaw v. United States, 75 F. 513 (Ninth Circuit Court of Appeals, 1896).

"Latest and Greatest Attempt to Raise the San Pedro Meets with Poor Success." *Daily Colonist,* August 5, 1892.

Lewis, Captain Joseph. Letter from Captain Lewis, T. A. Scott & Company, December 5, 1914, regarding schooner Alice Lennoner. Papers in the G. W. Blunt White Library.

Maclay, Mira. "Dean of the West Coast Divers." *Sunset 54* (April 1925): 26–28.

MacMillen, Robert D. *Black Horse of the Sea.* New York: Merritt-Chapman & Scott Corporation, 1929.

Mailler, Roger T. "Iberia," http://dis.cs.umass.edu/~mailler/index.html; http://www.cs.cornell.edu/~rmailler (accessed June 12, 2006).

"Marine News: Thomas Whitelaw, veteran head...." *San Francisco Chronicle,* September 10, 1918.

"Maritime History of the Great Lakes: Shipwrecks: Cayuga, 1895," http://www.hhpl.on.ca/GreatLakes/Wrecks/Details.asp?ID=19664 &n=6 (accessed May 20, 2008).

"Maritime History of the Great Lakes: Shipwrecks: Moreland, William C.,"http://www.hhpl.on.ca/GreatLakes/Wrecks/Details.asp?ID=5798&n=1 (accessed May 20, 2008).

"Martin Lund, a diver for the Pacific Coast Wrecking Company." *San Francisco Chronicle,* September 28, 1908.

Mason, Arthur. "The Wreckmaster." *Woman's Home Companion 51* (April 1924): 27–28.

Massachusetts Office of Coastal Zone Management. "Ardandhu," http://www.mass.gov/czm/buar/shipwrecks/ua-arda.htm (accessed November 1, 2007).

Masters, David. *The Wonders of Salvage.* London: John Lane, The Bodley Head Ltd., 1924.

———. *When Ships Go Down: More Wonders of Salvage.* New York: Henry Holt, 1935.

McCurdy, James G. "Salvage of the Schooner Minnie A. Caine." *Scientific American* 87 (July 26, 1902): 52

McNairn, Jack, and Jerry MacMullen. *Ships of the Redwood Coast.* Stanford, CA: Stanford University Press, 1945.

"Meigs Family History and Genealogy," http://www.meigs.org/Henry_Meiggs526.htm (accessed October 15, 2007).

MetroWest Dive Club. "Ardandhu," http://www.mwdc.org/Shipwrecks/Ardandhu.html (accessed August 15, 2006).

Michigan Family History Network. "The Men Ruled by the Great Lakes: Captain James S. Dunham," http://www.mfhn.com/forum/topic.asp?TOPIC_ID=16&ARCHIVE = (accessed May 25, 2008).

Moeran, Edward H. "The Circassian Tragedy." *Long Island Forum,* September 1942, p. 69–172.

Morris, Paul C., and William P. Quinn. *Shipwrecks in New York Waters: A Chronology of Ship Disasters from the 1880s to the 1930s.* Orleans, MA: Parnassus Imprints, 1989.

"Motor Car's Buoy Starts for China: Mermaids Out Joy Riding." *San Francisco Examiner,* December 1912.

"Mrs. Whitelaw Taken by Death." *San Francisco Examiner,* January 19, 1931.

Mystic Seaport. "Records of T. A. Scott Company, Inc. (Collection 1)," http://www.mysticseaport.org/library/manuscripts/coll/coll001/coll 001.html (accessed October 15, 2007).

"Nelson—One More Victim of Progresso Found." *San Francisco Examiner,* December 15, 1902, p. 8.

Newell, Gordon, ed. *The H. W. McCurdy Marine History of the Pacific Northwest.* Seattle: Superior Publishing, 1966.

"No Lives Lost in Collision, but Ships Damaged." *New London Telegraph,* October 11, 1915.

Nordhoff, C. "Wrecking on the Florida Keys." *Harper's Weekly* 18 (1874): 577–86.

"Nothing Worries Aged Mariner." *San Francisco Chronicle,* October 25, 1929, p. 9, col. 2.

"On Fire at Sea: Burning of the P.M.S.S. Constitution." *Alta California,* October 6, 1877, p. 1, col. 3.

"On the Beach: The 'Costa Rica' and Her Present Situation." *Alta California,* September 19, 1873, p. 1, col. 3.

"Perilous Job of Raising Wrecked Ships (The)." *The Literary Digest* 86 (July 11, 1925): 39–48.

Peter, Henry S. "Ship Wrecker's Crop Crowds Him Out of Quarters." *San Francisco Call,* November 18, 1926.

"Pilot of Steamer Held Responsible for Collision." *New London Day,* December 15, 1915.

Quinn, William P. *Shipwrecks Along the Atlantic Coast.* Beverly, MA: Commonwealth Editions, 1988.

"Race Rock, New York, Lighthouse." Harbour Lights Lighthouses, http://www.harbourlights.com/catalog/2002/hl_race_rock.htm (accessed October 15, 2007).

Reinstedt, Randall A. *Shipwrecks and Sea Monsters of California's Central Coast.* Carmel, CA: Ghost Town Publications, 1975.

"Report Covering Operations on Schooner, 'Maggie Ellen,' Owned by Horace Sarcent, Portland, Maine, Ashore South Side of Fishers Island, Wednesday, November 13, 1912." Papers in the G. W. Blunt White Library.

"Report of Operations, Schooner 'Estelle,' Owned by Capt. J. B. Phillips, Sag Harbor, New York, Ashore South Side of Fishers Island, Wednesday, November 13, 1912." Papers in the G. W. Blunt White Library.

"Resurrected: The 'Costa Rica' Gets off the Rocks." *Alta California,* September 25, 1873, p. 1, col. 3.

Ringuette, Janis. "Offshore Reefs: 1891–1892 Efforts to Refloat the San Pedro," http://www.islandnet.com/beaconhillpark/contents/appendix_D.htm (accessed May 27, 2008).

Robertson, Morgan. "Modern Methods of Saving Ships." *The World's Work* 5 (January 1903): 2946–54.

Rudmann, Brent. "The SS Pomona: The History and Archaeology of a California Steamship and the Industry that Built Her." Master's thesis, University of San Diego, 2002.

"Salvage of the Oregon." *Scientific American* 83 (September 1, 1900): 136–38.

"Salvaged Winds of Wrecked Ships Served at Feast: Captain and Mrs. Whitelaw Celebrate Golden Wedding from Long-Lost Cargos." *San Francisco Call,* March 25, 1920.

"Salvaging the San Pedro." *Daily Colonist,* January 10, 1892 (p. 5), January 26, 1892 (p. 5), April 20, 1892 (p. 1), August 5, 1892 (p. 6), August 22, 1893 (p. 8), November 18, 1893 (p. 3), September 25, 1896 (p. 8), May 8, 1897 (p. 7), May 16, 1897 (p. 5), and June 22, 1897 (p. 7). This series of articles deals with the salvage attempts by Whitelaw.

"San Diego History," http:www.sandiegohistory.org/journal/78summer/asama.htm (accessed May 26, 2008).

"Saving the Steamer Jose." *Scientific American* 107 (August 31, 1912): 178.

"Sea Captain Sues Over Old Ship Seizure." *San Francisco Examiner,* July 15, 1924.

"Sexton of Ship Graveyard Completes Fifty Years of Service, Lists Sea Toll." *San Francisco Call,* February 21, 1925.

Shanks, W.F.G. "Wreckers: Policemen of the Sea." *Harper's Weekly* 38: 433–48.

Shaw, William J. Letter to Honorable E. O. Crosby, January 6, 1864. Quoted in Charles B. Turrill, "Foreign Population Held Balance That Placed City on Side of Anti-Slavery," The Virtual Museum of the City of San Francisco, http://www.sfmuseum.net/hist5/civwar.html (accessed May 27, 2008).

"Sixty-One Phantom Vessels Make Captain Rich." *San Francisco Bulletin,* January 29, 1929.

"Skipper Wins Seal Claim 33 Years Old." *San Francisco Examiner,* September 29, 1925.

Smith, F. Hopkinson. *Caleb West Master Diver.* New York: Grosset & Dunlap, 1898.

Smith, Horace. *A Captain Unafraid: The Strange Adventures of Dynamite Johnny O'Brien.* New York and London: Harper & Brothers Publishers, 1912.

"Snappy Shots: Captain T. P. H. Whitelaw." *San Francisco Examiner,* September 5, 1925.

Squires, Harry B. *Memoirs.* Bridgehampton Historical Society.

"S. S. City of Milwaukee—History," http://www.carferry.com/history.htm (accessed May 25, 2008).

"Statement by Capt. M. S. Goodale Relative to Operations in Floating Steam Yacht 'Warrior,' July 19, 1916." Papers in the G. W. Blunt White Library.

"Statement of a Custom-House Inspector." *New York Times*, December 31, 1876, p. 2.

"Steamer Torn in Collision at Night; Wrecked Cabins; 10 Sleeping Persons Hurt." *New York World*, October 11, 1915.

"St. Paul, 1895–1923." The Great Ocean Liners, http://www.greatoceanliners.net/stpaul.html (accessed May 27, 2008).

"Tall Ships of San Francisco," http://tallshipsofsanfrancisco.com/index.html (accessed May 25, 2008).

"Tears Fortune from Clutches of Greedy Sea: Dean of Divers Tells of Adventure Under Ocean." *San Francisco Chronicle*, June 29, 1924.

"The Circassian Wreck." *New York Times*, January 1, 1877, p. 8.

"The 'Costa Rica' Ashore: A Magnificent Steamer Wrecked for the Lack of a Few Barrels of Water." *Alta California*, September 18, 1873, p. 1, col. 4.

"The 'Costa Rica' Docked." *Alta California*, September 26, 1873, p. 1, col. 2.

"The Eastland Disaster," http://www.prairieghosts.com/eastland.html (accessed May 27, 2008).

"The Famous Overland Voyage of Lightship No. 50." *Columbia Magazine*, Summer 1988, p. 30.

"The Great Lakes Marine. *Detroit Tribune,* June 10, 1886, http://www.hhpl.on.ca/GreatLakes/Documents/DT86/default.asp?ID=c005 (accessed November 1, 2007).

"The Law of Salvage: The Accidents to the Machinery of the Steamships 'Colima' and 'Costa Rica." *Alta California*, November 16, 1874, p. 1, col. 3.

"The Pomona." *Weekly Humboldt Times*, September 13, 1888.

"The steamer 'Constitution' was raised yesterday." *Alta California*, October 15, 1877, p. 1. col. 3.

"The steamer 'Etta White.'" *Morning Journal*, August 21, 1890.

"The Warrior Goes on Rocks: Party Rescued." *New York Herald*, July 20, 1916.

"The World Still Looks Bright." *San Francisco Examiner,* December 6, 1928.

"The Wreck of the Circassian." Journal of Georgica Life Saving Station, Long Island, regarding the Circassian tragedy. Bridgehampton Historical Society.

"The Wreck of the Circassian." Journal of Mecox Life Saving Station, Long Island, regarding the Circassian tragedy. Bridgehampton Historical Society.

"The Wreck of the Circassian." New York Times, January 2, 1877, p. 2.

"'The Wrecker,' Capt. Thomas Whitelaw Dies: Noted Salvager of Ships Passes Away in 87th Year; Wrested Many Fortunes from Sea." San Francisco Chronicle, November 9, 1932.

"Thirteen-Thousand-Ton Vessel Righted by Rolling and Lifting." Engineering News-Record 81, no. 17 (November 2, 1918).

"Those Who Helped." Eastland Disaster Historical Society, http://www.eastlanddisaster.org/thosewhohelped.htm (accessed May 25, 2008).

Toronto Marine Historical Society, "Ship of the Month, No. 4 Parkdale," The Scanner 2, no. 3 (December 1969), http://www.hhpl.on.ca/GreatLakes/Documents/Scanner/02/03/defa ult.asp?ID=c004 (accessed last, October 15, 2007).

Turrill, Charles B. California Notes. San Francisco: E. Bosqui & Co., 1876.

United States Lighthouse Society, Long Island Chapter. "Captain Thomas A. Scott, Master Diver," http://www.lilighthousesociety.org/historicalcollection/master-diver/default.htm (accessed May 25, 2008).

"Vaterland/Leviathan, 1914–1938." The Great Ocean Liners: St. Paul, http://www.greatoceanliners.net/stpaul.html (accessed October 15, 2007).

Virtual Museum of the City of San Francisco, "Foreign Population Held Balance That Placed City on Side of Anti-Slavery," http://www.sfmuseum.net/hist5/civwar.html (accessed on May 27, 2008).

Walsh, George E. "Evolution of Wrecking." Cassier's Magazine 12: 563.

"West Coast shipwrecks," http://channelislands.nos.noaa.gov/ship-wreck/shiphome.html (accessed October 15, 2007).

West, Victor. "Shipwrecks of the Southern Oregon Coast (Vol. I–VII, including Index)." Unpublished manuscript, Southwestern Oregon Community College Library, Coos Bay, Oregon.

Wheeler, Captain G. J. Ship Salvage. London: George Philip and Son, Limited, 1958.

White, Magner. "Captain Whitelaw Has Raised Hundreds of Wrecks from the Seas." *American Magazine* 99 (June 1925): 24–25.

_____. "Why I Am Doing What I Am Doing: Capt. Thos. P. H. Whitelaw." *San Francisco Daily News,* September 14, 1926.

Whitelaw, Capt. T. P. H. "Cheating the Sea." *Popular Mechanics* 50 (November 1928): 770–75.

"Whitelaw Is Sued." *San Francisco Chronicle,* November 4, 1904, p. 13, col. 6.

Whitelaw, T. Kenneth. Interview with grandson, T. Kenneth Whitelaw, June 26, 1968, about grandfather, Captain T. P. H. Whitelaw. Audiotapes. San Francisco Maritime Museum.

"Whitelaw to Retire." *San Francisco Chronicle,* May 30, 1920, p. 62, col. 1.

Wilkinson, Jerry. "Keys History: History of Wrecking," http://www.keyshistory.org/wrecking.html (accessed October 15, 2007).

"Word was received...." *San Francisco Chronicle,* April 25, 1894.

"Wrecked San Pedro to Be Blown Up." *San Francisco Chronicle,* March 3, 1896.

"Wrecked Ship Destruction Sought in Clean-Up Week." *San Francisco Examiner,* April 29, 1929.

"Wrecking Vessels," http://www.melfisher.org/reefswrecks/wreckingvessels.htm (accessed November 15, 2007).

Wright, E. W., ed. *Lewis and Dryden's Marine History of the Pacific Northwest.* New York: Antiquarian Press, 1961. Reprint of first edition published Portland, OR: Lewis & Dryden Printing Co., 1895.

Young, Desmond. "Salvaging of the Ulidia." *Blackwood's Magazine* 208 (July–August 1920): 1–26; 243–61.

_____. *Ship Ashore: Adventures in Salvage.* London: Jonathan Cape, 1932.

INDEX

ABOUT THE AUTHOR

Dennis M. Powers is an established author, frequent media guest, and conference speaker. He was a business law attorney in private practice before joining the faculty and becoming a Full Professor in the School of Business at Southern Oregon University in Ashland, Oregon. He is a graduate of the University of Colorado, the University of Denver Law School, and Harvard Business School. His interest in the engaging stories about sea voyages, sailors, and ships in the seven seas has been ongoing for years.

He began concentrating on his writing fifteen years ago, and is the author of ten books in total, the last four about maritime subjects: *The Raging Sea* (2005) chronicles the crushing 1964 tsunami that ravished the U.S. West Coast; *Treasure Ship* (2006) is about the loss, legend, and legacy of the S.S. *Brother Jonathan,* a side-wheel steamer that sank off northern California with millions of dollars of gold—and was finally discovered 125 years later; *Sentinel of the Seas* (2007) tells the story of the most remote, dangerous, and expensive lighthouse built in this country's history, St. George Reef Lighthouse; and *Taking the Sea* (2008), which recounts the maritime age of wrecking, or ship salvaging, of vessels as the world changed from wooden clipper ships to the huge steamships of today.

Dennis Powers participates at writers' conferences as a workshop leader and speaker, as well as also writing fiction, short stories, and published poetry. Now a Professor Emeritus, Mr. Powers resides in Ashland, Oregon, with his wife Judy, three cats, and libraries of books.

More information about the author and his books is available at his website *www.dennispowersbooks.com.*